Netaji: Collected Works
Volume 10

THE ALTERNATIVE LEADERSHIP

Speeches, Articles, Statements and Letters
June 1939–January 1941

Subhas Chandra Bose with Rabindranath Tagore and Sarat Chandra Bose, Calcutta, 19 August 1939

Netaji Collected Works Volume 10

THE ALTERNATIVE LEADERSHIP

Speeches, Articles, Statements and Letters June 1939–January 1941

Subhas Chandra Bose

edited by

Sisir Kumar Bose and Sugata Bose

Orient BlackSwan

THE ALTERNATIVE LEADERSHIP: SPEECHES, ARTICLES, STATEMENTS AND LETTERS JUNE 1939–JANUARY 1941

ORIENT BLACKSWAN PRIVATE LIMITED

Registered Office
3-6-752 Himayatnagar, Hyderabad 500 029, Telangana, India
e-mail: centraloffice@orientblackswan.com

Other Offices
Bengaluru, Chennai, Guwahati, Hyderabad, Kolkata, Mumbai, New Delhi, Noida, Patna, Visakhapatnam

First published by the Netaji Research Bureau in 1998
First paperback printing 2004
Second impression 2016
This edition published by Orient Blackswan Private Limited 2023

ISBN 978-93-5442-442-7

037598

Printed in India at
Yash Printographics, Noida

Published by
Orient Blackswan Private Limited
3-6-752, Himayatnagar, Hyderabad 500 029, Telangana, India
e-mail: info@orientblackswan.com

Contents

Preface to the 2023 Edition

Sugata Bose

'With such a phenomenon in history,' Sisir Kumar Bose asked in his preface dated 21 October 1961, to *Crossroads*,[1] 'where does one begin and where does one end?' He decided to begin with the works of Subhas Chandra Bose between 1938 and 1940 as the very first book published by the Netaji Research Bureau (NRB) on 23 January 1962. The anthology represented 'the peak period in Netaji's political career in India'. As Rabindranath Tagore put it inimitably in his evocative 1939 address[2] hailing Subhas as '*Deshnayak*':

> I have watched the dawn that witnessed the beginning of your political *sadhana*. In that uncertain twilight there had been misgivings in my heart and I had hesitated to accept you for what you are now … Today you are revealed in the pure light of midday sun which does not admit of apprehensions. You have come to absorb varied experience during these years. Today you bring your matured mind and irrepressible vitality to bear upon the work at hand. Your strength has sorely been taxed by imprisonment, banishment and disease, but rather than impairing, these have helped to broaden your sympathies—enlarging your vision so as to embrace the vast perspectives of history beyond any narrow limits of territory.

'A clear and alternative leadership, defiant of all inhibitions,' Sisir Kumar Bose argued, 'is seen to emerge on the Indian political scene in the

[1] Subhas Chandra Bose, *Crossroads: Being the Works of Subhas Chandra Bose, 1938–1940*, compiled by Sisir Kumar Bose (London: Asia Publishing House, 1962), p. v.

[2] For the full text of Tagore's *Deshnayak* address, see Sisir Kumar Bose and Sugata Bose (eds.), *Netaji Collected Works Volume 7 Congress President* (Calcutta: Netaji Research Bureau, 2016), pp. 247–249.

beginning of 1940—fighting simultaneously on two fronts.' The battle against an intractable and cunning British imperialism had to contend with a vacillating right-wing of the Indian National Congress prone to compromise. After the outbreak of World War II most Congress leaders behaved as 'His Majesty's Opposition'; Subhas Chandra Bose alone stood forth as 'His Majesty's Opponent'.

Once NRB launched its 12-volume *Collected Works* project, the period covered in *Crossroads* was divided after adding more materials into volumes 9 and 10, with Bose's resignation as Congress President providing the temporal threshold between the two. Volume 10 titled *The Alternative Leadership* brings together Subhas Chandra Bose's speeches, writings, and letters at a time when Indian anti-colonial politics stood at the crossroads of history. The speeches include his welcome to Tagore at the foundation-laying ceremony of Mahajati Sadan in Calcutta on 19 August 1939, and his famous Ramgarh Address at the Anti-Compromise Conference in March 1940. The essays provide fascinating glimpses of Bose's political tours across the length and breadth of India between May 1939 and June 1940. In addition to the major political and personal correspondence with Mahatma Gandhi, Jawaharlal Nehru, Rabindranath Tagore, Sarat Chandra Bose, Jaya Prakash Narayan, and Linlithgow, the letters exchanged with M.N. Roy, Dr Satyapal, Mian Akbar Shah, N.G. Ranga, Indulal Yagnik, Swami Sahajanand Saraswati, Gaganvihari Lal Mehta, Agatha Harrison, Meghnad Saha, M.A.H. Ispahani, Sardul Singh Caveeshar, Arthur Greenwood, and Arthur Moore cover a broad range of topics spanning peasant movements, science education, municipal affairs, and international relations. Bose's prison letters from July to December 1940 are exceptionally valuable. They include the stirring document titled 'My Political Testament' of 26 November 1940, on the eve of launching his hunger-strike in Presidency Jail. 'What better reward can a soul desire than the certainty that his message will be wafted over hills and dales and over the broad plains to distant lands?' he wrote with unswerving conviction. 'What higher consummation can life attain than peaceful self-immolation at the altar of one's Cause?' He urged his own compatriots: 'Forget not that the grossest crime is to compromise with injustice and wrong.'

The 'Editors' Introduction' that Sisir Kumar Bose and I wrote a quarter of a century ago places the volume in historical context. It also identifies the principles of uncompromising anti-imperialism and undiluted socialism as two pillars of the alternative leadership on offer. From the perspective of 2023 it is imperative to stress Subhas Chandra Bose's position on equality and unity of all religious communities in the period before his *'Mahanishkraman'* or great escape to lead India's army of liberation abroad. He was aware that not so long ago in the 1920s Lala Lajpat Rai had been leader of both the Congress and the Hindu Mahasabha and the Ali brothers, Shaukat and Mohammad, and Maulana Akram Khan had bridged the Congress and the Muslim League. While stating his ideological opposition to 'communalism', he was not prepared to disregard the influence of 'communal organizations'. He identified Mohammad Ali Jinnah as leader of 'the progressive sections' of the Muslim League and met him in June 1940 to urge him to put up a joint fight against the British. In Calcutta he had negotiated with M.A.H. Ispahani in the spring of 1940 to forge the Bose-League Pact to share power in the Calcutta Corporation elections that was reminiscent of Deshbandhu Chittaranjan Das's Bengal Pact of 1923. With Bose's support Abdur Rahman Siddiqui of the Muslim League became Mayor of Calcutta. He regarded this agreement as 'a great achievement not in its actuality, but in its potentiality'. In May 1940 he advocated 'unity among Congressmen and a Hindu-Muslim settlement'. 'National unity,' he asserted in his Nagpur address of June 1940, 'will presuppose unity within the Congress on the basis of a dynamic program of struggle and at the same time unity between the Congress and other organizations like the Muslim League.' Later that month he demanded national cabinets based on broad-based coalitions at the centre and the provinces, which 'will ensure internal peace and harmony during the transitional period and will pave the way to a lasting Hindu-Muslim settlement'.

On the eve of Deshbandhu's 15th death anniversary on 16 June 1940, Subhas Chandra Bose wrote feelingly of 'that rare combination of Idealism and Realism which constitutes the essence of leadership and which was the secret of his greatness'. 'We want that unbounded love,' he continued, 'which made him a friend of the people and which drew the Muslims and the backward classes so close to him.' It was very much in tune with that generous and broad-minded political tradition that Bose embodied when he gave the call for a movement to commence on 3 July 1940, for the removal of the Holwell monument from Dalhousie Square in order to restore the honor of Siraj-ud-Daula, the last independent Nawab of Bengal. He was arrested the night before under the Defence of India Rules for his final spell of imprisonment in India.

After he was sent home on 5 December 1940, following his hunger-strike, Subhas Chandra Bose called his nephew Sisir Kumar Bose to his side and asked him in Bengali: '*Amaar ekta kaj korte parbe?*' The immediate *kaj* that Sisir was assigned was to help his Rangakakababu plan and execute his great escape from India. Uncle and nephew left Calcutta in Sisir's Wanderer car on the night of 16–7 January 1941, on the first stage of Netaji's global odyssey.

In bringing this new edition to readers, I must once more remember those who made certain that future generations would be able to learn from Netaji's book of life. Sisir Kumar Bose never stopped doing Netaji's work from the moment he helped his uncle escape from India in the quest for freedom until he passed away in 2000. He founded the Netaji Research Bureau in 1957 to preserve and disseminate the best traditions of India's freedom movement. He was ably supported throughout by Krishna Bose who helmed the Netaji Research Bureau with utmost grace and dignity as its Chairperson from 2000 until her own passing in 2020. In the early decades, the NRB publications department was run by the indefatigable Benode C. Chaudhuri and the archives cared for by the devoted Naga Sundaram of the Indian National Army. In my current responsibility as NRB Chairperson, I am very glad to be helped by Sumantra Bose, Director, Amitava Deshmukh, Treasurer, and members of the NRB Council. I would also like to record my gratitude to two senior staff members, Kartik Chakraborty, now retired, and Netai Sundar Thakur, who served for decades. Anirban Bhattacharjee, Anirban Chatterjee, Manohar Mandal, and Saswata Bandyopadhyay worked diligently in the library and archives of Netaji Research Bureau and Debangana Pal at Orient BlackSwan competently handled the production process. I would like to thank Nandini Rao, Uday Rao and Nilanjana Majumdar of Orient BlackSwan for their professionalism and dedication in partnering with the Netaji Research Bureau in making Netaji's works accessible to the new generation.

Editors' Introduction

Sisir K. Bose and Sugata Bose

Between his resignation as Congress President in Calcutta on 29 April 1939 and his escape from his Elgin Road home on the night of 16–17 January 1941, Subhas Chandra Bose sought to provide the Indian people with an alternative leadership at the national level in place of the old guard represented by the Gandhian High Command. This alternative was based on a commitment to uncompromising anti-imperialism in the current phase of Indian politics and undiluted socialism once freedom was won. Volume 10 of his *Collected Works* brings together the writings and speeches of this crucial phase in Bose's political life immediately prior to his emergence as the Netaji of India's army of liberation. The themes dealt with in his articles and speeches include the role of the left within the Indian independence movement, the Second World War as a conflict between rival imperialisms, and the need for Hindu-Muslim unity and Congress-Muslim League understanding in presenting a joint national demand to the British. Among the letters is his 'political testament' written just before undertaking a fast-unto-death in prison in November 1940, a set of candid letters from prison to his elder brother Sarat Chandra Bose giving his assessment of the moral failings of the Congress leadership and his final correspondence with Mahatma Gandhi in the month before his escape.

Having resigned as Congress President, Bose set up the Forward Bloc of the Indian National Congress. It is clear from his articles and speeches that he considered his Bloc to be an integral part of the Congress and his political aim was to convert the majority within the Congress to a radical point of view. He differed, therefore, from other leftist leaders like M.N. Roy who wanted a clean break from the Indian National Congress and also those who in the name of unity would not take the risk of pressuring the Congress leadership towards greater internal democracy. Since the various leftist groups — the Congress Socialist Party, the National Front (the communists) and the Radical League — refused to give up their distinct identities, Bose tried initially to unite the leftists, despite their differences, on the basis of a common minimum programme. Reacting to the news of 'disciplinary action' against him by the High Command barring him from holding elective office within the Congress for three years, he wrote on August 19, 1939:

> I shall cling to the Congress with even greater devotion than before and shall go on serving the Congress and the country as a servant of the nation. I appeal to my countrymen to come and join the Congress in their millions and to enlist as members of the Forward Bloc. Only by doing so shall we be able to convert the rank and file of the Congress to our point of view, secure a reversal of the present policy of Constitutionalism and Reformism and resume the national struggle for Independence with the united strength of the Indian people.[1]

On the same day he joined Rabindranath Tagore at the foundation-laying ceremony of 'Mahajati Sadan', House of the Nation, which he hoped would become 'the living-centre of all those beneficial activities [for] the emancipation of the individual and the nation'.[2]

A week before the outbreak of war in Europe Bose wrote that 'if war broke out between Germany and Poland the sympathy of the Indian people would be with the Poles'. But he then posed the question: 'Whatever our subjective reactions in this international conflict may be, what are we to do as a nation?' He wanted the Congress to emulate the European phenomenon of national cabinets and establish a composite rather than a homogeneous Working Committee. Bose was clear about the duty of the national leadership in the event of war:

> Great Britain and her apologists are now talking of self-determination for the Poles and if she goes to war, she will do so with the word 'Self-determination' on her lips. Is not this the time to remind our British rulers that east of the Suez Canal there is a land inhabited by an ancient and cultured people who have been deprived of their birthright of liberty and have been groaning under the British yoke? And is not this the time to tell the British

[1] See item 3 'Statement on Disciplinary Action' below.
[2] See item 4 'The House of the Nation — Mahajati Sadan' below.

> people and their Government that those who are slaves at home cannot fight for the freedom of others.[3]

After the outbreak of war Bose offered a series of sharp analyses of the unfolding international situation. At any critical moment of decision Bose felt a need to combine intuitive perception with rational understanding. As he put it, 'Where reason fails, instinct can guide us. Where instinct misleads by creating a mystical haze, reason can put us on the right path.'[4]

During the months of October and November 1939 Bose traversed the length and breadth of the country in an attempt to bring about a confluence between what he called the individual-mind and the mass-mind. He gave a fairly detailed account of his tour in a series of essays.[5] By December 1939 Bose was denouncing the vacillating policy of Congress leadership and warning against the Congress proposal of 'a Constituent Assembly under the aegis of an Imperialist Government' which he likened to the Irish Convention of Lloyd George. It was a 'stunt' to 'stave off a struggle' since 'behind the facade of a party-struggle within the Congress there [was] in reality a class-struggle going on all the time'.[6] A genuine Constituent Assembly, he argued, could only be convened after the seizure of power. In his Presidential address to the All-India Students' Conference in Delhi in January 1940, he decared:

> The silver lining in today's cloud consists of the fact that while the Congress leaders have been deliberating and vacillating, the Majlis-i-Ahrar of the Punjab has been acting. Nevertheless, there are people — and stay-at-homes at that — who do not scruple to cast aspersions on the patriotism of Indian Muslims as a body.

The Congress High Command, he charged, could 'think of a compromise with the Fascist British Government' but were bent on 'war to the bitter end' against the leftists. In an allusion to Gandhi's call at the time of the non-cooperation and Khilafat movement, he reminded his audience of 'a message once given to 'Young India' by one of our erstwhile Leftist leaders' who had said, 'Freedom comes to those who dare and act.'[7]

[3] See item 6 'The Need of the Hour' below.
[4] See item 8 'Heart Searcing' below.
[5] See item 9 'Glimpses of My Tour' below.
[6] See item 16 'The Correct Line' below.
[7] See item 18 'An Address to Students of India' below.

On the question of a Constituent Assembly Bose held up before his followers the examples of the Bolshevik withdrawal from the Russian Constituent Assembly in 1917 and the Sinn Fein rejection of Lloyd George's Irish Convention.[8] One thorn in the path of compromise, Bose noted, was the British penchant for using the minorities 'as a lever against the Congress'. But he felt that if a compromise with the Congress High Command could be worked out the Government 'would be prepared to let down the Muslim League':

> Should the British Government come to an understanding with Gandhiji behind the back of the Muslim League, it appears to us inevitable that both the Congress and the Muslim League will split. Within the Congress, Gandhiji and all those who stand by him will line up with British Imperialism. On the other side, the loyalist elements in the Muslim League, being under the thumb of the British Government, will break away from Mr Jinnah and the progressive section who are influential in the League Council today.

In case the Congress High Command compromised with British imperialism, Bose hoped for 'the voluntary withdrawal or expulsion from the Congress of the compromise-wallahs'. 'Why should we secede from the Congress,' he asked, 'and allow the backsliders to inherit the name and the traditions of that body.'[9]

When the next Congress session met at Ramgarh in March 1940, Bose held his own, mammoth Anti-Compromise Conference close to the site of the official meeting. 'The age of Imperialism,' he declared, 'is drawing to a close and the era of freedom, democracy and Socialism looms ahead of us. India, therefore, stands at one of the crossroads of history.' He launched a scathing attack in his Ramgarh address on the indecisive nature of the existing leadership at that fateful moment. He issued a call for a political consolidation of all genuine leftists. 'In the present phase of our movement,' he explained, 'Leftists will be all those who will wage an uncompromising fight with Imperialism . . . In the next phase of our movement, Leftism will be synonymous with socialism . . .'[10]

From April 1940 onwards, as the 'old imperialist power' — Britain — seemed to be discomfited by the 'new imperialist power'

[8] See item 19 'Danger Ahead' below.
[9] See item 22 'Stem the Rot' below.
[10] See item 26 'The Ramgarh Address' below.

— Germany,[11] Bose's attention turned more emphatically to ways of forging unity among the religious communities. March 1940, it must be remembered, had seen not only the rival Ramgarh meetings but also the passage of the Lahore Resolution by the All-India Muslim League. While being sharply critical of 'communalism', Bose does not seem to have been entirely persuaded by the mainstream Congress discourse on a singular nationalism. In a key essay published on May 4, 1940, he recalled that not so long ago 'prominent leaders of the Congress could be members and leaders of communal organizations like the Hindu Mahasabha and the Muslim League'. Lala Lajpat Rai, he pointed out, had been a leader of both the Congress and the Mahasabha, just as the Ali brothers were at one point leaders of the both the Congress and the League. In Bengal Maulana Akram Kkan had served as president of the Bengal Provincial Congress Committee while also being a leader of the Muslim League. He, therefore, did not wish to treat the 'communal organizations' as untouchable. He then went on to explain how the Bose group of the Bengal Congress had reached a pact with the Muslim League in the Calcutta Corporation which had infuriated 'a certain number of communally-minded Hindus'. He noted that for the past three years futile attempts had been made for an understanding between the Congress and the Muslim League. His own attempts to negotiate with Jinnah and the Muslim League in 1938 had been blessed by the Congress Working Committee and Mahatma Gandhi. 'Those who had not objected to that attempt which failed ultimately,' he wrote, 'now strongly object to the present attempt, because it has succeded.' His overall assessment of the Bose-League pact was as follows:

> We regard the present agreement with the Muslim League as a great achievement not in its actuality, but in its potentiality. During the last three years, we have been groping in the dark, but without success. Every time we have come up against a dead wall of communal prejudice and passion and we have been frustrated in our efforts. This time we have broken through the wall and through the fissure, a ray of light has poured in. There is now some hope that we may ultimately succeed in solving a problem which has proved well nigh insoluble to many. Great achievements are often born out of small beginnings.[12]

[11] See item 31 'The New Parade' below.

[12] See item 32 'Congress and Communal Organizations' below.

As Britain suffered reverses in the war, Bose noted in May 1940 that the problem of 'fighting British Imperialism' was likely to give way to the more pressing problem of 'internal unity and consolidation'. He wrote:

> There is today dark uncertainty before us as to our future fate. But all this will vanish in no time, if we can achieve two things — unity among Congressmen and a Hindu-Muslim settlement.[13]

Bose saw no prospect of enslaved India coming to the rescue of England. 'India,' he asserted, 'has first to save herself. And she can save herself only if the Hindus and Muslims put forward a joint demand for a provisional national government to whom all powers should be immediately transferred.' Only after India was 'strong eneough to save herself', could she 'lend a helping hand to other friendly countries'. 'Can the Congress and the Muslim League,' he asked, 'agree on this issue [of a joint Hindu-Muslim demand]?'[14] India, he felt, needed Deshbandhu C.R. Das's 'unbounded love which made him a friend of the people and which drew the Muslims and the backward classes so close to him'.[15]

It was in his Nagpur address as President of the second All-India Forward Bloc Conference in June 1940 that Subhas Chandra Bose provided the most elaborate statement on the duty of anti-imperialists in the context of 'the war between rival Imperialisms'. He stressed the need for national unity and solidarity. 'National unity,' he declared, 'will presuppose unity within the Congress on the basis of a dynamic programme of struggle and at the same time unity between the Congress and other organizations like the Muslim League.' He called for the establishment of 'a Citizen's Defence Corps organized on an all party basis' aimed at 'preserving internal peace, harmony and goodwill'. Defence of subjugated India against any foreign power should 'concern the Government only and not the people'. 'What interest can we have in fighting for the perpetuation of our own slavery,' he asked, 'for that is exactly what is implied in fighting to defend an enslaved India.'[16] At the end of June 1940 he re-iterated his demand for national cabinets at the centre and the provinces which 'will ensure internal peace and harmony during the transitional period and will pave

[13] See item 34 'Act Quickly' below.
[14] See item 37 'A Provisional National Government' below.
[15] See item 38 'Long Live Deshbandhu' below.
[16] See item 41 'The Nagpur Address' below.

the way to a lasting Hindu-Muslim settlement'. If it were not possible to set up a national cabinet at the Centre immediately, Bose was in favour of trying the experiment of national cabinets in the provinces. 'In the present dynamic situation,' he believed, 'national cabinets in the provinces will be a great help not only in maintaining internal harmony, not only in establishing Hindu-Muslim unity—but also in winning power at the Centre — should there be obstacles in the path of attaining Swaraj.'[17]

In his pursuit of Hindu-Muslim unity in Bengal Subhas Chandra Bose launched a movement on 3 July 1940 for the removal of the Holwell Monument from a public sqaure in Calcutta. Although the movement was successful, the British seized this opportunity to place Bose behind prison bars. During this, his last, spell in prison from July to early December 1940 he wrote a number of important letters and essays. In his letters to Sarat Chandra Bose he criticized the moral failings of the Congress leadership in a frank and forthright manner. In one letter he condemned Gandhism for its 'sanctimonious hypocrisy' and 'outrage on demoracy'.[18] In another he wrote:

> The more I think of Congress Politics, the more convinced I feel that in future we should devote more energy and time to fighting the High Command. If power goes into the hands of such mean, vindictive and unscrupulous persons when Swaraj is won, what will happen to the country . . . .We should concentrate on fighting the Congress High Command now and to that end, we should make alliances with other political parties wherever and whenever possible.[19]

But it was his determination to fight British imperialism by taking advantage of the international war crisis that led Subhas Chandra Bose to go on an indefinite hunger strike in an attempt to force the government to release him. The letter he wrote to the Governor of Bengal on 26 November 1940 before commencing his fast remains one of the most stirring documents of sacrificial patriotism. ' . . . [N]obody can lose,' he wrote, 'through suffering and sacrifice. If he does lose anything of the earth earthy, he will gain much more in return by becoming the heir to a life immortal.'[20]

[17] See item 42 'Task before the Country' below.
[18] See letter to Sarat Chandra Bose, 24 October 1940, below.
[19] See letter to Sarat Chandra Bose, 31 October 1940, below.
[20] See 'My Political Testament' below.

The government released Bose on 5 December 1940, having decided to play 'a cat and mouse policy' of rearresting him as soon as he recovered his health. His home on Elgin Road was put under round-the-clock surveillance. Between his release from prison and his escape on 16–17 January 1941 he received an interesting letter from Jayaprakash Narain and wrote a couple of important ones to Viceroy Linithgow. By far the most fascinating, however, is his final exchange of letters with Mahatma Gandhi. When Bose wrote to Gandhi on 23 December 1940 offering cooperation in any future movement, he had already finalized plans for his escape from India. 'You are irrepressible,' Bapu replied to Subhas on 29 December 1940, 'whether ill or well. Do get well before going in for fireworks.'[21] By this time Subhas Chandra Bose had already completed preparations for his fireworks and was simply waiting for the right moment to light the fuse.

[21] See letter from Mahatma Gandhi, 29 December 1940, below.

Speeches, Articles and Statements

1
Why Forward Bloc

Signed editorial in the *Forward Bloc*, 5 August 1939

The Indian National Congress represents a movement which has sprung from the soil of India. It is the political organ of the Indian people and embodies their hopes, aspirations and ideals. It is an organization which has unlimited potentialities of growth and development-potentialities which are as limitless as those of the Indian nation itself. The growth and development of the Congress has taken place as the result of an inner urge though it has been stimulated by external factors. It is this inner urge which is primarily responsible for the birth of the Forward Bloc. Neither personal factors nor accidental circumstances can account for this new phenomenon in Indian politics. The Forward Bloc has appeared because the Congress must enter on a new phase in its evolutionary process.

Now, how does this growth and development of the Congress take place? What is the law underlying it? Several theories may be put forward by way of explanation, but the one that appeals to me most and which in my view approximates to reality more than any other — is the Hegelian Dialectic. Progress is neither unilinear, nor is it always peaceful in character. Progress often takes place through conflict.

Out of the conflict between 'thesis' and 'antithesis', 'synthesis' is born. This 'synthesis' in its turn becomes the 'thesis' of next phase of evolution. This 'thesis' throws up an 'antithesis' and the conflict is resolved by a further 'synthesis'. Thus the wheels of progress move on and on.

Those who in season and out of season talk of unity and appeal for unity under all circumstances and at any price, lose sight of the fundamental law of evolution. We have to distinguish between real unity and false unity — between the unity of action and unity of inaction — between the unity which makes for progress and the unity which brings stagnation. Today the slogan of 'unity at any price and under all circumstances' is a convenient slogan in the mouths of those who have lost dynamism and revolutionary urge. Let us not be led astray by its fascinating appeal.

In every movement that is living or dynamic, there is a latent Left — a latent 'antithesis', if you will. This latent Left Wing becomes manifest in the fullness of time and through it, further growth and development takes place. To determine how best the Left Wing could be nurtured under a given set of circumstances requires political, and sometimes philosophical, insight. It often happens that through compromise and co-operation with the Right Wing, the Left Wing gathers strength and extends its influence. In a different set of circumstances, this may not prove possible. It may then be necessary for the Left Wing to differentiate itself from the Right and consolidate and expand its strength and following. In such circumstances, a sharp conflict, though painful for the time being, may in reality be conducive to progress and be, in fact, unavoidable. Organizational development invariably necessitates the appearance and growth of a Left Wing. Through co-operation with the Right or through conflict with it, the Left must continue to grow till it succeeds in capturing the organization or in winning the Right over to its side. When this is achieved and the possibilities of the Left Wing (now the majority party) are exhausted, history must repeat itself and a new Left Wing must emerge and ultimately oust the Left Wingers of yesterday. The Gandhiites of 1920 were the Left Wing in the Congress, but it does not follow therefrom that they are the Left Wing today. The Leftists of yesterday often, if not always, become the Rightists of tomorrow. To say that there should be no differentiation between Right and Left within the Congress of today and to argue that this Congress as a whole is Left — is talking arrant nonsense. It is time we faced facts — however unpleasant they may be.

Between 1936 and 1938 the Left Wing of the Congress has grown and developed as a result of co-operation with the Right. In September, 1938, the cry was first raised on behalf of the Right that co-operation with the Left was no longer possible and that the Left was becoming too noisy and troublesome to collaborate with. This new cry ultimately reached climax in 1939, when the Right Wing deliberately decided to end co-operation with the Left. What else is the deeper significance of the present-day insistence of the

Rightists on a homogeneous Cabinet or Working Committee? For three years they could cooperate with the Left, but they cannot do so any more. Why? Because the Right Wing can no longer view with equanimity the growing strength of the Left in the Congress.

When the All-India Congress Committee met in Calcutta on the 29th April 1939, to settle this problem of the new Cabinet or Working Committee it was found that the Left wanted to cooperate with the Right and their slogan was that of a composite or mixed Cabinet. The Right, however, were not prepared to cooperate with the Left and their slogan was that of a homogeneous Cabinet. Consequently, it was the Rightists who ended compromise, co-operation and unity. The Right Wing today want nothing less than complete surrender on the part of the Left. Should the Left agree to it on the score of unity? If they do so, what would the consequences be? Would we thereby lubricate the wheels of progress or would we buttress reaction within our ranks?

The Right Wing having refused co-operation with the Left we Leftists would be justified in surrendering to them on the plea of unity, only if the Right Wing still had a dynamic role to play. But it is unfortunately clear from the correspondence I had with Mahatma Gandhi in March and April last that he no longer thinks in terms of a coming struggle. The Ministers and their guides who now dominate the Congress do not contemplate a struggle either. To surrender to the Right under such circumstances and preserve the external facade of unity would in reality amount to perpetuating stagnation and reaction within the Congress. We cannot do so. We should not do so.

The time has therefore come for the Left Wing to differentiate itself from the Right and proceed to consolidate itself. When this is done, the Left will secure a majority within the Congress and then proceed to resume the struggle for independence in the name of the Indian National Congress. This is the task of the Left Wing today. To fulfil this task the Forward Bloc has come into existence.

It was open to the existing Leftist parties to accept this role of Left consolidation, but for some reason or other, they did not do so. Last year, when the proposal to form a left Bloc was being discussed by Left Wing Congressmen — it looked as if the Left Wing parties would accept this idea and try to put it into effect. But later on, they changed their mind. It then became indispensably necessary to inaugurate the Forward Bloc with the help of fresh elements from the Left. The Forward Bloc is therefore not only the creature of an inner urge within the Congress, but it is also the product of historical necessity. Moreover, the circumstance of the present day warrant its emergence. Having been born in this manner and under such circumstances, the Forward Bloc cannot die. It is an inevitable phenomenon in our political evolution. It has come to stay and it will grow from strength to strength as the days roll by. Let those who doubt the truth of what I say have patience and watch the future history of the Congress and of the Forward Bloc.

2
The Role of Forward Bloc

12 August 1939

After a number of preliminary skirmishes, the Left Wing under the leadership of Mahatma Gandhi succeeded in capturing the Indian National Congress in 1920. That was the signal for several of the erstwhile leaders like Messrs. Jinnah, B.C. Pal and B. Chakravarti to walk out of the Congress. The Left Wing became the dominant party in the Congress and for a time commanded an overwhelming majority. With the suspension of the Civil Disobedience Movement in 1922, a rift occurred within the majority party and, over the issue of carrying the fight into the Legislatures, it split into two groups — the Swarajists and the No-changers. After a time the differences were made up through the Congress accepting the Swarajist plan of extending the fighting front to the Legislatures.

With the publication of the Nehru Committee's Report in 1928, in which the majority of the members advocated a Constitution for India based on Dominion Status, a Left Wing emerged in the form of the Independence League. At the annual session of the Congress held in Calcutta in December 1928, the members of the League endeavoured but failed to induce the Congress to alter its creed so that Independence would be declared in unmistakable language to be the goal of the Congress. The opposition to this move came from the main body in the Congress led by Mahatma Gandhi. The conflict with the Independence League went on for a year, till at the Lahore session of the Congress held in December 1929, the Congress at the instance of Mahatmaji, adopted Independence as its goal.

This compromise enabled all sections in the Congress to join hands and march shoulder to shoulder in the Civil Disobedience Campaign which was launched in 1930.

The suspension of struggle in 1933 and the adoption of a parliamentary programme by the All-India Congress Committee in 1934 provoked a revolt from the Left. The Congress Socialist Party then came into existence and, thanks to its timely appearance and its dynamic activity, the drift towards Constitutionalism was checked to a large extent. The Congress Socialist Party soon became the rallying-centre for the Leftist elements in the Congress.

From 1934 to 1937, the Congress Socialist Party made considerable headway both in numbers and influence. But in 1938, at the Haripura Session of the Congress held in February, it was found that the C.S.P. was no longer forging ahead. In my Presidential Address at the Haripura Congress, I observed that the role of the C.S.P. within the Congress should be an anti-imperialist Left Wing role and not a Socialist role and only by playing the former role, would it continue to make headway.

Socialist and Communist friends with whom this matter was discussed after the Haripura Congress agreed with this view. It was generally felt that all progressive, radical and anti-imperialist elements in the Congress, who might not be ready to join the Socialist or Communist Party, should be organized on the basis of a common minimum programme. I felt, further, that only by that means could the onslaught of the Right be resisted and the soil prepared for the growth of a Marxist Party.

The Gandhi Seva Sangh, which may be regarded as the 'steel frame' of the present majority party (or Gandhi Party) in the Congress, held an important Conference at Delang, in Orissa, in March 1938. At this Conference the Gandhi Seva Sangh decided to launch an offensive against the Left. The Sangh decided, among other things, to send its agents into the labour field with a view to ousting those trade-unionists who stood for a class-conscious trade-union movement in this country. It decided also to depute its prominent members to capture provincial and other Congress organizations in the country.

The parliamentary programme adopted by the All India Congress Committee in 1934 found its culmination in the acceptance of ministerial office in the provinces in 1937. This enabled the Right Wing to so consolidate its position and strengthen its influence and prestige as to launch an offensive against the Left in 1938. Against this determined attack, the Left could hope to preserve its existence, only if it were consciously organized and disciplined.

If all the progressive, radical and anti-imperialist elements in the Congress had rallied together on the platform of the Congress Socialist Party, then matters would have been greatly simplified. But this did not happen. Because of this, the idea of a Left Bloc for organizing all the Left elements on the basis of a common minimum programme was mooted after the Haripura Congress. If the existing Leftist Parties had undertaken the responsibility of developing the Left Bloc (now renamed as the Forward Bloc) — then the task of Left-consolidation would by now have proceeded apace.

But though individuals or groups may fail us, the cause cannot be allowed to suffer to be neglected. Hence the Forward Bloc has been formed with such Left elements as are now available. There is no doubt that the Bloc will grow and expand with unprecedented rapidity, despite the many obstacles that beset its path. And the time will soon come when even those who are hesitating to join today, will shake off their vacillation and take the plunge. Left-consolidation, winning over the majority in the Congress, and resumption of the national struggle — these represent the three-fold task before the Forward Bloc and before the Left in the Congress. Let those who criticize us or pick holes produce a better alternative. We shall not hesitate to accept it. We are afraid, however, that no other alternative is possible.

The Congress has to be saved from the clutches of the Right which has given up the idea of a struggle and is now thinking in terms of Constitutionalism and Reformism. Only the Left can preserve the revolutionary character of the Congress and bring about an early resumption of the fight for national freedom.

Today, in certain quarters, the word 'Socialism' has become cheap. One can even find Socialists in some provinces who are the henchmen of the Ministers. Let us therefore beware of Rightists who masquerade in the cloak of Socialism. What is wanted is deeds, not words. Genuine Socialists must play an anti-imperialist Left Wing role in their day to day activity. Uttering Leftist slogans and making spicy speeches will not suffice by themselves.

Forward Bloc will rally all progressive, radical and anti-imperialist elements in the Congress, whether they be Socialists or not. Through this consolidation, the people will equip themselves for the anti-imperialist struggle that will bring India her birthright of liberty. But the attainment of political Independence will not mean the dissolution of Bloc. It will only mean a new phase in its life and activity. And that phase will undoubtedly be a Socialist one.

3
Statement on Disciplinary Action

19 August 1939

I welcome the decision of the Working Committee virtually expelling me from the Congress for three years. This decision is the logical consequence of the process of 'Right-consolidation' which has been going on for the last few years and which has been accentuated by the acceptance of ministerial office in the provinces. The action of the Working Committee has served to expose the real character of the present majority party in the Congress and the role they have been playing. The punishment accorded to me is, however, thoroughly justified from their point of view. By trying to warn the country about the continued drift towards Constitutionalism and Reformism, by protesting against resolutions which seek to kill the revolutionary spirit of the Congress, by working for the cause of Left-consolidation and, last but not least, by consistently appealing to the country to prepare for the coming struggle — I have committed a crime for which I have to pay the penalty. The sentence meted out to me may have come as a shock to the vast majority of our countrymen, but not to me. It has appeared as a perfectly logical development in the struggle between Constitutionalism and mass struggle and as an inevitable phase in our political evolution. Consequently, I do not find within myself the slightest trace of bitterness or anger. I am only sorry that the Working Committee did not realize that this sort of action should hurt them more than it should hurt me.

To members of the Forward Bloc, to Leftists in general and to the public at large I would appeal to remain calm and collected in face of the above provocation and to continue working with increasing patience and perseverance. What does it matter if I am victimized today? I shall cling to the Congress with even greater devotion than before and shall go on serving the Congress and the country as a servant of the nation. I appeal to my countrymen to come and join the Congress in their millions and to enlist as members of the Forward Bloc. Only by doing so shall we be able to convert the rank and file in the Congress to our point of view, secure a reversal of the present policy of Constitutionalism and Reformism and resume the national struggle for Independence with the united strength of the Indian people.

In conclusion, I would request the public not to forget that what has happened today is but a repetition of history. Years ago, Left Wingers were once expelled from the Congress, But they came back in large numbers before long and the Congress then had to accept their policy and programme. I feel no doubt in my mind that the cause which we Leftists represent is a just cause and it will prosper more through such action on the part of the Working Committee than otherwise. The wonderful response that the Forward Bloc has received from one end of the country to the other makes me feel confident that before long we shall be able to rejuvenate the Congress, restore to it its revolutionary character and role and resume the struggle for Independence in the name of the Indian National Congress.

4
The House of the Nation — 'Mahajati Sadan'

Speech made in Bengali at the foundation-laying ceremony of 'Mahajati Sadan' by Rabindranath Tagore on 19 August 1939

Today we assemble here to witness the beginning of the fulfilment of a long-cherished dream. Those who for years have toiled and suffered — laboured and sacrificed — so that India may be free, have long wished for an abode to provide shelter and protection for their activities and to serve as a visible symbol of their hopes and ideals-dreams and aspirations. More than once has the attempt been made to give us the home that we have wanted, but it has failed and it has been left to you to lay the foundation stone of the 'House of Nation'. It is indeed a rare piece of fortune that we have you here in our midst this afternoon to sow with your hands the seed that will bear the fruit with which our nation will be nurtured in the days to come.

On this auspicious occasion we cannot help casting our eyes towards the past and the future of our people. From this soil sprang the movement that was at once the Reformation and the Renaissance of modern India. It was a movement which knew no provincial boundaries and which transcended the national frontier of India as well. Was not the message of Ram Mohan and Ram Krishna — a message for humanity? Was it not the voice of awakened India that spoke through them? We are the heirs of their spiritual and cultural heritage and we are conscious of it.

The liberated soul of modern India wanted to manifest itself in action, but found itself enchained by the state on the one side and society on the other. Then emerged the movement for the political and social emancipation of the Indian people. For this movement, our soil was not less fertile than it was for the earlier movement — the Reformation and Renaissance of modern India.

Twenty years of agitation after the birth of the Indian National Congress in 1885, ushered in a new era in our political history — the age of self-help and self-reliance, of Swadeshi and Boycott. The pressure of governmental repression on the one side and of the Partition of Bengal on the other soon broke down the walls of prudence and the maddened youths of India sought inspiration along another path — the path of armed revolt so well-known in history. Before the lapse of a decade, we again entered on a new age — the age of non-violent non-cooperation and Satyagraha (or Civil Disobedience).

Today clouds have darkened our political firmament and the Congress stands at one of the crossroads of history. Shall we hark back again to the days of Constitutionalism which we thought we had discarded in 1920? Or shall we continue along the path of mass-movement which ends in mass-struggle? I shall not enter into a controversy. I shall only say this that the awakened masses of India cannot give up the method of self-help and self-reliance, of mass-organization and mass-struggle which has given them the success they have won and which will bring them the greater success that is yet to come. Above all, they cannot give up their birthright of freedom for a sordid bargain with alien Imperialism.

Today our people dream not only of a free India, but also of an Indian State founded on the principles of justice and equality and of a new social and political order which will embody all that we hold noble and sacred. With the voice of eternity, you, Sir, have all along given passionate expression to the hopes and aspirations of our regenerate nation. Yours has been the message of undying youth. You have not only written poetry and produced art — but you have also lived poetry and art. You are not only India's poet but you are also the poet of humanity. Who can understand better than yourself what surges within us today as we assemble to witness the beginning of the fulfilment of a dream? Who else can perform this sacred ceremony for which we have gathered in your presence. Gurudev, we welcome you as the high-priest in today's national festival; proceed to lay with your hands the foundation stone of 'Mahajati Sadan'. Give us your blessings so that we may be able to make this the 'House of the Nation' — the living-centre of all those beneficial activities which will bring about the emancipation of the individual and of the nation, as well as the all-round development of India's personality and nationhood. Bless us that we may hasten along the path that will lead to India's liberty and to our national self-fulfilment.

5
Our Critics

Signed editorial in the *Forward Bloc*, 19 August 1939

Standing as we do for the right of legitimate criticism and believing as we do that healthy criticism is indispensable for growth and development, we welcome the criticisms that have been hurled at the Forward Bloc since its very inception. We have carefully examined them and have endeavoured to profit by them. We have also tried to answer them to the best of our ability. We are gratified to find that, in consequence thereof, several of our erstwhile critics are now our supporters.

But it appears that a certain class of critics are determined not to be satisfied and are going on repeating their charges. Most of them are Rightists, nevertheless among them are to be found men who are generally looked upon as Leftists. It is not difficult to imagine what motives inspire such incorrigible Rightist critics, but it is difficult to understand those who call themselves Leftists, yet seem to find a peculiar pleasure in attacking the Forward Bloc.

In the earlier stages, it was urged that the birth of the Forward Bloc was due to personal factors and factional differences — that the Bloc did not have a positive programme and was in reality an 'anti-Bloc' — that the Forward Bloc accepted the Gandhian policy and programme and still wanted to set up a new organization within the Congress in order to create unnecessary split and that the Forward Bloc was set up with the sole object of fighting the Congress Working Committee or its inner circle, the Congress High Command. Since the All-India Conference of the Forward Bloc held in Bombay on the 22nd June, such criticisms have been virtually silenced as the principles, policy and programme of the Bloc have been clarified beyond the shadow of a doubt. But criticisms of a different type have been persisting, despite effective replies repeated from many a platform.

These criticisms can be classed under two heads. The burden of one set of criticism is that the Forward Bloc is drawing into its fold opportunists and fascists. To accuse the Forward Bloc of opportunism is amusing indeed. A member of the Bloc has to fight on two fronts — British Imperialism and Congress bureaucratism and has to suffer persecution at the hands of both. From the personal point of view he has nothing to gain, but everything to lose. The line of least resistance and the path of opportunism, however, takes one straight to the Rightist camp. There you find Congress Ministers who had been openly working against the Congress, till the Congress eschewed Satyagraha (or Civil Disobedience) and took to parliamentarianism. You find men who never went within miles of a British jail. You find multi-millionaires who pose as patriots, because they can call themselves Gandhiites. You find Congressmen who accept nomination to local bodies through the mercy of Congress ministers (as in Central Provinces) though acceptance of Government nomination to local bodies was definitely banned by the Congress. And you find Congress ministers (as in Bombay), making J.P.s by the score in order to rope in more opportunists, though the Congress had long ago advised Congressmen not to become J.P.s or Honorary Magistrates. What are the zeminders (landlords), industrial magnates and multi-millionaires who now hang about our Congress ministers, if they are not opportunists? And are not the British-owned newspapers of Bombay and Madras, that have overnight become ministerial organs, blatant and undisguised opportunists? Verily, verily, one can urge and maintain that it is the Rightists and their allies who are the real opportunists.

And referring to our so-called Leftists, may it not be pointed out that, to talk as a Leftist and act as a Rightist — to seek to overthrow Gandhism by words and then succumb to the first Rightist rebuke — to boycott the Working Committee and yet take part in its deliberations — are perhaps brilliant examples of opportunism.

And now about the fascists. It is difficult to understand what exactly is meant by 'fascists' in an Indian context, if the word is used in its scientific or technical sense. Nevertheless, if by 'fascist' is indicated those who call themselves Hitlers, super-Hitlers, or budding Hitlers, then one may say that these specimens of humanity are to be found in the Rightist camp.

The burden of the other set of criticisms is that the Forward Bloc is associating with the anti-Congress elements in the country and will soon break away from the Congress and set up a parallel organization with their help. Those who intend condemning the Forward Bloc in this indirect manner as an anti-Congress organization, know full well that without being a member of the Congress, one cannot be a member of the Bloc and that one has to be a radical, besides being a Congressman, in order to be a member of the Forward Bloc. Moreover, I have repeated from any number of platforms that in no circumstances are we going to break away from the Congress. Our task is to convert the Congress — not to desert it. Our critics know this as well as we do, but they go on repeating their accusation, hoping that if there is sufficient mud-slinging, some of it will stick in the long run.

It may perhaps be that our critics are jealous of the fact that while their Rightist friends are unable to attract the minorities and other sections of the Indian community to their fold, the Forward Bloc has, from the very beginning, succeeded in winning their sympathy to a large extent. These sections, who are outside the Congress, have comparatively speaking, more faith in the Left Wing of the Congress than in the Right Wing. And if they come into the Congress in the near future, it will be a Congress under the aegis of the Left Wing. This is perhaps because the Left Wing fights for Democracy, stands for a mass-movement and a programme which will benefit the masses, and declares uncompromising hostility to the Federal Scheme.

But this game will not do. You cannot deceive even the Indian public today in this way. They are no longer as unsophisticated as you would wish them to be. Consequently, these critics notwithstanding, the Forward Bloc is forging ahead and will continue to forge ahead. The only alternative to Right-consolidation and

Constitutionalism is the programme of the Forward Bloc. The three-fold task of the Bloc is Left-consolidation, winning over the majority in the Congress to our viewpoint and resumption of the national struggle in the name and with the united strength of the Congress. If you can suggest a better alternative than that offered by the Forward Bloc, by all means do so. We have an open mind and are ready to be convinced. But it is no use indulging in the negative role of a carping critic. That way lie futility and disaster.

6
The Need of the Hour

Signed editorial in the *Forward Bloc*, 26 August 1939

As I write, who knows what is happening in Europe? There are reports that Herr Hitler has delivered an ultimatum to Poland. This is quite possible — nay, probable. If this has happened, how is Poland going to react? With the Russo-German Non-Aggression Pact staring them in the face, will the freedom-loving Poles fight for their sacred soil? Or will they go the ways of the Czechs? If Marshal Pilsudski had been alive, one could have safely predicted war despite the Non-Aggression pact and despite the German ultimatum. But the first Marshal of Poland is no more and it remains to be seen how his people will act in his absence. If the Poles had not been as emotional as they actually are, one should have banked on peace based on surrender to Germany. But today, no safe forecast is possible, though it is quite on the cards that under diplomatic pressure from Great Britain and France, Poland may finally decide that discretion is the better part of valour.

It would be correct to say that if war broke out between Germany and Poland the sympathy of Indian people would be with the Poles. It would take Germany a lot to convince us that the Polish Corridor or any territory over which there may be war is now inhabited by more Germans than Poles. But so far as Danzig is concerned, the German claim is certainly indisputable and if war breaks out over the issue of Danzig alone, Germany will have an unanswerable case before the bar of world opinion.

Whatever our subjective reactions in this international conflict may be, what are we to do as a nation? Are we to go on cogitating and wrangling while the conflagration spreads from one end of the world to the other? If Russians and Germans, who till yesterday were sworn enemies, can bury the hatchet when confronted with a world-crisis, cannot the two wings of the Congress sink their differences and join hands for leading the nation towards Purna Swaraj? Will non-party 'national' Cabinets remain an exclusively European phenomenon? In such emergency, will not Congressmen learn to discard homogeneous Cabinets and form composite Cabinets instead? The answer to this can be given only by the members of the Congress Working Committee and their mentor, Mahatma Gandhi. The Leftists have always stood for the principle of a composite Cabinet, but they have been ignored so far.

It would be well for all concerned to realize that if the majority party in the Congress and its leaders do not rise to the occasion and give the proper lead to the nation in this critical hour, they would be lending confirmation to the belief that is now widely held that the Right Wing of the Congress is aiming at a compromise with British Imperialism. Great Britain and her apologists are now talking of self-determination for the Poles and if she goes to war, she will do so with the word 'Self-determination' on her lips. Is not this the time to remind our British rulers that east of the Suez Canal there is a land inhabited by an ancient and cultured people who have been deprived of their birth right of liberty and have been groaning under the British yoke? And is not this the time to tell the British people and their Government that those who are slaves at home cannot fight for the freedom of others?

It is time to inform Britain in the simplest language possible that India is not going to allow her resources in men, money and material to be exploited for an imperialist war. The Congress is pledged to war-resistance, though that resistance must necessarily be of a non-violent character. It is therefore not enough to say, as the Working Committee has recently done, that we shall not assist British Imperialism in a war-emergency. We have to go further and reaffirm our resolve to non-violently resist enforced participation in an imperialist war.

The Working Committee has called upon the members of the Central Legislature to abstain from attending the next session of the Central Assembly and the Council of State. This is, of course, better than doing nothing — but it is utterly inadequate. The members of the Central Legislature should resign their seats forthwith as a protest against the war-preparations of the Government of India and should appeal to the electorate for a fresh mandate on this issue. This would stimulate political consciousness among the masses and would make the question of India's participation in war a live issue with even the man in the street.

If war does not break out during the next few days and if the present storm blows over, we should not be so foolish as to think that the crisis has been finally resolved. International tension may increase once again over the issue of Roumania or the German demand for colonies. Moreover, if Herr Hitler wants a war, he will never suffer from want of a convenient issue. Consequently, we, in India, should realize that the present international tension is a continuous one and we should prepare ourselves accordingly.

In a statement which has appeared in today's papers I have made an offer to Mahatma Gandhi and the Working Committee. I have stated therein that if they adopt a bold policy and take up with the British Government the issue of India's National Demand, we shall sink all our differences and line up as humble camp followers. And if the need arises, we shall gladly surrender all the posts that we Leftists may now be occupying. We shall anxiously await their answer.

Meanwhile let us tell the British Government in unmistakable language that only a free India can determine what our policy should be in the event of war. War or no war, we demand our freedom and we must have it.

7
The Friend's Voice

Signed editorial in the *Forward Bloc*, 2 September 1939

'The Friend of India' — better known as '*The Statesman*' — has for some time past been writing brilliant articles on foreign policy and the present international situation. It has also been giving estimable advice to the people of India as to how they should behave at this critical juncture. The writer is particularly thankful to 'The Friend of India' for the attention and importance it has been pleased to bestow on a small man like himself.

It is strange world that we live in and a world that is changing from hour to hour. Time was when Moscow was a bugbear to our

'Friend' and the story was deliberately propagated that Moscow gold was regularly passing into the hands of political malcontents in India. Since the rise of Herr Hitler to power, he has displaced both Stalin and Trotsky, and in recent months, the bogey of Berlin — and along with Berlin, of Rome and Tokyo — has seized our 'Friend' and caused it many a sleepless night. Simultaneously, Moscow has become a good boy and Moscow gold been transferred to Berlin, Rome and Tokyo. Our 'Friend's' imagination has, of late, begun to conjure up scenes of gold from Berlin-Rome-Tokyo pouring into India and poisoning the minds of the docile and good-natured people of this country. But one wonders what 'The Friend of India' will think or say now. Will Moscow remain a good boy or will it fall from favour because of association with vile Berlin after the Russo-German Non-Aggression Pact?

'Friend' has made the remarkable discovery — or should one say, invention? — that the moment war breaks out, Indian malcontents will declare for Herr Hitler and line up behind him and the Berlin-Rome-Tokyo Axis. The British people are not particularly reputed for their imagination, but our 'Friend' is evidently an exception — for exceptions prove the rule. His theory is interesting indeed and deserves credit.

Since disgruntled Indians will begin shouting 'Heil Hitler' as soon as there is war in Europe, 'Friend' has recommended capital punishment for them. Failing capital punishment, they should be safely lodged behind prison bars. Then all will be well both in India and Europe. India should certainly be grateful to such a 'Friend'.

Though these fulminations of 'The Friend of India' have afforded us considerable entertainment, we must confess that they have, nevertheless, a sinister significance. This paper often functions as the mouthpiece and apologist of the Government of India and enables us to have a peep into the official mind of Great Britain. What 'Friend' has said should not therefore be lightly dismissed as merely a piece of amusement.

In a recent article we are told by 'Friend' that the outbreak of war should not mean the postponement of Federation. The journal has, of course, been a consistent advocate of the Federal Scheme as the one thing which will solve the Indian problem. It has been considered unnecessary to enquire as to what the Indian people themselves think about this solution of their own problem. Perhaps our 'Friend' was distressed to hear it being mooted in certain official circles that with the advent of war, the Federal Scheme should automatically stand postponed and this appeared to 'Friend' as nothing short of a calamity. Consequently, it has been at pains to convince people that on the contrary, war should expedite the inauguration of Federation. The point that will strike everybody is as to how Federation could be introduced when the Leftists are running up and down the country. This difficulty was previously solved by 'Friend' through the suggestion that capital punishment or incarceration should suffice to silence the mischief-mongers and thereby pave the way for the easy advent of the Federal Scheme.

If the above suggestion finds favour with the British Government or if they are an indication of the official mind, then what will happen in the event of war is that all the Leftists will be given short shrift by the British Government — not metaphorically but literally. When the coast is found clear, Federation will steam in and will be welcomed by the prospective ministers with drums beating and colours flying — not the colours of the Indian National Congress, but of the British Empire which stands for peace, democracy and progress.

But there is after all, nothing fundamentally new in this scheme. It is just another illustration of the timeworn method of repression-cum-conciliation, with the only difference that this time the method to be adopted is more drastic than before.

Now what have we to say to such a course of treatment? The patient must, of course, have a say in the matter. In this present case, we might as well tell our 'Friend' that if this superb method has failed every time in history, is there much hope that it will go down with the Indian people this time? They are not quite like dumb-driven cattle today and they may refuse to fit into the scheme prepared for them by others. Moreover, one cannot ignore altogether the temperament of the people. A drastic dose of repression applied to one section of the people may not necessarily frighten the rest of the people or another section thereof. It may, indeed, have the opposite effect of making them truculent. In that event, who will welcome Federation with drums and colours? A preliminary treatment of repression may make it impossible for even pro-federationists to feeling to accept the Federal Scheme, with or without modification, owing to feeling of revolt in the popular mind.

No, 'Friend'! the solution is not so simple as you may think now, or as Lord Willingdon once thought. The Leftists are not such a negligible factor in the country as you would like them to be.

Suppression of the Leftists may be possible, but it may upset your apple-cart also. Thank you for revealing your plans and for forewarning us. We assure you that we, on our part, are prepared for all contingencies and we are confident of winning our liberty, with or without the 'Friend's' help.

8
Heart Searching

Signed editorial in the *Forward Bloc*, 28 October 1939

In the life of every nation there come occasions when momentous decisions have to be taken which may make or mar its future. It often happens that on such occasions the final decision has to be made by a few individuals or even by one individual. What would have happened to Russia if Lenin had given a different lead in 1917 is today a matter for speculation or conjecture.

How is this tremendous responsibility to be discharged by those who hold the future of their nation in the hollow of their hands? They have naturally to think and think deeply. They have to look fore and aft — to consider possible alternatives and to weigh the probable consequences. But even then it may be difficult to decide. Not every leader can make a bold and clear decision when face to face with a crisis. But even if one has that capacity, the human intellect may fail to supply us with all the facts and considerations that are necessary for arriving at a definite conclusion.

We are sometimes told that where reason fails, instinct or intuition succeeds. The great heroes of history have felt their way through impenetrable darkness and their decisions, based on instinct or intuition, have been justified by subsequent events.

There is a great deal of truth in this assertion. Within the ken of our limited experience, we have seen leaders make striking decisions in crucial moments, being guided solely by unerring political instinct and such decisions have proved to be correct in the light of subsequent developments. Now what is this elusive instinct or intuition? Is it something mystical — something beyond one's comprehension — something which is inborn? To a certain extent it is inborn. The successful painter or musician has a delicacy of touch and a fineness of perception which cannot be wholly explained by education or training. If he does not start with an innate artistic tendency, he can never reach the heights of artistic excellence. So also in the case of the political fighter. He must have a political sense at the very outset.

But instinct has to be sharpened by training and that training has to be continuous. If instinct or intuition has served as an unerring guide on half-a-dozen occasions, that is no guarantee that it will always do so. Now what is it that can help to make one's political instinct as faultless as possible?

It is absolutely necessary, in the first place, that one should be perfectly selfless in his pursuit. If instinct is warped by selfish considerations, whether conscious or unconscious, it will not lead — but mislead. And when self dominates instinct, disaster is ahead of us. Consequently, when playing with the destinies of a nation one should endeavour to be as selfless as humanly possible.

Secondly, one should try to merge one's individual consciousness in mass-consciousness — so that the mass-mind may speak through our individual instinct or intuition. This is not an easy thing for the ordinary man. Fortunately, some people can merge their identity more easily in the life of the people than others and they can accordingly have a better understanding of the mass-mind. We know from our own experience that, all things being equal, that leader is more influential, more powerful and more successful, who has a better appreciation of mass-psychology. This appreciation is not possible through reason alone, but requires the help of instinct as well.

It is possible to so discipline and train one's mind that one can be in tune with the mass-mind. But this entails continuous effort and vigilance. Imagine a torrential stream breaking through a mountain gorge. Cannot the drops composing that cataract merge their identity in and put themselves in tune with the stream as a whole? Imagine the elan vital of Bergson. Cannot the human spirit plunge into the heart of reality and identify itself with its unceasing flow? Imagine the Absolute Idea of Hegel unfolding itself through a world-process. Cannot the individual merge himself in that evolutionary development and thereby comprehend it? Imagine the 'Divine Shakti' manifesting itself in a kaleidoscopic creation. Cannot the human soul seek to attain oneness with it in thought and feeling?

In short, it is possible for the individual mind to put itself in tune with the mass-mind. But this instinctive or intuitive perception may go wrong and may lead us on to the blind alley of mysticism if we are not mentally fortified with a rational understanding of the evolution of the world and of man. We must therefore, in the third place, have a rational understanding — based on analysis, criticism and extensive study — of history. Where reason fails, instinct can guide us. Where instinct misleads by creating a mystical haze, reason can put us on the right path.

Fourthly, we must have a correct appreciation of international events and developments. We are living in an age when frontiers have, in a way, been obliterated. The world is today one unit. What happens in one corner has far-reaching repercussions throughout our globe. Consequently, even if we are in tune with the mass-mind, even if we have a correct understanding of historical development, we may still go wrong if we lack the international sense.

We are now passing through a most critical period in the history of India and of the world. The All-India Working Committee of the Forward Bloc at its meeting at Wardha on the 8th September and the following days made a momentous decision which was duly conveyed to the Congress Working Committee. Was the decision a correct one? Will it pass the four tests mentioned above? The future alone can give a convincing reply. Meanwhile let us give effect to that decision to the best of our ability. Whatever happens we can certainly claim that we have no other wish, no other desire, but to serve the cause in the best possible manner.

9
Glimpses of My Tour

Signed articles in the *Forward Bloc*,
28 October – 25 November 1939

I

Since the formation of the Forward Bloc early in May 1939, I have toured, though in a rather hurried manner, practically the whole of British India. During the course of this tour, I have passed through a number of Indian States and have addressed large crowds of States' subjects at wayside stations. It is now time to take stock of what I have seen and learnt during the last few months and draw conclusions therefrom for our future guidance.

At the outset I should say that the events and experience of the last few months have eminently justified the inauguration of the Forward Bloc and nobody can have the shadow of a doubt today that the Bloc has come to stay in order to fulfil its historical role. In what follows I shall endeavour to substantiate this statement.

In most places that I visited I had no co-operation or assistance from Congress organizations or Congress leaders. The exceptions to this rule were few indeed. In some places the attitude of the official Congress was one of neutrality or indifference — but in others, there was hostility, open or covert. In Andhra and Tamil Nad Provinces (i.e., Madras Presidency), an appeal was made by the Presidents of the two Provincial Congress Committees asking people to boycott me. Similar public appeals were made elsewhere as well. In other places, as in Gujarat, covert propaganda was carried on and some of my political opponents did not hesitate to calumniate me in the most malicious and unabashed manner. In Patna, provincial sentiment was exploited as far as possible by a group of people and along with shouts of 'Long live Gandhism' shoes and stones were hurled. After the 9th of July incident when disciplinary action was taken against me, I was openly proclaimed a rebel against the Congress. There was variety in the propaganda conducted against me by my political opponents. Sometimes they would say that I was organizing a new party with the help of anti-Congress elements like the Hindu Mahasabha and Dr Ambedkar's Independent Labour Party. On other occasions they would say I had joined the Muslim League. This type of propaganda one could put up with. But what about that scurrilous propaganda carried on secretly from mouth to mouth by the votaries of truth and non-violence, against which it was impossible to take action.

In such circumstances and in the face of such obstacles I had to conduct my tour. Moreover, almost all the known leaders, from Mahatma Gandhi downwards, were ranged against me. What credentials I carried with me can be better imagined than described. Nevertheless, from beginning to end, the tour was like a triumphal march. As I moved from province to province, more and more surprises were in store for me. And today it is really difficult to say which province gave us the most enthusiastic reception.

When I resigned the Presidentship of the Indian National Congress at the meeting of the All-India Congress Committee in Calcutta, on the 29th April 1939, I took a leap in the dark. Among my co-workers and friends, some approved of it but others considered it a blunder. In making that fateful decision, I was guided in the last resort by my own instinct and political sense. It was, however, a pleasant surprise to discover soon after, that through my resignation I had succeeded in rallying public opinion round us to an unimaginable degree. Bengal, in particular, stood solidly behind us and there the Forward Bloc had the best start possible.

But what about the rest of India? I could find that out only by travelling extensively. My first visit was to the United Provinces — or rather to Unao and Cawnpore. At both places, Forward Bloc had very good reception. Some misunderstanding had been created about the policy and programme of the Bloc by interested parties and through my speeches I was able to remove it. When I left, I felt hopeful that the reaction outside Bengal would be favourable to us.

After U.P. — Punjab. When I alighted at Lahore, there was a seething mass of humanity before me and enthusiastic shouts of 'Forward Bloc zindabad'. It was not the Lahore I had visited last year as Congress President. I realized in a trice that Forward Bloc has caught the imagination of the masses. But how did the miracle happen? Who had carried the message of the Bloc to remote Lahore? No human messenger probably but the cloud messenger of the poet or the time spirit of the historian.

Punjab crowds usually bubble with enthusiasm, but this time I had an overdose of it. I was all the more elated and from there I proceeded to the North West Frontier Province. This was a place I had never visited before and I had no idea whatsoever as to how our Pathan brothers would react to the call of the Forward Bloc. One had heard so much of the wonderful hold of the Khan Brothers over the Frontier people that a doubtful frame of mind was but natural in the circumstances. Reports had reached me in Lahore that word had already been sent round on behalf of Khan Abdul Gaffar Khan Sahib that the Congress should have nothing to do with me. But I was assured that nevertheless a warm welcome awaited me. As soon as I entered the Frontier Province all doubts vanished. There were huge crowds at wayside stations and Red Shirt volunteers (or Khudai Khidmatgars) figured conspicuously among them. As we approached Peshawar the crowds began to swell and at Peshawar there was a right royal reception.

I was in Peshawar for hardly a day. But that was enough to assure me that the freedom-loving Pathan could not but be a

Forward Blocer in spirit. The public meetings in Peshawar city and in the cantonment were a great success. The cantonment authorities had banned our meeting at first, though Mahatma Gandhi and Pandit Jawaharlal Nehru had been allowed to lecture there — but when we resolved to defy the ban, the authorities relented and the order was withdrawn. The discussion I had with Congress workers and sympathizers proved very helpful and we were able to inaugurate the Forward Bloc forthwith. In Mian Akbar Shah Shahib of Nowshera, the Forward Bloc found a doughty fighter and organizer.

After my flying visit to the Frontier Province it was clear that so far as northern India was concerned, the Forward Bloc could count on enthusiastic public support. It had caught the imagination of the masses and 'Forward Bloc zindabad' was already a mass slogan. But northern India was not India. The Rightist strongholds were at Bombay, Madras and elsewhere and until they were stormed, no generalized statement could be made for India as a whole. I therefore took the Frontier Mail at Peshawar and went straight to Bombay, where Sjt. K.F. Nariman had been organizing the All-India Conference of the Forward Bloc.

II

In February 1938, I had visited Bombay as Congress President. Coming straight from the Haripura Congress, I was given a magnificent reception on my arrival. All sections co-operated in the function and that accounted for the unique demonstration. This time (June, 1939) it was different. I was no longer president. I was touring on behalf of the Forward Bloc and was therefore marked down by the Congress High Command as rebel no. 1. I could not be proclaimed public enemy, because Mahatma Gandhi had observed in one of his statements — 'After all Subhas Babu is not an enemy of the country'.

How could Bombay — the Gandhian stronghold — welcome such a man? What would happen to the All-India Conference of the Forward Bloc which was to meet there on the 22nd and 23rd June? These questions were naturally stirring my mind when I was speeding towards the 'Gateway of India'. But I was optimistic. The reports from Bombay pointed in that direction. Moreover, the reception I was receiving at the wayside stations, notably at Delhi, Jubbulpore and similar places, enabled me to feel the public pulse.

It was not merely the large crowds at the stations that interested me but the exuberant enthusiasm which inspired them, the expression on their faces, the gleam in their eyes. I was not sailing under false colours. They knew exactly under what auspices I was travelling — but they had nevertheless come and come of their own accord. There was hardly any organization at my back at the time. But the Forward Bloc was undoubtedly the expression of the time-spirit, it was giving vocal expression to the vague feelings, hopes and aspirations which stirred the masses — so it had captured their imagination spontaneously and to such unprecedented degree.

The reception I received in Bombay on arrival did not come up to last year's level, so far as numbers were concerned. But the enthusiasm was very much greater and altogether spontaneous. The attitude of the Congress organization was one of non-co-operation and perhaps, to some extent, of underground hostility — but that did not have any appreciable effect. The public meeting we had at Azad Maidan was a mammoth one and judging from the applause of the audience, the public were entirely with us. After this big demonstration we had a round of meetings covering every quarter of the city. Many were surprised to find that the meetings in the quarters, generally regarded as Gandhian strongholds, were attended by large and enthusiastic crowds and it was widely remarked that they were reminiscent of the glorious days of 1930. There was not the slightest doubt that we had captured the imagination of the Bombay public. The Cowasji Jahangir Hall was packed to overflowing by an eager and enthusiastic audience when the All-India Conference of the Forward Bloc met there. In fact, loudspeakers had to be fitted on the street to serve the huge crowd who could not find any room inside. The Conference was attended by delegates from all provinces and with their help and co-operation the constitution and the programme of the Bloc were laid down. Till then the Bloc had been a target for cross-fire. The Rightists would condemn it as a revolt against the Congress. Certain Leftists (or pseudo-Leftists) would malign it as a Gandhian party in reality, though not in form. A running criticism was carried on the supposed ground that the Bloc did not stand for a definite policy and programme and that it had become a refuge for opportunists and diverse disgruntled elements. When the constitution and programme of the Forward Bloc were adopted and given wide publicity in the press, much of this propaganda — and particularly that part of it which was bona fide — was automatically silenced.

The principal problem which we had to tackle in Bombay was the relation of the newly formed Forward Bloc to existing Leftist Parties and groups. We naturally wanted all Leftists to merge their separate entity in one organization for the purpose of working an agreed minimum programme. None of the existing Leftist parties or groups need be dissolved and they may function for the purpose of working any extra programme. Unfortunately, this was not possible. Partly due to mutual distrust and partly due to other factors, it was not possible to bring about a merger on the basis of an agreed minimum programme. Nor would liberty be given by any party or group to its members to join the Forward Bloc individually. Left-consolidation had therefore to be attempted on the assumption that the existing parties and groups would maintain their separate identity.

That was the next best alternative and no better solution was possible. So the Left Consolidation Committee was formed. The units comprising it were the Congress Socialist Party, the National Front Group, the Radical League and the newly constituted Forward Bloc. These units would have the same status and the Left Consolidation Committee would act only when there was unanimous agreement among them.

The device was more effective in practice than it would appear on paper. The Left Consolidation Committee made its presence felt at the meeting of the All-India Congress Committee, because there was effective collaboration among all Leftist elements and though they were numerically in a minority, they were able to exert a marked influence on the deliberations of the A.I.C.C. When the A.I.C.C. meeting was over, the L.C.C. met and formulated its future plan of action.

A word about the A.I.C.C. meeting. Though some resolutions were carried in the teeth of Leftist opposition which was in a minority, the organized Left in the A.I.C.C. made a good impression on the visitors' galleries. Leftist leaders, and particularly the leaders of the Forward Bloc, were warmly applauded whenever they rose to speak.

After a successful tour in Bombay, I went to Poona. I was not a stranger there and Poona has never been a Gandhian stronghold. Consequently, I was assured in advance of a warm and enthusiastic response. I met workers from different districts of Maharashtra and addressed a huge meeting in the evening. We were lucky in getting Senapati P.M. Bapat, the renowned leader of Maharashtra, to join the Forward Bloc. After securing his co-operation we were assured of the rapid progress of the Bloc in Maharashtra.

After Maharashtra came Karnatak where I was a perfect stranger. I had no idea as to what was in store for me there. But the actual results surpassed my fondest expectations. And before I left Karnatak a bombshell was thrown into Rightist circles, with the announcement that the President of the Karnatak Provincial Congress Committee, Sjt. S.K. Hosmani, M.L.A. (Central), had joined the Forward Bloc. But of this, more in my next.

III

From Poona I took the night train to Dharwar and Hubli. When morning dawned, I found the train winding its way through mountain scenery at several places. It was wet and chilly — but in spite of it, I felt enchanted by the surrounding countryside. The wayside stations had expectant crowds who demanded short speeches. We went straight to Dharwar where we alighted.

I had a busy programme for Karnatak and I covered the major portion of the province — excluding the Bijapur District — partly by train and partly by car. While the province was new to me, I could not claim personal intimacy with most of our comrades there. Nevertheless, they were exceedingly cordial and enthusiastic. As a matter of fact, the volume of mass support which I found for the Forward Bloc came as a pleasant surprise to me. Along with many outsiders, I was under the impression that since Sjt. Gangadhar Rao Deshpande was the outstanding leader of the Karnatak Congress, the Bloc would not perhaps make much headway there. But, as in other provinces, things had changed beyond recognition there also. Owing to the progress of mass awakening, new forces and new elements had come into our movement. Moreover, other anti-imperialist organizations had come into existence during the last few years. Those who could not keep pace with the march of time, could not adapt themselves to the changing composition of the Congress and could not link up with other anti-imperialist organizations, were gradually being eclipsed by more progressive and dynamic personalities. It appeared to me — and I hope I am not misjudging the situation — that older leaders like G.R. Deshpande, in spite of their past service, were getting out of touch and out of tune with the rising generation who will, after all, make India's future. Many of us are liable to forger that politics is after all something dynamic and ever-changing. If you rest on your oars and on the strength of your past sacrifice and service, claim a position for yourself for all time, you will surely land yourself in disaster. You will have to move forward all the time if you want to be always in the forefront.

Again and again throughout my all-India tour did I feel how rapidly the composition of the Congress was changing and new anti-imperialist forces were springing up and how quickly the political aspect of India was changing along with them. If this had been equally realized by the older leaders, perhaps our political progress would have been more speedy and simultaneously devoid of internal frictions.

I do not know if it will be generally admitted that the character of a revolution in a country is determined by the nature of the forces opposing and resisting progress and that the latter in turn is determined by the psychology of the leaders and of the existing Government. Where the psychology of the leaders or of the Government is inelastic or static, the obstacles to progress are more formidable and the reaction to them is consequently more strong and stubborn. There are signs that the opposition within the Congress to further progress is growing from day to day and this should give rise to serious concern in every quarter. If this opposition is somehow removed, then India will march forward with rapid strides and with one sweep will pass through both political and socio-economic phases of her movement. Otherwise much sorrow and suffering will be in store for us.

To come back to our story, beginning at Dharwar I finished my tour at Belgaum. The weather was not altogether favourable. Nevertheless, when we reached Belgaum, there was wild enthusiasm. The educational institutions had all closed down for the day and excitement in the town was at its height. After a mammoth gathering of students I went to the public meeting. It was raining cats and dogs but the huge concourse though drenched to the skin, despite umbrellas, hardly moved. It was a sight that could not but thrill a living soul.

As far as my recollection goes, the meeting was presided over by Sjt. S.K. Hosmani, President of the Karnatak Provincial Congress Committee and member of the Central Assembly. In any case, I clearly remember that he was sitting at my side. After the function we had a closed-door conference of the sympathizers of the Bloc which Sjt. S.K. Hosmani attended. He was unanimously offered the Presidentship of the Provincial Organising Committee of the Bloc which he kindly accepted. The news came as a bombshell to Rightist circles in the province who had never expected that a sane, sober prudent and elderly person like Sjt. Hosmani would join a group of 'rebels' like Forward Bloc. Most interesting was the remark he made to me to the effect that if disciplinary action was taken against the President of the Bengal Provincial Congress Committee, then another President was needed to stand by him. Besides Sjt. Hosmani we found enthusiastic workers in Sjt. Mandgi and Sjt. Idgunji.

From Karnatak I returned to Bombay via Poona. On reaching Bombay I found that a storm had broken out over my statement on the Prohibition Scheme of the Bombay Government, which I had issued early in July when I left for my Poona and Maharashtra tour. My statement had been misrepresented in certain circles and political capital was being made out of it. Some hostile papers did not have the decency to publish the whole of it before proceeding to attack me. Since its inception the Forward Bloc had been making such headway that it had caused consternation in certain circles. How were they to arrest its progress — was the question. My statement on the Prohibition Scheme gave them a convenient stick to beat me with.

IV

From Karnatak the scene shifts to Gujarat but before I invite the reader thither, I have to indulge in a digression. Early in July, before leaving Bombay for Maharashtra and Karnatak, I ran up to Jubbulpore on a flying visit. A conference had been organized there by our sympathizers and supporters and that was the occasion for my going there — the real object being to popularize the Forward Bloc in Mahakoshala Province (i.e. C.P. Hindustani Province.) On that occasion, there was something like a rally of Forward Blocers from different districts of Mahakoshala and we were able to make a good start with our organization there.

I had been to Jubbulpore in 1932 but only as a prisoner and I had lived in Jubbulpore Jail for some months. My next visit there was in the capacity of Congress President, but I went to the Tripuri (near Jubbulpore) Congress as an invalid and returned as such. As a matter of fact, I had to be carried on a stretcher and in an ambulance car and saw practically nothing of Jubbulpore or Tripuri or the Tripuri Congress. I was only informed by friends that the

Presidential procession was a magnificent affair and my absence was keenly felt by the multitude from the surrounding countryside. But it was one thing to go as a Congress President and with all the halo that surrounds him. It was quite a different proposition to go as a mere Congressman and with the label of a rebel against the Congress High Command. Till then I had not done anything which could be stigmatized as an act of rebellion — I had simply resigned the Congress Presidentship and joined the Forward Bloc. Nevertheless, in official Congress circles it was regarded as a revolt and proclaimed as such. Jubbulpore was the first place I visited after the All-India Conference of the Forward Bloc and consequently there was an added significance in my experience there.

As soon as my train steamed into the Central Province I realized what sort of welcome I would have there. There were crowds — enthusiastic crowds — at the wayside stations and it was clear that the stigma given by the official leaders of the Congress had not affected them in the least. The slogan 'Forward Bloc zindabad' (Long live Forward Bloc) was vociferously shouted everywhere and when we reached Jubbulpore, there was a seething mass of humanity. All doubts were set at rest.

There was no procession from the station, but it had been fixed for a later hour. Ordinarily I dislike processions immensely — they are a waste of time and often cause considerable strain and discomfort, especially in the daytime. But in another sense they are useful. They afford us a peep into mass psychology and with all my political preoccupations, I have not been able to abandon my interest in Psychology or in Philosophy. Perched on a throne-like chair in a lorry or on the hood of a car or in a gaily decorated horse-drawn vehicle, one has a rare opportunity of watching crowds of men and women and studying their psychology. No doubt perhaps as a doll in a showcase would, if imbued with life. Nevertheless, at times the experience is worth having.

And so it was in the case of Jubbulpore. The mammoth procession revealed in an unmistakable manner the affection of the crowds and their spontaneous response to the cause I was advocating. The public meeting was also an undoubted success and according to local friends, both the procession and the meeting were on a par with the best records of Jubbulpore.

Not less important than these demonstrations was the small closed-door conference of workers from different districts of the province. A skeleton organization was set up there and we had the satisfaction of leaving behind something permanent. From Jubbulpore I paid a hasty visit to Mandla by car. There, under the scorching midday sun of May, was a large and expectant crowd. It was perhaps midsummer madness to wait under the scorching sun for hours to hear a rebel, but there was something noble, something sacred in this type of madness which makes one oblivious to sun or rain.

Coming back to Bombay from Jubbulpore I found once again eager crowds at intermediate stations where short speeches had to be made. I could not help regretting that the visit to Mahakoshala had to be so short.

On reaching Bombay on 7th July a surprise was in store for me. This was the statement of the Congress President, Dr Rajendra Prasad, virtually banning the All-India demonstrations we had planned for 9th July. As the reader will remember, the All-India Congress Committee which had met in Bombay towards the end of June had passed two resolutions to which we Leftists had taken serious exception. One of them had prohibited Congressmen from offering Satyagraha or Civil Disobedience without the previous sanction of the Provincial Congress Committee, while the other had made the Congress ministries in the province virtually independent of the Provincial Congress Committee concerned. In the view of the Leftists, these resolutions were calculated to strengthen the position of the Rightists and to take the Congress away from the path of mass struggle and it was consequently felt desirable and necessary to voice our protest against them. The observance of an All-India Day on the 9th July for this purpose had accordingly been decided on by the Left Consolidation Committee — and not by the Forward Bloc alone.

Behind the statement of Dr Rajendra Prasad was the veiled threat of disciplinary action and nobody could miss it. As soon as I read the statement, it appeared necessary to convene a meeting of Left Consolidation Committee to consider it. Representatives of the Socialist Party, National Front Group, Radical League and Forward Bloc, accordingly met and considered the statement and reviewed the general situation. We found no reason to alter our previous decision. Arrangements were therefore set on foot for a proper observance in Bombay.

An attempt was thereafter made by Mr M.N. Roy to countermand this decision on behalf of the Radical League and also to influence the Congress Socialist Party to that end, through the medium of Pandit Jawaharlal Nehru — but in Bombay, as in most places in India, the demonstration was held under the joint auspices of the above four organizations and of the Kisan Sabha.

This was the first open clash between the Left and Right after the formation of the Left Consolidation Committee and people in Bombay were exceedingly curious and anxious to see how the general public would respond to the call of the Left. There were also vague rumours of the supporters of the Rightists coming to break up our meetings. But nothing untoward happened. All the meetings held in Bombay were eminently successful. I attended the one at the Franji Cowasji Hall which was packed to its fullest capacity with a large overflow of crowd waiting outside. The enthusiasm of the public was at its highest pitch.

So we crossed the first hurdle.

10
Looking Back

Signed editorial in the *Forward Bloc*, 4 November 1939

Last week we tried to do a bit of heart-searching. This week we shall attempt to look back and take stock of the changes on the political chessboard since last year. We shall then endeavour to dive into the future and to comprehend the role we have yet to play.

It will be remembered that at the annual session of the Indian National Congress held at Haripura in February 1938, the most important resolution adopted was that pertaining to the Federal Scheme embodied in the Government of India Act of 1935. The policy enunciated therein was one of uncompromising hostility to the proposed Federation. At that time it was seriously apprehended that the British Government would force Federation down our unwilling throats and the extraordinary interest evinced by H.E. the Viceroy, Lord Linlithgow, in the Federal Scheme lent colour to this apprehension. As the months rolled by, many of us began to feel that the acceptance of ministerial office in the provinces had begun to demoralize a section of Congressmen by engendering a purely constitutionalist mentality in them. Simultaneously, one began to get reports of insidious attempts being made by the agents of the British Government to canvass support for the Federal Scheme either in its original form with certain modifications.

Consequently in July 1938, I felt constrained to draw public attention to the danger of a compromise with British Imperialism over that Scheme. I added that I felt so strongly over that issue that if by any chance the Congress by a majority approved of a compromise over the Federal Scheme, I would deem it my duty to resign the Presidentship of the Congress and initiate a campaign against it. This statement caused annoyance in Gandhian circles — not so much because of my strong views on federation, but because of the clear hint given therein that a decision by a majority over such an all-important problem would not necessarily gag the minority or reduce it to inaction. This was perhaps the beginning of the storm that was subsequently to break out. It appeared strange to me that while no annoyance or embarrassment was caused in Gandhian circles by the utterances of certain Rightist Congressmen openly advocating acceptance of a modified Federal Scheme in defiance of the Congress policy of uncompromising opposition, my statement which was more in line with that policy was regarded with disfavour and annoyance. As a matter of fact, we Leftists could not help noticing that in spite of the clear and unequivocal stand taken by the Congress on the issue of Federation, which was the burning problem of the day, a strenuous campaign against it was never launched by any of the Rightist leaders.

In October 1938, at a conference of Congress Ministers of Industries held at Delhi and presided over by myself, it was unanimously decided to appoint a National Planning Committee. Though several prominent members of the Congress Working Committee, including the General Secretary, were present there and no one struck a discordant note, circles in close touch with Mahatma Gandhi disapproved of this step and regarded the National Planning Committee as a menace to the aims and objects of the Village Industries Association which was a creation of Mahatma Gandhi. Some went so far as to opine that the National Planning Committee would undo the lifework of the Mahatma. Another item was thereupon added in the charge-sheet against me.

Since my July pronouncement on Federation the political situation in India and abroad was undergoing a change and many of us began to feel that Federation was no longer an immediate danger for our people. It was quite on the cards that the British Government would in its own interest shelve Federation for a number of years till the international tension was eased. Thereby the Government would lose nothing. From their standpoint, provincial autonomy was working satisfactorily and at the Centre, the old autocratic Government was also running smoothly. If the inauguration of Federation meant popular resistance and perhaps a Civil Disobedience Movement at a time when the international horizon was so clouded, the Government would, in fact, stand to gain by postponing Federation. The problem for India then would be as to what we should do if the postponement did really take place.

I mooted this question publicly in November last year when I toured a part of the United Provinces and the Punjab. I declared emphatically that if the British Government chose to shelve the Federal Scheme, we could not postpone the national struggle till the day when Federation would once again become a live issue. We should raise the issue of India's National Demand ourselves — give the British Government time to reply to it — and meanwhile prepare for the eventuality that the Demand may at first be turned down. The mass response to this suggestion was enthusiastic but it did not move the Rightist leaders at all and later on, was even ridiculed by them. Nevertheless, the Bengal Provincial Conference at its annual session at Jalpaiguri in February, 1939, adopted a resolution on these lines and a certain amount of propaganda was carried on with a view to popularizing it.

Towards the end of January 1939, the election of the Congress President for the year took place. The decision to offer myself for re-election was an act of dare-devilry, the majority of Congressmen being of the view that the chances of success were remote. My justification for standing was the belief that by doing so I would strengthen the anti-Federation cause, no matter what the result of the contest might be. There is no doubt that the result while it brought disappointment to the Rightists, sent a thrill of joy and self-confidence to all Leftists in the country. 'Federation is now as dead as a doornail' — was the universal comment on my re-election. 'The work of twenty years has been undone overnight' — was the remark at Wardha.

But the Gandhians were not to be discomfited so easily. Mahatma Gandhi was stirred to activity, proclaiming to the world (and quite wrongly, in my humble opinion) that Dr Pattabhi's defeat was his own defeat. The party machinery set to work with full force and preparations were made for a battle royal at the

* The terms Gandhian and Rightist are interchangable when we talk of Congressmen.

annual session of the Congress which was to meet at Tripuri in March last.

In my presidential speech at Tripuri I pleaded for a bold policy including the presentation of India's National Demand to the British Government, fixation of a time-limit of six months for a reply and preparation for all eventualities during the intervening period. My suggestions received scant attention. The question of Swaraj receded to the background and the one thought and endeavour of the Gandhiites was to avenge their defeat at the Presidential election, about which they were optimistic, having won over Pandit Jawaharlal Nehru in the meantime. They succeeded, but at what cost to the national cause, we can now realize.

After the Tripuri Congress the All-India Congress Committee met at Calcutta towards the end of April last. The main problem before that Committee was the formation of the Working Committee (or Cabinet) of Congress. As the public already know, when I was not allowed to have a composite Cabinet consisting of both Rightists and Leftists with the inclusion of some fresh blood, I resigned. Till then the Left Movement in the country was being conducted on the basis of co-operation with the Right. At Calcutta, the latter definitely took the stand that a composite Cabinet was unworkable and that co-operation between the Left and Right Wings was no longer possible. There were then but two courses open to us — either to surrender to the Right or to stand on our own legs and organize the Left. I chose the latter course.

But why? It was clear from the correspondence I had with Mahatma Gandhi after the Tripuri Congress that there was no hope of the Right Wing leading a national struggle. Consequently, a surrender to the Right Wing meant a surrender to Constitutionalism and to compromise with British Imperialism. My final submission to the Mahatma was that if he would stand for a struggle, we would sink our differences and line up behind him. His reply disappointed us and the Forward Bloc had to be launched.

The three-fold task of the Forward Bloc was: (1) Left-consolidation, (2) establishment of real and effective unity within the Congress, and (3) resumption of the national struggle in the name of the Congress. This three-fold task was popularized by us throughout the country. But we were charged with creating disruption and split. The fact was that the real disruptors were the Rightists who refused to co-operate with the Leftists and thereby forced them to attempt Left-consolidation in isolation from the Right.

Left-consolidation was the natural antithesis to Right-consolidation which had been going on for the last two years. There was no objection to Right-consolidation and no voice was raised when the Gandhi Seva Sangh was transformed into a political party. But when the Forward Bloc was formed and Left-consolidation was attempted the cry of disruption and disunity was raised.

According to the Forward Bloc, the existing programme of the Congress in so far as it is beneficial to the national cause, has to be worked with a dynamic spirit. Over and above that, a supplementary programme is needed to prepare the country for all eventualities. And in order to work either programme, a fighting mentality is essentially necessary instead of a constitutionalist mentality. It is one's mentality which supplies the motive power to all his activities.

Various criticisms have been made against the Forward Bloc and its programmes — some genuine and some malafide. Now, no human institution can claim infallibility. Hence, the Forward Bloc cannot be free from shortcomings either. But the point is — has any better alternative or substitute been suggested whereby we can attain our national objective most speedily and with the minimum of sacriface? If such an alternative be proposed, we shall gladly accept it. After all, the Forward Bloc is for the Cause and not the Cause for the Forward Bloc. But we are afraid no better substitute can be offered.

Looking back on past events, one cannot help observing how different things would have been today if our suggestions of the past had been duly accepted and given effect to. Six months after the Tripuri Congress, war broke out in Europe and India was dragged into it. The whole world had prepared for the crises which has overtaken us, but not the Indian National Congress. Such incompetent leadership can rarely be found anywhere in the world.

Even after the outbreak of war, leaders have been cogitating and cogitating. There is hesitation, vacillation and weakness at every step. The resolutions of the Haripura and Tripuri Congress have been forgotten. If they had not been, then we would have seen — not hesitation and inaction, but decision and action.

Have we yet to realize that pilgrimages to New Delhi will not bring us to our goal? The key to Swaraj will not be found there but in our own souls.

But if you needs must cogitate, then consider for a moment

what the situation would have been to-day if the legacy of the late Vithalbhai Patel of revered memory had been properly utilized and India had set up unofficial embassies throughout the world. But perhaps to some people, more important than Swaraj is the drive against the Left and the vendetta against certain individuals.

11
Whither High Command?

Signed editorial in the *Forward Bloc*, 18 November 1939

Ever since the beginning of September, members of the public who usually look to the Congress for light and lead have been passing through mental bewilderment and confusion. The resolution of the Haripura Congress on War had formerly been regarded as an unerring guide and the natural expectation was that as soon as the crisis broke out, steps would be taken to implement it forthwith. But this did not happen. At first there was delay. This was followed by vague murmuring in Rightist circles to the effect that altered circumstances rendered that resolution inoperative. The result was vacillation and comparative inaction.

Surprise and bewilderment gave place to utter confusion. One can easily imagine the mental condition of those who had got into the habit of taking marching orders from the Congress. What were they to do? The Haripura resolution which should have served as their objective guide, was unceremoniously shelved and no substitute was given. No doubt in September the Congress Working Committee produced a long-winded resolution which some of our international experts hailed 'as a lead to the whole world' or as 'a charter of liberty for subject races' — but analysis of that resolution did not reveal much more than mere words. And in the midst of verbiage, the kernel was missing. What was the Congress going to do if the reply of the British Government on the questions of War aims and of India's political future was inadequate and unsatisfactory?

The heroic language of the resolution naturally led the unsophisticated reader to expect heroic deeds. But were the intentions of the authors equally heroic? In Rightist circles there were high hopes that a satisfactory response would come and a crisis would thereby be averted. One fails to understand, however, what justification there was for entertaining such hopes. Nobody claiming political sense should have felt optimistic in the given circumstances. The fact, nevertheless, was that there was considerable optimism which was dashed to the ground when the Viceroy's pronouncement was made in October. The statements of some of our ministers contained a note of wail and afforded distressing reading.

For once there was prompt action. The Viceroy's statement evoked a ready response from the Congress Working Committee and our ministers were instructed to vacate office. Though we hold a different view as to the manner in which this should have been done there cannot be the slightest doubt that ministerial resignation was an act worthy of an organization that had to vindicate the honour of a nation. It was the very least that the Congress could do, but it was not all that it should do.

The Viceroy's statement had disappointed and surprised our friends on the Right. It was now the turn of the Viceroy and of the British Government to feel likewise over the resignation of the Congress ministries. It is a moot question as to why ministerial resignation should have caused disappointment and surprise in Governmental circles and why, on the contrary, it was not regarded as an inevitable corollary. Whatever the answer to that question may be, the facts of the case are perfectly clear. It can be surmised, however, that a combination of factors had induced the British Government to think that the Congress would not show fight. The statement of Mahatma Gandhi early in September revealing an attitude of unconditional co-operation towards the Government, the feeling in Rightist and particularly in ministerialist circles, the absence of preparation in Congress Working Committee dominated by Rightists — these and other factors could have but one meaning and significance and it was natural for the authorities at Delhi and at Whitehall to infer that all would be quiet on the Congress front. This inference was legitimate but it contained one piece of miscalculation. The Congress was neither a static nor an utterly homogeneous body. It was, therefore; possible for elements within the Congress to bring their influence to bear on it and produce results which might appear to the outsider as a deviation from the official course or at least as a development wholly unexpected.

By the man in the street, ministerial resignation when viewed against the present national and international background, could not possibly be regarded as an isolated phenomenon. He has, therefore, been expecting this act to be followed to its logical conclusion — in accordance with his commonsense, 'native' logic. Transcendental logic — if we may use that expression — will not make him change his mind and this elementary fact should be grasped by the Congress Working Committee if it does not desire to betray India's cause at this critical juncture. All the excuses and extenuating considerations that may now be put forward in the name of prudence or caution or even truth and non-violence, will not weaken in the least possible degree the popular demand that however badly circumstanced we may be today, honour and self-interest alike demand that the Congress should march forward towards its goal. This elemental demand of the nation's soul can be ignored only at our own peril.

A forward policy and move as desired by the people has been consistently resisted by Mahatma Gandhi for the last twelve months or more. Stock arguments advanced in support of his view have been mainly two — firstly, the existence of corruption within the Congress and secondly, the inevitability of the outbreak of violence in the event of a national struggle being launched. We have often urged in the past that these arguments are of questionable validity and that in no case can they be used as an excuse for applying the brake to our forward march.

Since the beginning of September, the above arguments have been reinforced by a third one — viz. that the launching of civil disobedience will be followed by Hindu-Muslim riots, etc. A more worthless or erroneous argument cannot possibly be conceived. The Hindus and Muslims against whom such a serious reflection is made will, we have no doubt, emphatically repudiate such a charge. According to our understanding and information, a forward move on behalf of the Congress will appreciably improve the present intercommunal relations and bring the two parties nearer to each other than even before.

If you are not prepared for a forward move, why not say so frankly and without equivocation? Why cloud the issue by advancing arguments that will not hold water?

The position of the Left is perfectly clear and has been reiterated times without number. If the Congress Working Committee does not move forward, we shall do so. No threat hurled either by Mahatma Gandhi or by the Working Committee will deter. And if they resist us, we shall boldly face such resistance.

But if the Working Committee rises to the occasion, we shall be with it like loyal soldiers. Differences will be sunk within one moment and the Congress ranks will appear as one solid phalanx arrayed against the forces of Imperialism and Reaction.

12
Whom They Fight?

Signed editorial in the *Forward Bloc*, 25 November 1939

As I glanced through this morning's papers, certain incongruous things struck my eye. On the first page — and perhaps in order of importance — comes the resolution on the Congress attitude towards the British Government. Then follows the timetable of the Ramgarh Congress. Thereafter we come across a lengthy resolution on the Bengal Provincial Congress Committee.

The most significant sentence in the first resolution is as follows: 'The Working Committee will continue to explore all means of arriving at an honourable settlement, even though the British Government has banged the door in the face of the Congress.' Which when paraphrased should read: 'We shall continue to lick the feet of the British Government even though we have been kicked by them.'

This is not politics as we understand it or as the modern world understands it — but perhaps it is in accordance with Biblical or Vaishnavic traditions. Such a policy may appeal to one or to a few persons — but will it be acceptable to the nation that is more interested in freedom, which is a life-and-death question, than in the whims of individuals? It remains to be seen if the Indian people will repudiate a policy that demands that we should lick the feet that kick us.

In the same resolution appears the following: 'The Working Committee desire to make it clear that the true test of preparedness for Civil Disobedience lies in Congressmen themselves spinning and promoting the cause of Khadi to the exclusion of mill cloth and deeming it their duty to establish harmony between the communities by personal acts of service to those other than members of their own community and individual Hindu Congressmen seeking an occasion for fraternizing with Harijans as often as possible. The Congress organizations and Congressmen should, therefore, prepare for future action by promotion of this programme. . . .

When we came to this part of the resolution, we rubbed and rubbed our eyes and once again glanced at the date of the paper — 24 November 1939. So in the year of grace 1939, a political party of the stature and importance of the Indian National Congress can put forward such a wonderful plan for preparing the country for Direct Action. There is no reference to enlistment of volunteers — no talk of cadres for a programme of Direct Action. There is no appeal to one's higher self which can send a thrill through his nerves and steel him for suffering and persecution. There is not a word about collection of funds either, which are the sinews of war, whether violent or non-violent. There is no direction, either, to wind up other unimportant affairs and clear the decks for action. We are told instead that the preparations for the Ramgarh Congress, including the election of delegates, Presidential election, etc. are to go on apace — as if nothing has happened or is to happen. But the Indian people are no longer as politically ignorant or unsophisticated today as they were sometime back. Does not even a child know today that in a war emergency, the first step to be taken by any Government or Party is to postpone elections *sine die*?

Against this background stand in bold relief the statements issued from time to time by prominent members of the Working Committee, including Dr Rajendra Prasad, to the effect that they hope and trust that it will soon be possible for the Congress ministers to go back to office. What longing, tearful eyes they must still have to continue thinking of the vacant chairs in such an atmosphere and in the midst of such an emergency. One wonders if they are losing all sense of national self-respect. And one is surprised and pained beyond measure to be reminded that in the midst of this tragic scene stands the lone figure of the ex-revolutionary, ex-Leftist leader of India who had once emphatically declared to a worshipping world that in no circumstances would he accept a seat on a homogeneous Cabinet, whether of the Right or of the Left. Who can tell us if this solemn declaration could be reconciled with his present stand — his complete identification with the Rightist elements in the Congress and his complete disavowal of the Left movement in the Country?

Let us therefore be perfectly plain and brutally frank, despite the danger of treading on others' corns. Nothing will be gained by mincing matters in this fateful hour of our national history. Such resolutions of the Working Committee are mere verbosity, calculated to hoodwink and bluff the innocent people of this country.

Mahatma Gandhi has been consistently telling us for a year or more that a national struggle is out of the question and that the country is not prepared for it — though it is a moot question as to who is not prepared, the country or the shining lights of the Working Committee. If the Mahatma had stood for a struggle from the beginning, much of the present controversy and dispute between the Right and the Left would not have arisen at all. Consequently, it would be futile to hope that at this late hour he will go back on all that he has said and all that he has stood for, during the last twelve months. Pressure of events and the force of public opinion may make him do a lot, but they cannot induce him to launch a nationwide struggle. It is one thing to take a plunge and enter a swimming bout, it is quite a different thing to be pushed into the water from behind when the sight of it gives you cold hands and feet. Compare the inspiring articles of '*Young India*' of 1921 with the stuff that is nowadays served out by the weekly, '*Harijan*', and you will at once see the difference. It is a changing world that we are living in, and as the world changes, so do the personalities who dominate it.

The problem today is not merely one of launching Direct Action. This has to be done effectively — if at all — otherwise it will amount to 'sabotaging' and not launching Direct Action. There is also the further question of pursuing it to a victorious end and avoiding any half-way house along our path. Let us be perfectly frank once again and say that even if Direct Action is started by the present Working Committee, the Left will nurse the apprehension that Chauri Chura and the Harijan Movement, or rather new forms of them, may appear any time and scotch our movement when it gathers strength and volume.

Is this apprehension justified — we may be asked? Of course, it is — otherwise the drive against the Left would not have continued with unabated ferocity even after the declaration of War. From all provinces news continue to pour in of this drive against the Left and in the case of the Forward Bloc it amounts to a vendetta. Naturally, the wrath of the Working Committee is concentrated on Bengal and the Bengal portfolio has been taken over by the President himself. The word has gone round throughout the province that one has only to send in a complaint direct to the Working Committee or to the President from any remote corner and he can rest assured that the Provincial Congress Committee will at once be summoned to the dock. The impartial observer consequently finds lip homage paid to the ideals of unity and discipline in lengthy press statements but in actual practice, suppression and persecution of political opponents within the Congress. In the case of the British Government, you may undertake repeated pilgrimages to the Viceroy's House and lick the feet that kick you. In the case of your Leftist colleagues, you may nevertheless consistently, with your principles of truth and non-violence, refrain from any demonstration of toleration, goodwill and generosity and continue with full wrath and ferocity a policy of vendetta.

What is the moral of this sordid story? It is this that for the Rightists, British Imperialism is a lesser enemy than Indian Leftism. You can compromise with the former, but in the case of the latter, war to the bitter end. And perhaps if British Imperialism strikes at Indian Leftism our Rightist friends will have no cause for regret.

'If India is to be freed, let her be freed by us or not at all' — so says a Bengali adage and so think our Rightists today.

13
Our Working Committee

Signed editorial in the *Forward Bloc*, 2 December 1939

The All India Working Committee of the Forward Bloc met at Calcutta on 24th November and the following days. Representatives of other Leftist organizations, like the All-India Kisan Sabha and the National Front Group, attended on invitation and their presence and advice were exceedingly helpful. Swami Sahajanand Saraswati who is a host in himself, besides being the General Secretary of the All-India Kisan Sabha, and who is a tower of strength to the Left Movement in India was good enough to visit Calcutta twice within a fortnight — his second visit being on the occasion of the meeting of our All India Working Committee. The Committee did a great deal of hard thinking and heart-searching and passed sixteen resolutions on questions of varying importance. These resolutions have already appeared in the daily press but they are also published in one lot in this issue.

The main resolution deals with the present situation in India. It examines in great detail the stand taken by the Congress Working Committee with regard to the major questions of War policy and

India's National Demand and adversely criticizes that Committee on some points. This resolution deserves the attention of the public. The central point in it is that the position and stand of the Congress Working Committee have not yet been clarified with the result that the people at large are left in considerable doubt. Some of the utterances, and statements of members of that Committee as also of Mahatma Gandhi create the impression that they mean a fight. Others create a contrary impression — as, for instance, the remark of Mahatmaji to the effect that he will resist Civil Disobedience if started and of Sjt. Rajagopalachari, ex-Premier of Madras, to the effect that the Congress ministers are on a three months' holiday. Over and above these remarks, news trickle in from time to time which tend to confirm the impression that the Congress Working Committee will not ultimately show fight. For instance, it is reported from Bihar that the advisers, who are carrying on the administration since the recent ministerial resignations, have in some cases been ordering that files are to be put up before the Congress ministers when they come back to office.

The Forward Bloc has made it clear more than once that in the event of the Congress Working Committee not giving the lead expected of it, it will endeavour to do so — though the best thing would undoubtedly be for the official call to go forth in the name of the Congress. The point at issue now is as to what the C.W.C. will ultimately decide. There should be no room for complaint that it was prepared to give the call and that somebody else butted in. So far, the C.W.C. has been asking others to wait and to give it a chance to satisfy the public demand. But there should be a limit to our patience. Consequently, the sooner the C.W.C. comes to a decision, one way or the other, and announces it, the better for everybody concerned.

As in many other cases double faced propaganda is now being conducted against us by our political opponents. We are being condemned for threatening to act independently of the C.W.C. and of Mahatma Gandhi. We are at the same time being adversely criticized for not declaring war on the British Government. Members of the C.W.C. are reported to have openly challenged us in public meetings to go ahead and launch a struggle. Either attack leaves us unaffected, for we have to determine the course of action that would be most conducive to our national welfare, regardless of the smiles or frowns of our critics.

The declared attitude of the Forward Bloc should not be construed as a threat or a challenge to the C.W.C. — for it is not so. That is why it has also been repeatedly stated that the most desirable thing would be for the C.W.C. to move forward and have an undivided Congress behind itself. Nevertheless, it has to be admitted that our attitude has had and will have a steadying effect on the C.W.C. Who can now tell what the C.W.C. would have decided after the outbreak of war in September or whether the Congress ministers would have resigned by now but for the bold stand taken by the Leftists on the issues of War Policy and National Demand?

The resolution on the international situation is also important since it defines clearly our attitude towards recent world developments. It is not generally recognized that the countries primarily responsible for the mess that we now see in Europe are Great Britain and France. Both these countries have encouraged Fascism in various forms out of an implacable hatred for Soviet Russia and have sought to eliminate the latter from European Politics. Further, Great Britain is responsible for undermining and ultimately breaking the elaborate systems of alliances which France, largely through M. Laval's efforts built up on the Continent with a view to encircling Germany. After France was thereby reduced to impotence, she naturally threw herself into the arms of Britain. In consequence thereof, Europe outside Russia, Germany, and Italy, is today being governed by British Foreign Policy. Russia had consistently and tenaciously endeavoured to secure an understanding with Great Britain and France and also with Poland. It was only after she was convinced of the utter hopelessness of this effort, that she decided to enter into a Non-Aggression Pact with Germany. The statements on Foreign Policy made in recent months by M. Molotov on behalf of the Soviet Government are remarkable for their clarity and transparent lucidity and should serve as an example to all Foreign Ministers.

The recent arrest of Pandit V. D. Tripathi, Secretary of the All India Committee and President of the Provincial Committee of the Forward Bloc is extremely significant. It has brought into prominence before the public eye what we had already known before — viz. that the repressive policy against the Forward Bloc is in full swing. To use a rather unhappy but very effective expression, Tripathiji is the uncrowned king of his own district of Unao in U.P. Besides his position in the Forward Bloc, he is the Chairman of the Unao Municipality, Member of the U.P. Legislative Assembly, member of the Executive Council of the Provincial Congress

Committee, of the All-India Congress Committee and of the War Council of the U.P. Provincial Congress Committee. The arrest of a leader of such outstanding position carries its own moral.

The other resolutions passed by the A.I.W.C. of the Forward Bloc will show that we are now under cross-fire. There is governmental repression on the one hand and unmitigated vendetta of the Congress High Command on the other. At the moment, the latter is causing more harassment than the former. But we shall survive both.

The resolution on the Bengal Political Prisoners was a timely one. It made it clear that the Forward Bloc stood by the Bengal Provincial Congress Committee in its pledge to the Political Prisoners. There is no room for apprehension that that pledge will not be redeemed. Whether as a separate issue or as an integral part of larger All-India issues, the Bengal P.C.C. will fight for the cause of the Political Prisoners and in this task it will have the wholehearted sympathy and support of the Forward Bloc.

The resolutions dealing with Muslims under different heads also deserve attention and perusal and particularly of Muslims themselves. They clearly illustrate our manner of approach to the Hindu-Muslim problem. A special resolution on the Majlis-i-Ahrar was absolutely necessary, because the Ahrars have not unfortunately received as much attention so far as they should really deserve.

In conclusion, let it be noted from now by all concerned that the next Independence Day on 26th January 1940, will have special significance. Our Working Committee has referred to this matter as well.

14
At It Again

Signed editorial in the *Forward Bloc*, 9 December 1939

After a temporary lapse from its customary role, 'The Friend of India' has once again appeared in its true colours. During a temporary lapse, it shows balance, dignity and sense of proportion in dealing with affairs both internal and external. But when it comes back to its own, it appears as rabid as a mad dog. In one matter, however 'The Friend of India' has been consistent throughout, viz.

its deep dislike and hatred for the present writer. Unlike most Britons, it cannot stand straightforwardness in politics, but fancies those who can cringe and fawn.

One can only hope that 'The Friend of India' does not really reflect the mind of Britons in India — whether official or non-official. For if it does, then one must indeed have a poor opinion of them. It is difficult to conceive that they are so erratic and eccentric, changing their views as quickly as a political weathercock. For months, our 'Friend' had been advocating a liberal and progressive policy with regard to India. But on the eve of the Viceregal statement in October, it suddenly assumed a die-hard complexion. Subsequently, thereto, it has been blowing hot and cold alternately.

In foreign affairs, 'The Friend of India' was, prior to the War, remarkably well-informed, though its foreign policy might not have met with approval in all quarters. In the old days it was anti-Soviet to the core. But the rise of the Nazis to power served to blunt the edge of its hatred for Russia and things Russian. A soft corner for the U.S.S.R. gradually became noticeable and the wrath of the paper was directed against Nazi Germany. This tendency persisted even after the outbreak of war in Europe and the absorption of Eastern Poland in the U.S.S.R. But since hostilities broke out between Finland and Soviet Russia, our 'Friend' has gone off its head and its writings have been more like the raving of a lunatic than the arguments of intelligent and responsible journalism. Owing perhaps to this stroke of lunacy it has drifted along the path of dishonest journalism. When the All-India Working Committee of the Forward Bloc was holding its deliberations in Calcutta on 24th November and the following days, all the papers published its resolutions and also reprinted the editorials of '*Forward Bloc*', our official organ, but 'The Friend of India' did not. Nevertheless on 4th December, it commented editorially on the above in the course of a very significant article under the caption 'You have been warned'.

That 'The Friend of India' has always had a specially soft corner for us — who in India does not know? And this affection deepened since it had to appear and answer before a Court of Law. But in spite of all this, should there be no honesty in journalism? In the old days, Indian nationalists who had to be denounced used to be painted red, as agents of Moscow. Communism was the bogey that had to be raised every now and then and the picture of Red gold flowing into India then used to be dangled before the public eye.

After sometime the Rome-Berlin-Tokyo Axis supplanted Moscow and Russia became respectable for a while. Whether it was Soviet association with Genega or Stalinite repudiation of Trotsky or superior hatred for Berlin on the Friend's part that accounted for this respectability, one does not know. But it was amusing to notice our 'Friend' fraternizing with Moscow in order to spite Berlin. It was no longer dangerous for an Indian nationalist to be called a friend of Moscow. To have any sympathy for the Nazis or for the partners of the Rome-Berlin-Tokyo Axis constituted the real danger. To out 'Friend's' eyes, the flow of Red gold into India ceased — and henceforth it was the Axis gold that began to poison Indian nationalists. Certain sentences in the writer's book, *The Indian Struggle* 1920–1934, taken out of their context, proved handy and a series of denunciatory articles appeared in the columns of '*The Statesman*'. This tirade was reminiscent of a similar campaign directed against the writer about eight years ago, preparatory to his incarceration without trial under Regulation III of 1818.

After a short lull the attack has started again, the spearhead being its leader of 4th December. There is, however, one difficulty before our 'Friend' on this occasion. What is the scare it is to raise? Moscow or terrorism or Berlin revolution or what? To solve this obvious difficulty, the Frankenstein it is trying to create is the Hitler-Stalin combination. And to prepare the necessary background for the panic it has to rouse in this country, it has made a medley of all possible bogeys in two articles on 'Communism in India' in its issues of the 6th and 7th December. In this motley crowd the villain of the piece is no longer Hitler — it is now Stalin.

Perhaps there is one piece of miscalculation on the part of our 'Friend'. The Indian public are no longer as unsophisticated as they were some years ago. They can now see through 'The Friend of India's game and through the elaborate official propaganda conducted in its column'. We would, however, like to know if this is cricket as generally understood.

Coming events cast their shadows before. So do these articles. We know what is coming, but we are not disturbed. Everything has its price, so has liberty. We have to pay the price of liberty, but it is as well for Britishers to remember that browbeating and bullying — with or without gloves — will no longer do. It is a changed India that we live in.

And the Europe that India faces today is also a changed Europe.

15
A Reminder

Signed editorial in the *Forward Bloc*, 16 December 1939

It may be remembered that soon after the inception of the Forward Bloc we had declared that in addition to working out of the detailed programme adopted by it, the Bloc would aim at achieving a three-fold objective in the immediate future — firstly, Left-consolidation; secondly, conversion of the Congress to its own point of view and the establishment of real unity within the Congress; and thirdly, the resumption of the national struggle in the name of the Congress. No occasion has arisen for altering this immediate objective in the light of subsequent events and in particular, the developments since September last. But a slight modification has become necessary. Owing to the pressure of events the tempo of our movement has perforce been accelerated. We cannot therefore wait till we can convert the majority in the Congress to our point of view and initiate a forward move in the name of the Congress. On the one hand, speedy action has become absolutely necessary, and on the other, the task of winning over the Congress majority has been made more difficult by the persistent drive against the Left and by various constitutional devices as well as executive acts of the Rightist leaders. The endeavour to convert the Congress majority will undoubtedly continue, as also the attempt to get the Congress to launch a forward move. But what if they do not fructify at once? Time and tide wait for no man and the world today is now advancing like a roaring cataract. In the present critical situation the Forward Bloc must be prepared to launch a forward move and to act in a dynamic way in the event of the Congress Working Committee holding back or staying its hands. We cannot afford to wait on the doorstep of time for the day when we shall secure a majority in the Congress or succeed in having a forward move adopted by the Congress itself. It sometimes happens in history that the vanguard has to act in advance of — and perhaps in temporary isolation from — the rest. Desperate situations need desperate remedies at times.

Two arguments will be advanced against such a policy. It will be argued by doctrinaire disciplinarians that if the Left Wing or the vanguard acts in this manner it will violate discipline and destroy organizational unity. By pseudo-pragmatists it will be argued that if the vanguard acts thus it will isolate itself and thereby reduce itself to impotency — whereas it should in reality seek to isolate the Right Wing leadership from the rank and file.

To the first argument, our reply is that unity and discipline are not ends in themselves but means to an end. They have value in so far as they strengthen us for action and struggle and they are meaningless if they reduce us to inaction. To the second argument, our reply is that while there is a possibility that the vanguard may isolate itself from the rank and file if it adopts a dynamic policy — it is equally possible that in a crisis when action is paralyzed owing to the influence of political Hamlets, a bold move on the part of the Left Wing may break the stalemate, bring the eager ranks and file into the vortex and thereby isolate the Right Wing leadership from its erstwhile following. It would be a mistake to suppose that the isolation of the Right Wing leadership can come only through steady propaganda or through local struggle in different parts of the country. It would be equally wrong to suppose that we should first bring about the isolation of the Rightists before we can look up to the Left Wing to launch a forward move on a national scale. We should never forget that under certain circumstances, the isolation of the Right Wing leadership can best be brought about by the Left Wing taking a leap in the dark, as it were, and initiating a dynamic policy. This may be an adventure of some sort — but not necessarily adventurism.

But how are we to judge if an adventure of this kind will lead to the isolation of the Left Wing? It is difficult to answer such a question. It is largely a question of political instinct or intuition.

Today it is possible for us to cogitate as to what would have happened if Lenin's adventure had failed in 1917. What would have happened, we may also ask, if the Irish adventurers of 1916 had brought about their own political death by their rash and hasty action, instead of digging the grave of the Redmondite Party?

Consider again Mahatma Gandhi's Satyagraha of 1919 which not only misfired but landed the country in the Jallianwallabagh tragedy. And what about Hitler's Munich Putsch of 1923 which was ridiculed by the whole world including the Germans themselves?

There is no similarity between such variegated scenes as those of Moscow, Dublin, Delhi and Munich — but the underlying moral is the same. There is no royal road for isolating an effete leadership. More often than not, bold action on the part of the vanguard becomes indispensable for bringing about such a consummation.

And without the isolation of a worn-out leadership further progress is impossible of achievement.

For the newborn Forward Bloc the ninth of July was a formidable hurdle. There were many who apprehended an early death for the Bloc when it faced this hurdle so early in its career. But we were optimistic because we could feel the public pulse. Our anticipations were justified. The Forward Bloc emerged out of the ordeal with added strength and prestige. Subsequent persecution of our members has only speeded up our progress. The Bloc has come to stay and it has already become a factor in the public life of India which cannot be ignored — not even by 'The Friend of India'.

We had declared at the outset that the Forward Bloc was the product of historical and dialectical necessity. So it really is. But the 'Forward Bloc' has to be forward in policy and in action if it is to justify its existence in future as well. And if the 'Forward Bloc' continues to be forward, everything will be well for the country and for itself.

16
The Correct Line

Signed editorial in the *Forward Bloc*, 26 December 1939

In life and particularly in politics there is nothing so harmful or dangerous as an attitude of indecision. This is more so when indecision masquerades in a borrowed mantle. Let us consider the attitude of the Congress Working Committee since September last. Mahatma Gandhi's initial stand on War policy was perfectly intelligible, though it was not in consonance with public opinion in the country. He advised unconditional co-operation with the British Government on the question of war, but this was in direct opposition to repeated resolutions of the Congress and particularly of the Haripura Congress of 1938. The Congress Working Committee, which invariably follows the lead of the Mahatma, did not venture to do so in the present crisis. Instead, it passed a lengthy finely-worded resolution which gave the man in the street the impression that the Congress was on the warpath, but which in reality camouflaged a mind that was altogether undecided about the future. On one pretext or other, the Committee has been putting off its final decision from meeting to meeting. The first time it postponed a decision, namely in September, it sought to ascertain from the British Government their war-aims as well as their policy regarding India. But after the Viceroy's reply which was nothing less than a slap on the face of the Congress Working Committee, there has been no valid excuse for indecision or procrastination.

Several leaders of the Gandhian Party, headed by the ex-Premier of Madras, expressed their profound disappointment at the Viceregal pronouncement. Their deep disappointment presupposed a hopeful outlook at the start, but we wonder what had led them to expect anything else from the Government. We, on our part, had correctly predicted what was coming; consequently neither surprise nor disappointment overtook us when the reply of the British Government became known.

Smarting under an unexpected blow, the Congress Working Committee promptly decided to direct the Congress Cabinets in the provinces to resign. In the prevailing atmosphere the decision was good so far as it went, but it was not in keeping with what we regard as sound tactics. Instead of throwing up the sponge, the Congress ministers should have stuck to their posts, should have gone on implementing the Congress programme and should have invited dismissal while discharging their legitimate duties. If this policy had been followed, then by the time the last ministry was dismissed, public feeling would have reached the boiling-point.

Nevertheless, we welcomed the resignation of the Congress Cabinets, hoping that it would prove to be the first step in a forward policy. In 'Real Politik', there can be no such thing as marking time. One has to move either forward or backward. Consequently, we hoped that once the ministries were out of our way, the pressure from below would force the Congress Working Committee into a bold and dynamic policy.

The mass-pressure is there all right, but the Committee, including our erstwhile Leftist Leader, Pandit Jawaharlal Nehru, has, under the Mahatma's leadership, succeeded in resisting it so far. The Committee today has no existence of its own — it is but the shadow of Mahatma Gandhi in whose favour it has voluntarily abdicated. But Mahatma Gandhi is no longer the dictator of the Indian National Congress. He is the dictator only of the Right Wing of that great institution and of some erstwhile Leftist leaders — for the Left Wing will most definitely not take orders from him blindly.

To examine how the Congress Working Committee has so far succeeded in resisting mass pressure would be indeed an interesting study. Having suspended the fight with Imperialism it has been conducting a ruthless and continuous drive against the Left and particularly against the Forward Bloc. This serves to divert public attention from the path and the duty that lie ahead of us. To bewilder the public and thereafter scare it away from the path of struggle, bogeys have been created from time to time. Before the war, we were told that a forward move was impossible, because there was corruption within the Congress and because a forward move, when launched, would lead to an outbreak of violence. Since September last, they have had a brain-wave and we are now told that if the Congress starts a 'Satyagraha' campaign, Hindu-Muslim riots will inevitably follow. We are awaiting the invention of fresh arguments for desisting from a dynamic policy. The tragedy that has overtaken the upper ranks of Congress leadership is due primarily to demoralization that followed in the wake of office-acceptance. This demoralization was altogether unexpected. Who had ever expected that even those who have fought for years for India's freedom and who have braved the rigours of prison-life would thus fail us in the most fateful hour of our history?

While carrying on the drive against the Left and inventing bogeys of the above sort, the Congress Working Committee has not failed to keep up appearances. Leftist phraseology it has never stinted and hopes are consistently held out that the Congress will soon be on the move. Reports that we are receiving from several provinces and particularly from ex-ministerial circles belie such hopes. On all sides there are whispers that the Congress Cabinets will stage a comeback and that negotiations are going on behind the scenes for that purpose. It is a hard thing to make the allegation — but we are reluctantly compelled to do so — that the Congress Working Committee and Mahatma Gandhi are today out of touch with radical and progressive elements in the country.

The tension and the struggle between the Right and the Left in this country are important and interesting as a historical phenomenon. Lust for power has seized the upper ranks of our leadership — not the power that follows from Independence, but such power as will come through a compromise with Imperialism. Consequently, the Right Wing will not shrink from a compromise when the opportunity appears but will not think of an understanding with the Left, in spite of a national crisis which demands national unity.

This is 'Macht-Politik' or 'Power-Politics' at its worst. We have no doubt that behind the facade of a party-struggle within the Congress, there is in reality a class-struggle going on all the time.

The latest stunt which has been devised to stave off a struggle and which may in time prove to be the greatest fraud perpetrated on the Indian people by their own leaders, is the proposal of a Constituent Assembly under the aegis of an imperialist Government. We have made some serious study of History and Politics and in our view, a Constituent Assembly, if it is not a misnomer, can come into existence only after the seizure of power. If, for instance the Congress and the British Government are engaged in a struggle over the Indian Problem, the Congress will first have to come out victorious and form a provisional Government to take over power. Only such a Provisional National Government can summon a Constituent Assembly for framing a detailed Constitution for India. The Assembly that is now being proposed by the Congress Working Committee may be a glorified All-Parties Conference, but it is certainly not a Constituent Assembly. It will meet with the fate of the Irish Convention which was the Creature of Mr Lloyd George. The Indian people should have nothing to do with such an Assembly, the only purpose of which would be to sidetrack us from our principal task, as the Harijan Movement did in 1932 and 1933.

Our own path is clear. We are now passing through the anti-imperialist phase of our movement. We have to rally all uncompromisingly anti-imperialist elements for the next move. The problem today is not merely to force the hands of the Congress Working Committee. That we must do. But even if we succeed therein, with Mahatma Gandhi at our helm, there will always be the danger of another Chauri-Chaura, or another Harijan Movement or another Gandhi-Irwin Pact. For that danger we must prepare in advance, so that we may be able to meet it successfully when the time comes.

Let the Congress Working Committee have the leadership of the nation for all time — we have no objection to that. But a leader must lead. We still hope against hope that the Committee will soon make a move. But if they do not, then, we must act. We are confident that the masses will follow, no matter who gives the lead.

When Imperialism is ended, the Socialist phase of our movement will commence. Those who win power must undertake the task of post-struggle reconstruction.

17
Leaders Misleading

Signed editorial in the *Forward Bloc*, 30 December 1939

The ordinary, unsophisticated man who is not politically-minded generally believes that the hero who won several battles will go on winning till the end. Rarely, if ever, does he remember that the victory of Austerlitz may terminate in the debacle of Waterloo. When the tragedy does take place he is overwhelmed with surprise. It is always painful to discover that one's god has, in reality, only feet of clay. When this discovery is once made, the spirit of the people rises in revolt in anger and disappointment, and ruthlessly repudiates the erstwhile god. This is how Sir Surendranath Banerji — once known as Surrender-not Banerji and one of the fathers of Indian nationalism — was discarded by his own countrymen, his erstwhile worshippers.

It would be unfair and improper to conclude from this that the public are ungrateful or that public memory is short. It only means that while a nation feels grateful for a leader's past services and may love him for the same, it will follow him only so long as he moves with the times and marches at the head of his countrymen. Past suffering and sacrifice can never be a passport to future leadership under all circumstances.

In living and progressive nations there is a link between the old and the new. The wisdom and experience of age is made available to the rising generation without being obstructive. Youth, on the other hand, which is naturally radical and progressive, seeks advice and guidance from grey hairs without giving up its dynamism. Ex-Premier, Lord Baldwin, gave up his office when he was at the height of his power and glory and has been living in comparative seclusion since. He is no longer an obstructive force, but as an elder statesman he wields tremendous influence still and may perhaps be regarded as the power behind the throne.

In a nation that has been enslaved or suffers from a slave-mentality, it is somewhat different. Once leaders ascend the pedestal, they do not feel like retiring voluntarily. They have to be pulled down as Sir Surendranath Banerji had to be and this is a painful operation indeed. In such a country, the people are more prone to blind hero-worship and take more time to be disillusioned than elsewhere. But the evil day can nowhere be put off indefinitely. In the fulness of time, the naked truth ultimately stands unmasked.

In the present case it is so very difficult for a grateful, admiring and emotional people to believe that those who have held the reins of leadership for two decades, have fought many a battle with varying success and have braved many a storm in life's path will fail us when the supreme moment has arrived. But is there any other conclusion that we can possible draw? Through warned over and over again since last year, these leaders of ours did not move their little finger to prepare for impending developments. Instead, they ridiculed us. At the Tripuri Congress they were more anxious to wreak vengeance on us and to rehabilitate their lost prestige than to look after the nation's interests. Thanks to them the Indian National Congress has proved to be the only major political organization in the world that deliberately refrained from preparing for the approaching international crisis.

This is but the beginning of the indictment. How did they behave when the storm actually broke out in September? The inconvenient resolutions of the Haripura Congress of 1938 and Tripuri Congress of 1939 were quietly and unceremoniously shelved. We were told that the Supreme Executive of the Congress had started deliberating. But what was there to cogitate over? Since 1927, the Congress has been deliberating over the war-crisis and has embodied its decision in successive resolutions. There was nothing to reconsider — all that remained was to implement the resolutions already passed and reiterated. But all kinds of subterfuge have been resorted to, in order to evade the issue.

The two classic arguments against the adoption of a forward policy have, since September last, been reinforced by a third argument, viz. that a Satyagraha campaign will culminate in Hindu-Muslim riots. This is not only a subterfuge, but a dishonest subterfuge. What has happened since the Majlis-i-Ahrar of the Punjab launched their campaign in September? Moreover, what does it matter if mischief-mongers, here and there, succeed in creating communal trouble? Did not such stray riots occur in 1921 and 1930 and 1932? If this argument is allowed to go unchallenged, it can always be thrown at us in order to frustrate a forward move.

The strangest thing that has happened since September is the virtual abandonment of the demand for Swaraj and the surreptitious substitution of the demand for a so-called Constituent Assembly in its place. In order to resist the mass-pressure from below, the Congress High Command has cleverly sidetracked the main issue of Swaraj and introduced a false issue.

In the last issue we examined this proposal of a Constituent Assembly and pointed out that what the Congress Working Committee was now demanding was certainly not a Constituent Assembly. Such an Assembly could not meet under the aegis of an imperialist Government. It could be summoned only by a National Government or a Provisional National Government after power had been transferred to its hands, following a successful fight. The National Demand has been whittled down by the Congress High Command in order to avoid a struggle and because its advisers in Great Britain say that there is a reasonable chance of such a demand being fulfilled.

We can only hope and pray that this demand will not be fulfilled by the British Government — for if it is, then the Congress will surely land itself in disaster. Thanks to separate electorate which has been conceded by the Working Committee, the proposed Constituent Assembly will have such composition that it will soon become the battleground of communal forces. It will ultimately break up in disorder and the enemies of India will point their fingers at the Congress as the real author of the tragedy.

Even if the above Constituent Assembly does succeed in framing a Constitution, it will always be open to the British Government to find an excuse or a plea for not conceding that Constitution to India. This will be the case if the present international storm blows over in the meantime. We feel astounded that it does not strike our elderly leaders that before they could sit down to frame a Constitution, they should first win the right to do so. Have they, we may ask, secured that right? No. That is why we say that a real Constituent Assembly can be summoned only by a National Government or a Provisional National Government.

One thing we cannot understand. If our leaders really do not want to move, why do they talk big? It would be more honest to follow the clear lead of Mahatma Gandhi, however erroneous it may be. Lengthy resolutions, high-sounding phraseology savouring of Leftism, frothy speeches, periodic doses of bellicose utterances, frequent references to a new world order that need not be fought for, but will fall from the skies — Imperialism crashing under its own weight without any onslaught from outside — all these fit in with what we know as Kerensky-tactics and ill accord with the demands of 'Real-Politik'. Soon after, the Congress ministries tendered their resignation, and the official organ of the Congress High Command declared that the hour had come 'to clear the decks'. Many such hours have passed since then, but nothing has transpired so far. While the decks were being cleared by the official organ, 'war-councils' were set up in some provinces. These 'war-councils', we are informed, are now busy spinning along with their commanders. Under the order of the Congress Working Committee we have to spin yarns and also spin our way to Swaraj. With such a potent weapon in our hands, Constituent Assemblies appear superfluous.

Now what is all this evasion and backsliding due to? What has really happened to Congress High Command and to the Generalissimo of Satyagraha? Why are they moving earth and heaven to avoid the straight path that leads to Swaraj?

They are afraid that if and when a struggle is launched, the leadership will pass out of their hands. New forces and new elements will come into the field and they may capture both the machinery and the leadership of the Congress. Hence, avoid a struggle by all means, try to keep whatever power you have already won and work for more through ante-chamber conferences and negotiation. Meanwhile, do all you can to suppress the Left Wing. You may one day come to a compromise with Imperialism — but with the Left Wing there must be war to the bitter end.

Can one explain this apparent inconsistency — this vendetta against the Left Wing and against the Forward Bloc in particular, when we are passing through a crisis of the first magnitude and when the leaders themselves have been making repeated appeals for national unity? Can one account for the unceremonious rejection of the innumerable appeals made for the withdrawal of disciplinary action against the Leftists — and particularly of the appeal of no less a person than Viswakavi Rabindranath Tagore? Yes, perhaps we can. This is 'Real Politik', where neither sentiment nor humanitarianism has any place. Behind the apparent party-struggle within the Congress, there is in reality a class-struggle going on all the time. And wherever there is class-struggle — there is ruthlessness, truth and non-violence notwithstanding.

A large section of our countrymen still think that the Congress Working Committee and Mahatma Gandhi will not be found wanting. With them we would fain say — Amen. But, after all, is this not wishful thinking? We are told that the Mahatma will produce a formula (perhaps a magic formula like Salt Satyagraha) at the next meeting of the Working Committee and that this formula will be presented to the next session of the Congress at Ramgarh in March. Congress elections preparatory to the Ramgarh Congress are to go on in the meantime. Consequently, the programme of the High Command till the end of March has been already fixed. During this period, people have to spin hard and have to create the usual dissensions in the wake of Congress elections. Excellent preparations for a forward move.

One thing more before we close. If the elders think that by avoiding a struggle, they will maintain their present position, they are mistaken. This may, in fact, undermine their position much more than if they march boldly ahead in the present crisis. So far as we are concerned, we have to go our way, come what may. The road to freedom is not strewn with roses. It is a path covered with thorns, but at the end of it, there is the full-blown rose of Liberty awaiting the tired pilgrim. Forward, therefore, and ever forward.

18
An Address to Students of India

Presidential Address at the All-India Students' Conference at Delhi in January, 1940.

Comrades,

It has become customary for the President of a Conference to preface his speech with the remark that the Conference is meeting at a most critical juncture. But if I were to use that expression today, I should not be speaking in the language of convention. If you have not summoned me in a light-hearted manner — as I am sure you have not — then there can be no doubt that you have done me a very great honour. Apart from the honour involved, I am deeply sensible of the confidence in and the affection for me which you have exhibited on this occasion. I am in your midst today to answer your call and I thank you most sincerely for honouring me by selecting me as your President.

The dawn of the new year has brought us all together with hearts throbbing with anxious expectation. The problem of problems today is as to how the Indian people should face the crisis that has overtaken them. An average student who in normal times may not look beyond the four walls of his institution is also being forced to put aside his books and his problems for a while and to think of that crisis and his duty in relation to it. You are aware that in such a grave emergency, it is the practice and the convention abroad to shut down the Universities and to hand over the entire student-population to the drill-sergeants. What are our students to do in India now?

The approaching war-crisis was looming in the horizon ever since 1927. The Indian National Congress dealt with it year after year and embodied its decision in successive resolutions. The last resolution, which has now become historic, was passed at the Haripura Congress in February, 1938. It was the natural expectation of the public that as soon as the expected crisis broke out, the Haripura resolution would be implemented.

This has not happened. The Congress Working Committee has been thinking for the last four months. But, in reality, there is nothing to deliberate over. The thinking has been done by the Congress already ever since 1927. And if any further deliberation were necessary, it should have been started and concluded before September last, when we were crying ourselves hoarse in asking the Congress to prepare in advance for coming eventualities. Does it not evince bankruptcy of statesmanship on the part of elders that, thanks to them, the Congress has proved to be the only major political organization in the world that has not made necessary preparations to meet the crisis?

The silver lining in today's cloud consists of the fact that while the Congress leaders have been deliberating and vacillating, the Majlis-i-Ahrar of the Punjab has been acting. Nevertheless, there are people — and stay-at-homes at that — who do not scruple to cast aspersions on the patriotism of Indian Muslims as a body.

During the last twelve months or more, our suggestions regarding the coming crisis have been pooh-poohed. Our idea of an ultimatum and preparation in advance was sneered at and ridiculed at the Tripuri session of the Indian National Congress in March, 1939. Our elders were more anxious to rehabilitate what was considered to be their lost prestige than to consider seriously urgent national problems. There can be no doubt that at Tripuri they failed to look after the nation's interests properly or to rise to the occasion, as was expected of them. They put self-interest and personal prestige above the interest and the prestige of the nation.

In passing, we may ask those who laughed at us at Tripuri if the resolution of the Congress Working Committee passed in September, 1939, was not in effect an ultimatum. But what a difference it would have made to us if the ultimatum had been presented in March last!

Prior to September last, two classic arguments used to be advanced by Mahatma Gandhi and his followers in order to resist the demand for a resumption of the national struggle. Firstly, there was corruption in the ranks of the Congress and secondly, the launching of a 'Satyagraha' movement would lead to the outbreak of violence. Since September, they have had a brain-wave and a third argument has been added, viz. the apprehension of Hindu-Muslim trouble. On previous occasions communal trouble did take place here and there — but that was never used as a plea for deterring us in our march towards our goal. Let us see what other arguments are invented by our elders in future.

It may certainly be argued that the Congress Working Committee has not been sitting idle since September. Long-winded resolutions have been passed and what is more the Congress ministries in eight Provinces have been withdrawn. War-councils have been set up in several Provinces and there is talk of volunteer camps and volunteer organization. True. But what is all this talk of a three months' holiday indulged in by an ex-Premier? Why whispers on all sides that the Congress Ministers will soon return to office? The man in the street is naturally confused and does not know what to do. To make confusion worse confounded, war-councils have been ordered to spin. We are now expected to spin our way to Swaraj, but how can we be convinced of the efficacy of this 'magic mantra' of Mahatma Gandhi when we know that a century ago when the Indian people knew nothing but Khadi and hand-spinning, they fell victim to foreign domination. No, it is time to call a spade a spade and to tell our people clearly that the idea of winning Swaraj through spinning is moonshine. Spinning has its place in our national economy, but let it not be exalted into the method of our national struggle. And let not the Independence Day pledge be vulgarized by introducing clauses about spinning, etc.

Frankly speaking, it is much more honest to follow the unambiguous lead of Mahatma Gandhi in the matter of unconditional support to Great Britain in the War, however erroneous that policy may be, than to resort to confused thinking or to pursue a zigzag course which will lead us nowhere.

It should now be clear from the programme outlined by the

Congress Working Committee that till the next session of the Congress is held at Ramgarh, i.e. till the end of March, 1940, no forward move is under contemplation. We know that wherever a grave emergency has arisen, elections have been postponed indefinitely. Not so in the case of the Congress, which is virtually working out a peacetime programme. And we know already that the Congress Working Committee has achieved the unique distinction of continuing its drive against the Left Wing, though in other countries faced with a similar crisis, party politics has been suspended *sine die.*

What accounts for this strange behaviour of the Congress High Command? They can think of a compromise with the fascist British Government, but there must be war to the bitter end, where the Leftists and Forward Blocists are concerned. I shall leave it to you to explain this phenomenon — but I shall just suggest in passing that the struggle between the Right and the Left within the Congress is not so much for today as for tomorrow and that behind the facade of party-struggle there is, in fact, a class-struggle — perhaps an unconscious class-struggle — going on all the time. The cold-blooded, determined and ruthless attitude of our High Command is an exhibition of complete lack of *ahimsa* or non-violence and is demonstration of 'Macht Politik' or 'Power Politics' under Indian conditions.

The problem is 'what are we to do when confronted by our High Command and their shrewd and zigzag policy?' Judging from past experience, particularly since January 1939, I have no doubt that they are past masters in political strategy in dealing with their own people. They will not easily allow themselves and their erroneous policy to be exposed, nor will they easily permit themselves to be isolated. Their latest stunt, viz. their demand for a fake Constituent Assembly, is a case in point. Most ingeniously and almost without being noticed, they have substituted the demand for a Constituent Assembly in place of our National Demand, our demand for Purna Swaraj. Perhaps they think that there is some chance of getting this fake Constituent Assembly and if they succeed therein, they will be able to stave off a fight. It seems as if they are capable of any subterfuge, if only they can put off a struggle.

But why are they thus shirking a struggle? What is the real truth behind this whole game? It is difficult to answer the question — but I presume that they are afraid that once a nationwide campaign is launched, the control and the leadership of the nationalist movement will pass out of their hands. Consequently, their strategy consists in retaining the power that they have already won in the Provinces and in working for some power at the centre, through negotiations with the British Government. Hence these rumours about the Congress ministries staging a comeback. Hence the endeavour to purge the Congress of the Leftists. Hence the vendetta against the Bengal Provincial Congress Committee. And hence the elaborate efforts that have been made for some time past to resist mass invasion of the Congress through increased membership and to convert the Congress into a close preserve of the Rightists.

The above apprehension is not altogether without foundation. The Rightists are out of touch with the new forces and the new elements that have come into existence during the last few years. What we may ask, are their contacts with the Kisan Movement, the Working-class Movement, the Student Movement, the Youth Movement and similar radical and progressive movements in different parts of the country? They have, moreover, lost ground among the States' subjects. Consequently, they may nurse the apprehension that in the event of a struggle, they will lose their hold over the movement and ultimately over the Congress.

But there is a fallacy in this logic which may be fatal to the Rightists. If they avoid a fight owing to this fear and apprehension, that in itself may make back-numbers of them.

This brings us to a consideration of Rightist tactics. It is possible that under pressure they may alter their broad strategy and actually launch a struggle and that should not mean that our problem has been solved. If the struggle is launched under such circumstances, then Rightist tactics will consist in prematurely ending the struggle by some means or other. We shall, therefore, have to remain alert and guard against another episode like the Chauri-Chaura episode of 1922, another diversion like the Harijan Movement of 1932 or another pact like the Gandhi-Irwin Pact of 1931. In the absence of close vigilance, a struggle launched by the Rightists may end in a debacle. The best course, therefore, would be for the Leftists to announce clearly in advance with what object and with what mental attitude they will enter a struggle, whether it is launched by the Right or by the Left.

A word about the Constituent Assembly is necessary here. A real Constituent National Assembly is one which is convened by a Government after the transference of power has taken place. An Assembly convened by and meeting under the aegis of an imperialist

Government and electorate will surely end in disaster to the Congress and to the Indian people. Let us raise our voice in protest against it while there is time and warn our countrymen in advance of the coming danger, in the event of this demand being fulfilled by the British Government in its own interest.

The immediate problem before us is the launching of the national struggle. Will it be launched by the Congress Working Committee? That is what we all want and that is what will bring a united Congress into the movement. But what if they hold back? Shall we, too, then hold back? The country is ours, as much as it is theirs, Each and every one of us has his or her duty to fulfil towards the common motherland. Consequently, we cannot hold back in this fateful hour of our history. If the leaders fail us, we have to march ahead with such strength and resources as we happen to possess.

Even if the struggle is launched by the Left, it will not mean that it will be a Leftist struggle. The struggle will be a national struggle — no matter who gives the call, the Right or the Left. It will be a fatal mistake to confuse the nature of the call with the nature of the struggle.

In this connection, I cannot help observing on the basis of indisputable facts that the Congress is much stronger today than it was in 1921 or 1930 or 1932. If we have fought thrice with less strength and resources — should we quail before the present crisis?

I, therefore, appeal to you to gird up your loins and prepare for the impending struggle. The struggle is coming — what does it matter who gives the call.

Standing today in the midst of a complex situation, it is just possible that you may feel perplexed for a while. The vacillating, zigzag policy of the Congress High Command increases one's bewilderment. The menacing attitude of some communal organizations adds to one's difficulties. The want of unity among the Leftists themselves well-nigh unnerves an ordinary mortal. But though you stand with your backs to the wall, do not for one moment lose courage or self-confidence. Remember, comrades, that the Left Movement today is on its trial. Its future will depend on how you and I come out of this ordeal. Remember, also, that we now have a supreme opportunity for winning liberty for India. Such a rare opportunity we can miss only at our own peril. Posterity will never forgive us if we do not rise to the occasion.

I confess that I am not one of those who suffer from an inferiority complex. I do believe that even if the call comes from the Left, the masses will readily respond. Though we may be comparatively weak from the purely organizational point or view, the united Left has undoubtedly a larger mass-following than the united Right. Why then should we hesitate if Mahatma Gandhi or the Congress Working Committee does not give the lead that the country has been expecting and awaiting? If the Left is called upon by the logic of history to act as the spearhead of the nationalist movement, let us not be sorry for it. Let us on the contrary, welcome the opportunity, should it come, of playing the role of the vanguard in our movement. We shall thereby help in winning Swaraj, in bringing about the isolation of the Rightists and lastly in establishing the Left Movement firmly in the hearts of our countrymen.

If any of you feel upset at the continued onslaught from the Rightists and at their diversionist tactics whereby the National Demand has degenerated into a demand for a pseudo-Constituent Assembly, I would appeal to you to keep up your faith and courage and launch the counter-offensive against the Right in the shape of a national struggle. Only by this means can one hope to frustrate the tactics of our Rightist friends.

In this fateful hour I am reminded of a message once given to '*Young India*' by one of our erstwhile Leftist leaders. 'Freedom comes', he said, 'to those who dare and act.' The time has come for all of us to dare and act and let not any of us flinch at this critical juncture. I am also reminded of the inspiring words addressed by a famous Italian General to his innumerable followers while the Revolution was still in progress. 'I shall give you hunger, thirst, privation, forced marches and death', said he, 'if you will follow me.' Let these words ring in our ears now and inspire us to march forward and to dare and act. Only then shall we win victory and Swaraj.

19
Danger Ahead

Signed editorial in the *Forward Bloc*, 6 January 1940

In our last issue we drew attention to the latest move of the Congress Working Committee, viz. their demand for a Constituent Assembly. Neither the idea of, nor the demand for, a Constituent Assembly is an innovation. The Congress has repeatedly referred to it in its resolutions. But the form of the present demand and the manner and the circumstances in which it is being put forward is a novelty and an undesirable novelty at that. And the most dangerous feature consists in the fact that this demand has slipped in unnoticed as a virtual substitute for our National Demand for Purna Swaraj. As a piece of political strategy the move is undoubtedly a masterstroke and will confound a large number of Congressmen, including Leftists, who may not be extra-vigilant.

In order to comprehend fully the dangerous character of the above move, we should clarify our minds as to what a Constituent Assembly really signifies. It means no doubt an Assembly elected for the express purpose of framing a Constitution. But who is to convene this Assembly? When and under what circumstances should it be convened or should it actually meet? How will effect be given to its decisions and by whom? These are pertinent questions to be answered in connection with a Constituent Assembly.

When the idea of a Constituent Assembly was first mooted by the Congress, those who have some knowledge of History and Politics naturally inferred that the idea was to have the Assembly convened after the conquest of power, following a national struggle. After a successful fight when power would be transferred to the representatives of the people, they would form the National Government, or the Provisional National Government. This Government would summon a Constituent Assembly for framing a Constitution for the people. Under the aegis of such a Government actually in power after a successful struggle, it would be difficult, if not impossible, for mischievous agencies, Indian or alien, to frustrate the object of the Assembly in any way. But what will happen if the present demand is fulfilled by the British Government now? The Constituent Assembly will be convened by the British Government. It will be elected on the basis of separate electorate. It will meet under the aegis of the present imperialist Government. There will be no guarantee that the decisions of the Assembly will be given effect to by the British Government and it will be a glorified Debating Society. The floor of the Assembly will become, moreover, the battleground for all the communal forces in the country. The present Government standing in the background will be in a position to do all the wirepulling that they consider necessary. Unless a miracle happens, the squabbles within the Assembly will end in a complete deadlock and the Assembly will prove to be abortive. The

British Government will then point their fingers at the Congress as the author of the tragedy and they will take credit for the fact that they responded to the Congress demand unreservedly. What answer will the Congress be able to give in such a predicament?

No, this move is a most dangerous one and we can only hope that the Government, for reasons of their own, will not agree to it. If they do, then the Congress will land itself in disaster.

For the man in the street it is difficult to understand how the Congress Working Committee could put forward a demand of this sort at this juncture. It has agreed to separate electorate, knowing what its consequences would be. It has not demanded that there should be a prior announcement that the decision of the Assembly would necessarily be implemented by the British Government. Consequently, even if the Assembly arrives at some agreed solution, it will be open to the British Government or the British Parliament to review, revise or alter it as in the case of the Round Table Conference on India.

Indications are not wanting that this demand has a reasonable chance of being accepted by the British Government. And why not? They do not stand to lose but to gain therefrom. Messengers from Great Britain who have recently visited India, have pleaded with the Congress authorities for a postponement of the struggle. They have also held out hopes that the British Government would be in a position to come to some settlement over the Indian issue within the next few months and that even conservative opinion is veering round now. In normal circumstances, this sort of allurement should fall flat on a nationalist leader, but not so in the case of the present Working Committee who are anxious to find any excuse or justification for postponing the struggle *sine die.* In future, we shall probably hear of more messengers coming from Great Britain with frequency and regularity.

There is another practical consideration which should further open our eyes to the danger that is ahead of us. After a victorious struggle the leaders of the nation always emerge with tremendous influence and prestige and are therefore able to guide the public and shape public opinion. The public, too, develop so much confidence in the leaders that it almost amounts to blind faith. In such circumstances, it is the leaders who can influence and control the deliberations of the Constituent Assembly and it then becomes impossible for mischief-mongers or reactionaries to frustrate the purpose of that body. A Constituent Assembly today demanded by the Congress, will most surely become a platform for intrigues and manoeuvres. It is extremely doubtful if there will be any individual or organization with so much influence and prestige as to be able to guide and control its deliberations. Among Congressmen themselves, the Rightists being in charge of the Congress machinery today will be returned in much larger numbers than the Leftists. If through good luck, a settlement is reached, the greatest common measure of agreement will be determined not by the most progressive but by the most moderate opinion. Considered from every point of view, therefore, the demand for a fake Constituent Assembly should be repudiated in the most emphatic manner.

While on this subject, we are reminded of a scene when the Constituent Assembly was meeting in Russia after the Revolution of 1917. It was a large gathering composed of all shades of opinion opposed to the Tsarist régime. The Bolsheviks, who were the most progressive group there, were in a hopeless minority. The heterogeneous Assembly was swayed more by platform orators and doctrinaire revolutionaries of the Kerensky type. The Bolsheviks watched and waited till they were convinced that nothing fruitful would come out of it. They then left the Assembly and ordered its dissolution. What followed is now history. The Constituent Assembly died but the Revolution lived. What would have happened if the Bolsheviks had stuck to the Constituent Assembly, one could easily imagine now.

In the case of the Russian Constituent Assembly, there was little or no danger from foreign agencies. The Bolsheviks only apprehended that Mensheviks, moderates and reactionaries would dominate the Assembly and manipulate the deliberations in their own way. Hence they felt called upon to dissolve it.

The Irish analogy is even more relevant and interesting than the Russian. After the Great War, when the Irish people — and particularly the Sinn Fein Party — were showing fight, the then Prime Minister of Great Britain, Mr Lloyd George, tried a similar experiment. He called upon the Irish people to frame their own constitution through an Irish Convention — an Irish variant of the Constituent Assembly now demanded by the Congress Working Committee. The Sinn Fein leaders, who were more clever and farsighted than our own, left the Irish Convention severely alone and continued their work outside. The Convention met and debated for sometime, but in the absence of the Sinn Fein Party, it proved to be a farce. The Convention broke up; the Sinn Feiners continued the fight and what freedom Ireland won was the result of their efforts.

Let us lose no time in raising our voice of protest against this dangerous move of the Congress Working Committee and let us repudiate the proposed Constituent Assembly in advance, while there is time to prevent its inauguration. And let us tell the Committee plainly that if they are unable to lead the country along the path of struggle, the least they can do is to refrain from adopting such harmful and dangerous tactics.

20
Ramgarh

Signed editorial in the *Forward Bloc*, 13 January 1940

The darkest hour is ahead of the Forward Bloc. It has from its inception been fighting on a double front, viz. alien Imperialism and Indian counter-revolution. The path it had selected was not an easy one, but it is doubtful if anybody had expected Indian counter-revolution to be so determined, ruthless and vindictive as it has in fact proved to be. We all know from personal experience that very often it is more difficult to combat reaction at home than Imperialism imposed from without. We have seen in recent months how so many comrades who would have fought foreign Imperialism bravely have succumbed to the onslaught from the Right.

Looking at the scene quite dispassionately for a moment, as a student of History would, one cannot but admire the Rightists who with all their lip-homage to non-violence and toleration are fighting a political game in a most downright manner. This is 'Real-Politik' as History knows it and the game is bound to thrill all political fighters — even those who are being subjected to persecution at present.

One of the immediate objectives of the Forward Bloc was the consolidation of all the Leftist elements in the Congress and in the country. Since this could not be achieved on the platform of the Bloc, the Left Consolidation Committee was brought into existence. The Committee has had a chequered career. The moment it showed its strength at the meeting of the All-India Congress

Committee, held in Bombay in June, 1939, the onslaught from the Right began — the first occasion being the 9th July demonstrations. Since then some of the Leftist elements have been steadily dropping off from the Left Consolidation Committee. The astute Rightist leaders have been pursuing a dual policy in their handling of the Leftists. Some of the compromising and 'reasonable' elements are being systematically wooed. But the harder nuts are being dealt with ruthlessly. The result has been a gradual thinning of the ranks of the Leftists. To make matters more difficult for the latter, governmental persecution has been steadily going on in several provinces and it was first resorted to under the Congress regime. Today, doubts are being raised as to whether Left-consolidation is at all possible any longer.

Left-consolidation can be achieved in either of two ways. The first method is the one already adopted by us, viz. rallying the Leftist elements on a common platform and on the basis of a common minimum programme. If this method fails, then another method is still open to us. The events of the last few months have put Leftists to a severe test — they have had to pass through a fiery ordeal. Some have succumbed in the process, but not all. Those who have stood the test bravely have proved to be genuine Leftists and Left-consolidation will now mean their consolidation. In nature, floods are often preceded by a drying up of the rivers. A thinning of the ranks is often a prelude to a dynamic expansion. This will happen to the Left movement in this country. Those who have not lost faith during the course of the past struggle, will agree with us that the darkest hour that is ahead of us will be followed by the rosy dawn.

The role of the Forward Bloc in Indian history is not that of His Majesty's Opposition. We have seen remarks to the effect that the aim of the Forward Bloc is merely to ginger up the present policy and programme of the Congress. There could be no greater misunderstanding than this. The Bloc stands for something positive and dynamic. The role of the antithesis in the dialectic of History is not a negative one. It is something positive and dynamic which has to carry us swiftly along the path of progress.

It is not outside the domain of possibility that as we approach the darkest hour, some of the elements in the Forward Bloc may quail before the ordeal. But there can be no going back for us — nor any marking time. Forward Bloc has to move forward without a pause, without a break. That is its historical role. Determination has to be met with greater determination and persecution with unflinching heroism. Only then shall we survive the ordeal — only then shall we succeed in our fight on a double front. Our cause is just and our role historic. Let us not therefore lose faith and courage, even if unrelieved darkness overcomes us for a while.

There are moments when reason fails to rend the veil of the future and on such occasions men who are weak in faith sometimes lose courage and self-confidence. But where reason fails, intuition steps in. Intuitive insight can pierce through impenetrable darkness and give us a glimpse of what is to come. Today, intuition tells us that no power on earth can vanquish us and our cause. The tremendous mass-response that greets us every where has but one meaning. Despite persecution on a double front, people realize that we are moving with the times — that we are thinking their thoughts and acting in consonance with them.

The air is thick with rumours of a compromise with the Government. Some fancy that the endeavour to conclude a settlement will be made before the annual session of the Congress meets at Ramgarh in March next. Others opine that the Ramgarh Congress will vest plenary powers in the Congress Executive and that the final attempt at a compromise will be made after March. So-called English friends of India have been advising the Rightist leaders to mark time till March next, when an agreement will become possible. There is not the least doubt that in the Rightist plan, Ramgarh Congress occupies an important place. How else can you explain the determined and ruthless attempt that is being made to exclude Bengal, real Bengal, from the Ramgarh Congress? The Rightist plan has to be put through at Ramgarh and Bengal with her contingent of 544 delegates may prove inconvenient to the Congress High Command. Therefore Bengal has to be eliminated by hook or by crook.

But this is not so easy. You can exclude Bengal from the Ramgarh Congress, but you cannot exclude her from the public life of India.

For the Leftists, Ramgarh may not have much importance — but the month of March will be important in the history of India. Leftists should therefore gather together during this month and prepare to meet the counter-revolutionary and compromising tactics of the Rightist leaders. In this connection it may be necessary to hold an All-India Conference somewhere in Bihar at about the same time as the Ramgarh Congress. Among others, Leftists who have been expelled from the Congress or subjected to disciplinary action for their political convictions should attend this conference and make a success of it. Such a Conference will have a salutary effect on both the Congress Right Wing and on the British Government and will tone up the militant Leftists in the country. Members of the Forward Bloc need not be so anxious about attending the Ramgarh Congress. With so many Leftist leaders under disciplinary action and with real Bengal out of the Ramgarh Congress, there will be little chance of influencing the decisions of that Congress. Members of the Bloc should rather concentrate all their energies on the task of winning Purna Swaraj as soon as possible.

21
Our Problem

Signed editorial in the *Forward Bloc*, 20 January 1940

The All India Conference of the Forward Bloc was held in Bombay on the 22nd June 1939, and the Constitution and programme of the Bloc were adopted there. We have, therefore, had a little more than six months to organize ourselves throughout the country. What have we been able to achieve within this period?

At the outset, it should be noted that from July last we have been the target of a vehement drive against us from the Congress Working Committee. They have not given us any breathing time and during the last six or seven months, we have been actually fighting on a double front.

There are occasions when it is comparatively easier to fight foreign Imperialism than Indian Reaction. This is perhaps one of such occasions.

Nevertheless, we can legitimately claim that today 'Forward Bloc zindabad' (long live Forward Bloc) has become a mass-slogan. Its message has reached the remotest villages and has roused the sympathy and support of the masses everywhere. The Forward Bloc has, moreover, an All India organization at its back today.

The mass-sympathy that the Forward Bloc has met with from the very start has been quite phenomenal and has surpassed our fondest expectations. One wonders how this has been possible, especially when one remembers that there has been persistent and widespread opposition from interested quarters. The only explanation available is that the masses have instinctively felt that the Forward Bloc stands for something bold and dynamic — something forward and progressive.

The Bloc has stopped the drift towards constitutionalism and compromise in the Congress and has thereby stemmed the rot that had set in. The Congress is consequently much stronger today than it would have been without the Forward Bloc. What is more, today it is possible for Forward Bloc to stand up before the British Government and the Congress High Command and tell them that in the last resort, the Forward Bloc is prepared to go ahead and launch a struggle, should the older leaders fail us in this crisis.

But the real problem that faces us is an organizational one. Our organizational development has not been able to keep pace with our growing popularity.

Perfecting an organization and building up a new cadre need time and money — perhaps time more than money. We have had very little time at our disposal and the international crisis overtook us very early in our career. But we cannot put off facing the crisis boldly, till we have perfected our organization. The crisis has to be met with such resources as we now possess. National struggle and organizational development must proceed hand in hand. There is no other option before us.

Meanwhile let us always remember that our chief problem today is an organizational one. We have to face the coming struggle boldly and at the same time go on with our task of organizational development as best as we can. Perhaps, with good luck we shall emerge out of the struggle with a perfected organization.

22
Stem the Rot

Signed editorial in the *Forward Bloc*, 10 February 1940

The air is thick with rumours of persistent efforts at a compromise between the Congress High Command and the British Government. Circles in close touch with our ex-ministers are greatly interested and feel optimistic about an early return of the Congress ministries. There are two theories afloat at the present moment.

Some surmise that the Ramgarh Congress will be presented with a '*fait accompli*'. Others hold that the Ramgarh Congress will vest the Working Committee or Mahatma Gandhi with plenary powers and that the compromise will follow and not precede the Congress session. The first theory appears to us to be improbable. Whether the second will fructify remains to be seen. What is certain is that both Mahatma Gandhi and the British Government are keen on a compromise. Gandhiji wants to win Swaraj without a fight. The Government would welcome a compromise before the spring offensive on the Western Front begins. At the time of writing it still appears unlikely that the British Government will concede the minimum that Gandhiji would demand for effecting a compromise. We are referring to Gandhiji alone because the Working Committee has made him the sole dictator.

What is troubling the British Government and is preventing it from going far enough in the direction of meeting the Indian demand is its impression that the Congress will not ultimately show fight. Despite the new situation created by the European war, the British Government has not discarded its age-long habit of making concessions too inadequately and too late. We also know from experience that even when concessions do come, they are granted half-heartedly and they consequently lack generosity and good grace. Consequently it is quite on the cards that despite the keenness of both parties, the proposed compromise may not come off.

Another thorn in the path of a compromise is the attitude of the British Government towards the Indian minorities. The former is not yet ready to give up playing with the latter or using them as a lever against the Congress. But the latest reports go to show that if a compromise with the Congress High Command could be arranged the Government would be prepared to let down the Muslim League. The recent editorial comments in the '*London Times*' and other British journals lend colour to this view. Should the British Government come to an understanding with Gandhiji behind the back of the Muslim League, it appears to us inevitable that both the Congress and Muslim League will split. Within the Congress, Gandhiji and all those who stand by him will line up with British Imperialism. On the other side, the loyalist elements in Muslim League, being under the thumb of the British Government, will break away from Mr Jinnah and the progressive section who are influential in the League council today.

It is high time that we seriously contemplated what would happen in the event of the Congress High Command compromising with the Government. It is but natural that in the name of unity and discipline, the Rightists should try to force the compromise down the throats of dissident members. The former hope that a majority decision will silence the latter, just as the campaign against the acceptance of ministerial office in the provinces was liquidated as soon as the All India Congress Committee decided in favour of office-acceptance. But what will the dissenting Leftists do on this occasion?

It would be hazardous now to make a prediction on behalf of the entire Left. For the present, we shall speak only on behalf of the Forward Bloc. The Bloc cannot accept a compromise with British Imperialism. This would be altogether inconsistent with our goal of Purna Swaraj. We shall, therefore be constrained to declare that we are not bound by the compromise and that we shall continue the fight for Independence. The compromise-wallahs will, in our view, be guilty of two crimes — firstly, abandoning the objective of Independence and secondly, giving up the method of non-cooperation and Satyagraha. We shall, therefore, be perfectly justified in declaring that the compromise-wallahs having given up the essentials of the Congress, automatically cease to be Congressmen Should they persist in their folly or in sticking to the Congress, we would be further justified in expelling them from the Congress.

For the Congress is essentially and fundamentally an organization which stands for complete Independence and the method it has adopted is that of non-co-operation and Satyagraha. If a Congressman abandons these essentials and fundamentals he automatically ceases to be a Congressman. And if the Congress tomorrow gives up its fundamental objective and method, it will cease to be the Indian National Congress with which we have been familiar since 1920. With the voluntary withdrawal or expulsion from the Congress of the compromise-wallahs, the Congress will be restored to its former status and will become once again the revolutionary organization that it should always be. Why should we secede from the Congress and allow the backsliders to inherit the name and the traditions of that body? The latter should be expelled and it will be for them to set up parallel organization if they so desire. The

Congress should belong exclusively to those who stand for Independence and carry on the struggle for it.

We realize that the compromise-wallahs may not voluntarily withdraw from the Congress and may, with the help of a packed majority, continue exploiting the name of that body. In that event one can visualize two Congresses. It will then be for the people — for the masses — to decide and declare which is their Congress. About their answer, we have no doubt in our minds — for the masses are with us. The united Left has a very much larger following than the united Right, despite the prestige of Mahatma Gandhi's name. What after all, is the following of the present Congress Working Committee without the support of the Left Wing. It does not command the confidence of the organized peasantry, of the organized workers, of the organized youths, of the organized students and of the minorities. Consequently, with such a slender following, can they deliver the goods on behalf of the Indian people? The answer is obvious.

Without waiting for the day when the Rightists will succeed in effecting a compromise, we should, from now, try our level best to frustrate all efforts in that direction. With a view to that end, an Anti-Compromise Conference is being arranged at Ramgarh at the time the Congress is to meet. All Leftists and Leftist organizations in the country should muster strong at Ramgarh on the 18th and 19th March and help to make the Anti-Compromise Conference a complete success. We have no doubt in our minds that if this Conference proves to be a success it will automatically put an end to all efforts at a compromise and it will thereby save the Congress and the country from a national calamity.

The Bihar Provincial Kisan Sabha is organizing a peasants' rally at Ramgarh which will be attended by two lacs of Kisans. It is also proposed to hold the All-India Conference of the Forward Bloc at Ramgarh at or about the time the Congress meets. The occasion may therefore be opportune for holding an All-India Anti-Compromise Conference. We hope that this Conference will be held and the Leftists and Leftist organizations all over India will muster strong with a view to make this Anti-Compromise Conference a complete success. This Conference will serve to end all talk of a compromise and stem the rot that has set in.

Meanwhile may we not appeal to Mahatma Gandhi to give up these long and tiresome journeys to Viceroy's House and to come and stand at the head of his countrymen as he did in 1920?

23
The Bengal Tangle

Signed editorial in the *Forward Bloc*, 17 February 1940

Friends who are not in intimate contact with Congress affairs are often bewildered at the recent developments inside the Congress. This is particularly the case with comrades in remote parts of the country. Commonsense logic argues as follows: 'The Congress stands for Independence. The members of the Congress Committee and of the Bengal Provincial Congress Committee are all public servants who have set out to achieve Independence for their country. Why then this family quarrel?'

Others speaking in quite a naive manner, appeal in the following terms: 'Please make up your differences with the Congress High Command and present a united front to the enemy.' As if it is we who have picked up a quarrel with the Working Committee!

Public memory is proverbially short. Hence a brief recapitulation of past events is called for.

In April 1939, when the All-India Congress Committee met in Calcutta under my Presidentship and the question of the constitution of the new Working Committee came up, we were confronted with the Gandhian theory of a homogeneous Cabinet. We were told in effect that in future, the Rightists could not work in cooperation with the Leftists. In fact, this non-cooperation had begun in February 1939, after my re-election as President, when the members of the Working Committee sent in their resignation.

Not only were we confronted with non-cooperation, but we were told by no less an authority than Mahatma Gandhi himself that a national struggle in the immediate future was out of the question.

In such a crisis, Pandit Jawaharlal Nehru argued that in spite of all internal differences, I should neither resign nor start a new organization within the Congress in view of the international crisis that was looming in the horizon. I argued that since an international crisis was unavoidable in the near future and there was no hope that the Congress High Command would rise to the occasion when it came, we should lose no time in setting up an organization of our own. This organization would enable us to face the international crisis boldly, even if the Working Committee then failed us.

So the Forward Bloc and the Left Consolidation Committee came into existence.

Let us next refer to the demonstrations of 9th July 1939. Under the auspices of the Left Consolidation Committee, public meetings were held all over India in order to protest against two obnoxious resolutions of the All-India Congress Committee passed at its Bombay meeting in June 1939. One of these resolutions virtually robbed individual Congressmen of the right to offer Civil Disobedience. The other resolution sought to make Provincial Ministries more powerful than the Provincial Congress Committees concerned. Following my lead, the Bengal Provincial Congress Committee participated in the 9th July demonstrations.

This was the signal for the onslaught on the B.P.C.C. I was removed from the Presidentship of the B.P.C.C. by a fiat of the Working Committee. The B.P.C.C. did not take this lying down and a long controversy ensued. During this controversy it became clear that a solid majority in the B.P.C.C. would adhere to me despite the frowns of the High Command. And this majority was a Leftist majority.

The above developments since June 1939, demonstrated that even if the A.I.C.C. passed by a majority a resolution which was objectionable on grounds of principle, the minority would not hesitate to revolt against it. In order words, there would not be smooth sailing for the Rightists as in the case of office-acceptance in the provinces, when the oppositionist minority silenced itself as soon as the All-India Congress Committee decided on office- acceptance by a majority.

The Rightist leaders, looking far ahead, decided that the minority should from now on be forced into loyalty and discipline — so that when ultimately a compromise with British imperialism was arrived at by a majority — no discordant voices would be raised by dissenting Leftists. As a matter of fact, the same consideration was responsible for strenuously opposing my re-election as President.

There was another source of anxiety for the Rightists. They wanted to have an easy time at the next Congress at Ramgarh in Bihar and were eager to avoid the uncertain atmosphere which had prevailed at the Tripuri Congress in March, 1939. It was clear to them that Bengal would send a strong contingent of Leftist delegates to the Ramgarh Congress — perhaps 450 in number. This had to be frustrated at any cost.

People who are not acquainted with Congress affairs in other provinces are under the impression that it is only the Provincial

Congress Committee of Bengal that is fighting the Congress High Command. The contrary is, however, the case. The Forward Bloc being an All-India organization, we are in touch with what is happening in every corner of the country. We are, therefore, in a position to state authoritatively that the Leftists in general, and the Forward Bloc in particular, have been the target of attack on the part of the Working Committee in every province. The attack has been harder where the position of the Leftists and of the Forward Bloc is comparatively stronger. And because our position is the strongest in Bengal, the Bengal P.C.C. has incurred the maximum wrath of the High Command.

Successive steps have been taken by the Working Committee to curb and humiliate the B.P.C.C. but to no avail. On a flimsy ground, a partisan Election Tribunal was foisted on the Bengal P.C.C. The rules for the Tribunal framed by the B.P.C.C. came in for special attention and interference at the hands of the Working Committee, unlike what happened in the case of other provinces. It was then discovered by the High Command that these devices would not help to reduce our majority in the new P.C.C. Then the Working Committee adopted the drastic and desperate step of virtually superseding the B.P.C.C. by handing over to a partisan ad hoc Committee the entire responsibility of running the election of delegates for the Ramgarh session of the Congress to be held in March, 1940. Once Leftist Bengal was out of the way, the Rightists would have an easy time at the Presidential election and at the Ramgarh Congress.

As an interesting interlude, an auditor was sent by the Working Committee to examine the accounts of the B.P.C.C. But his Herculean efforts ended in smoke. The Working Committee had been misinformed by its agents in Bengal who had reported that the All-India Forward Bloc was being financed by the funds of the B.P.C.C. and of the Bengal Parliamentary Party.

We have no doubt in our mind that the drive and the vendetta against the Leftists and the Forward Bloc will continue so long as the Rightists entertain hopes of a compromise with British Imperialism or of getting back to power in the provinces. At present we are witnessing an exhibition of power politics and no one need be surprised at what is happening.

Whatever steps we take in self-defence or as a reply to the onslaught from the Right, must be on an All-India front. The Forward Bloc offers an All-India front if no other organization will.

Let everybody rest assured that Leftist Bengal is not going to be isolated from Leftist India.

The conflict in Bengal is thus a conflict on an All-India plane — a conflict between the forces of reaction and of progress — a conflict between the Right and the Left — a conflict between the policy of compromise and of no-compromise. The ultimate solution of such a conflict cannot take place in the local or the provincial sphere. The solution will come only when reaction is overthrown — and when the policy of compromise is discarded in favour of an uncompromising struggle with imperialism. Till then, let us go on fighting bravely and boldly on a double-front, with the firm conviction that we are going to win and to win soon.

24
Towards Communal Unity

Signed editorial in the *Forward Bloc*, 24 February 1940

The annual session of the Congress is upon us and much depends upon what will transpire at Ramgarh when the Congress meets there. The Leftists will be in a hopeless minority in that Congress — thanks to the enforced absence of Bengal and to the drive against the Leftists conducted by the Congress High Command throughout the country during the past year. Bengal delegates who would, in normal circumstances, have attended the annual session of the Congress need not feel sorry for their enforced absence. Even if they could be present in full strength at Ramgarh, they would not be able to influence the decisions of the Congress. The heavens will not fall if the Leftists do not bother about the Ramgarh Congress. In fact, it may be better if they could help to convert the Ramgarh Congress into a Rightist Congress.

This year, more important than what will transpire inside the Congress is what will happen outside the Congress pandal. The Bihar Provincial Kisan Sabha has given the call for a mammoth peasants' rally to be attended by at least two hundred thousand peasants from the neighbouring districts. An All-India Anti-Compromise Conference is also going to meet at Ramgarh about the same time as the annual session of the Congress. If this Conference proves to be a success, it may eclipse the Congress in its political importance. In any case, it will bury once for all, the talks and the efforts at a compromise between the Congress High Command and British Imperialism.

It is imperatively necessary for the political advancement of the country that the Congress High Command should be forced to give up their attempt to arrive at a compromise with British Imperialism. When this is done, there will be but one path open to the Congress — namely, the path of uncompromising struggle leading to Purna Swaraj. All those who stand for the Independence of India will then be obliged to launch a national struggle.

The call for a national struggle will be an appeal to all anti-imperialist elements in the country and to all patriotic men and women. When the bugle is sounded, all those who hunger after freedom will naturally fall in line and resume freedom's march regardless of their religious faith and denomination.

When people become 'comrades-in-arms' in the struggle for liberty, a new '*esprit d' corps*' will develop — and along with it, a new outlook, a new perspective and a new vision. When this revolution comes about, Indians will be a changed people and a revolutionary people at that. It will then be easy for them to solve many of the questions which to-day appear difficult to solve.

Under present conditions it appears well-nigh impossible to destroy the canker of communalism and foster all-round nationalism in our public life. But how easy this task will become, once we develop a revolutionary mentality on a nation-wide scale.

Communalism will go only when the communal mentality goes. To destroy communalism is, therefore, the task of all those Indians — Muslims, Sikhs, Hindus, Christians, etc. who have transcended the communal outlook and have developed a genuine nationalist mentality. He undoubtedly has a genuine nationalist mentality who wages a war for national freedom.

In every fight a special responsibility devolves on the vanguard of the army. In the war against communalism, a special responsibility similarly falls on the shoulders of the front-fighters. It is their task to lay the foundation of inter-communal — i.e. national unity. Hindus and Muslims, Sikhs and Christians who fight for India's Independence must be specially commissioned to solve the communal problem. Once they solve this problem and announce it to the whole country — the atmosphere will automatically change and the death-knell of communalism will be sounded. If the front-fighters show the way, the nation will ultimately follow.

Let us not therefore sit with folded hands waiting for the day when the High Command of the Congress and of the Muslim League will bring about a solution of the communal problem. Let us rather see to it that the real fighters for freedom get together and solve this problem. It they succeed, the first and the most formidable hurdle will be overcome and the general public — the entire nation — will follow in their footsteps. Those who love freedom and will die for it can solve the communal problem more easily than anybody else. Forward, therefore, all front-fighters and fulfil the mission that today is yours.

25
A Word About Germany

Signed editorial in the *Forward Bloc*, 13 March 1940

It seems that in modern warfare speed and mobility are exceedingly important factors. There is an old saying — 'Well begun is half done'. One should in these days modify it and say — 'Quick begun is half done'. Germany has been practising this teaching with scrupulousness and precision. Whether in the military occupation of the Rhineland, or in the annexation of Czechoslovakia or in the invasion of Poland or in the latest inroad into Scandinavia, she has always acted with lightning rapidity. By attacking suddenly the enemy's nerve-centres she has tried to overwhelm or paralyze him before he could realize what had happened. Such swooping tactics presuppose careful planning over a long period and adequate preparation in accordance with it. Nazi Germany has been a past-master in this art of detailed planning and careful preparation.

Besides detailed planning and adequate preparation, energy and vigour are needed to fulfil a particular programme according to a timetable. All these qualities the Nazis certainly possess. Owing to their speed and mobility they have invariably caught the enemy napping and overpowered him without much difficulty.

The ease with which Czechoslovakia was overpowered and annexed by Germany came as a surprise to many. The conquest of Poland within three weeks was a still greater surprise, because Poland was reputed to have a powerful army with the necessary modern equipment and the Poles were known to be fearless fighters.

The annexation of Czechoslovakia was necessary on strategic grounds in view of the coming attack on Poland. The annexation of Poland, or at least of the Polish Corridor, was necessary in order to link up East Prussia with the main portion of Germany. The annexation of Austria, of Danzig, of Memelland — one can understand and account for on grounds of race and nationality among other reasons. But what about poor Scandinavia?

The small Scandinavian countries of Denmark and Norway never constituted a menace to powerful Germany. Why, then, did the latter violate their territorial integrity? The ostensible ground is that Great Britain had laid mines in Norwegian waters and Germany acted in retaliation.

But this answer is not an adequate one. If Britain was responsible for laying mines in Norwegian waters, Germany should have struck hard at her in retaliation. Why did she strike at Denmark and Norway instead?

The reason is that Germany had grounds for believing that Great Britain was planning to occupy Denmark and Norway — just as she had occupied Salonika in Greece during the Great War. So Germany forestalled her enemy and herself occupied the two Scandinavian countries. Because of greater speed and mobility, Germany could do that in advance of Britain. The occupation of Denmark was like a picnic and that of Norway was like a cakewalk. With careful planning and preparation all this could be accomplished with lightning speed.

The occupation by Britain of the Faroe Island, which belonged to Denmark, shows that German anticipation of the British occupation of Denmark and Norway was not ill-founded.

Both Denmark and Norway can now be used as a jumping-off ground for a future attack on the British Navy, as also on the British territory.

Germany may be a fascist or an imperialist, ruthless or cruel, but one cannot help admiring these qualities of hers — how she plans in advance, prepares accordingly, works according to a timetable and strikes with lightning speed. Could not these qualities be utilized for promoting a nobler cause?

26
The Ramgarh Address

Full text of the Presidential Address at the All-India Anti-Compromise Conference, Ramgarh, Bihar, 19 March 1940

Comrades,

You have done me a very great honour by inviting me to preside over the deliberations of the All-India Anti-Compromise Conference at Ramgarh today. At the same time the responsibility you have thrown on my shoulders is onerous to a degree. This Conference is intended to focus all the anti-imperialist forces in the country that are now determined to resist a compromise with Imperialism. To preside over such a Conference is by no means an easy task. This task becomes all the more serious and arduous when the Chairman of the Reception Committee is no less a person than Swami Sahajanand Saraswati. It is in response to Swamiji's clarion call that we have a assembled here today.

Comrades, I shall fail in my duty if before proceeding to discuss the problem of the day, I do not pay a tribute to those who are responsible for organizing this Conference. I happen to know something of the obstacles and the difficulties that had to be overcome before this Conference could meet and I can, therefore, speak with a certain amount of authority. These obstacles and difficulties were of a twofold character. In the first place, there were physical and material obstacles and difficulties to be overcome at Ramgarh before adequate arrangements for the Conference could be made. In the second place, persistent hostile propaganda all over the country had to be faced and counteracted by the organizers of the Conference. The most surprising and painful of this propaganda was the determined endeavour of a section of Leftists (or shall I say pseudo-Leftists) to make this Conference impossible by openly condemning it and also by trying to sabotage it. As a matter of fact, during the last few months it has become more and more evident that a number of Leftists have begun to play the role of apologists of the Rightists — but such a phenomenon is not new in history. Man lives to learn and the longer he lives, the more does he realize the aptness of the oft-repeated truism that history repeats itself.

It has been argued by the apologists of the Congress Working Committee that the Congress is itself the biggest Anti-Compromise Conference and that such a Conference is, therefore, unnecessary.

The resolution of the last meeting of the Congress Working Committee which met at Patna is held up before our eyes in order to demonstrate that the Congress has adopted an uncompromising policy. One cannot but admire the naivete of such an argument, but is it meet and proper for politicians and political workers to be so very naive?

One has only to go through the whole of the Patna resolution and particularly through the latter portion of it in order to realize that there are loopholes which detract from the intrinsic value of that resolution. No sooner was this resolution passed than Mahatma Gandhi came forward with the statement that the door had not been banged on future negotiations for a settlement. Mahatmaji's subsequent lengthy remarks on Civil Disobedience do not assure us by any means that the period of struggle has commenced. In fact, what has distressed and bewildered us during the last year and a half is the fact that while on the one hand red-hot resolutions are passed and statements issued by members of the Congress Working Committee, simultaneously other remarks are made and statements issued either by Mahatma Gandhi or by other Rightists leaders which create a totally different impression on the average mind. Then there is the moot question as to whether the Patna resolution would have been passed at all, but for the pressure exerted by the Left during the last six months.

The country eagerly awaits a clear and unequivocal declaration from the Congress Working Committee that the door has finally been banged on all talks of a compromise with Imperialism. But will the declaration be forthcoming? If so, when?

Comrades, those who aver that the Congress is the biggest Anti-Compromise Conference perhaps suffer from shortness of memory and their brains consequently need refreshing. Have they forgotten that as soon as the War began, Mahatma Gandhi proceeded to Simla without caring to consult the Congress Working Committee and informed His Excellency the Viceroy that he was in favour of rendering unconditional help to Great Britain in the prosecution of the War? Do they not realize that Mahatma Gandhi being the sole dictator of the Congress, his personal views necessarily have a far-reaching implication? Have they forgotten that since the outbreak of War, the Congress Working Committee has sidetracked the main issue — namely, our demand for Purna Swaraj — by putting forward a demand for a fake Constituent Assembly? Have they forgotten that some prominent Rightist leaders, including members of the Congress Working Committee, have been continuously whittling down the implications of a Constituent Assembly and that they have gone so far as to accept separate electorate and the existing franchise for the Legislative Assembly as the basis for electing the Constituent Assembly of their dreams? Have they forgotten that after the resignation of Congress ministries several Congress ministers have been showing an inordinate desire to get back to office? Have they forgotten the consistent attitude which Mahatma Gandhi has adopted during the last six months in the matter of a compromise with the British Government? And do they not know that behind the smoke-screen of hot phrases, negotiations for a compromise have been going on apace?

Unfortunately for us, the British Government have ceased to take the Congress seriously and have formed the impression that however much Congressmen may talk, they will not ultimately show fight. Since September 1939, there has not been any dearth of resolutions and statements. Some members of the Congress Working Committee opine that these resolutions have impressed the world. But whether they have impressed the world or not, they have certainly not impressed the British, who are essentially a realistic race. During the last six months we have offered them only words and words and we have received the timeworn reply that so long as the Hindu- Muslim problem remains unsolved, Purna Swaraj is unthinkable.

Since September last India has been passing through a rare crisis when men's minds have fallen prey to doubt and vacillation. The first to fall were the leaders themselves and the demoralization that seized them has been spreading as a contagion throughout the land. A determined and widespread effort is needed if we are to stem the rot. To make this effort really effective, our activities should be focussed at an All-India Conference of all those who are determined to have no truck with Imperialism.

The crisis that has overtaken us may be rare in Indian history, but it is nothing new in the history of the world. Such crises generally appear in periods of transition. In India we are now ringing down the curtain on an age that is passing away, while we are at the same time ushering in the dawn of a new era. The age of Imperialism is drawing to a close and the era of freedom, democracy and Socialism looms ahead of us. India, therefore, stands today at one of the crossroads of history. It is for us to share, if we so will, the heritage that awaits the world.

It is not to be wondered at that men's minds should be bewildered when the old structure is crashing under its own weight and the new is yet to rise out of the ashes of the old. But let us not lose faith in ourselves, or in our countrymen or in humanity in this hour of uncertainty. To lose faith would be a calamity of the first magnitude.

Such crises constitute the supreme test of a nation's leadership. The present crisis has put our own leadership to the test and the latter has been unfortunately found wanting. It is only by analysing and exposing the causes of its failure that we can learn the lesson of history and lay the foundation of our future effort and achievement. But such analysis and exposure will necessarily be painful to all concerned, though there is no means of avoiding it.

I may digress at this stage and draw an analogy with similar crises in other climes and ages. When the October Revolution broke out in Russia in 1917, nobody had a clear conception as to how the revolution should be directed. Most of the Bolsheviks were then thinking in terms of a coalition with other parties. It was left to Lenin to denounce all coalitions and give out the slogan — 'All Power to the Soviet'. Who knows what turn Russian history would have taken but for this timely lead of Lenin's during a period of doubt and vacillation? Lenin's unerring instinct (or intuition) which ultimately proved to be prophetic, saved Russia from disaster and from a tragedy similar to that which overtook Spain the other day.

Let us now take a contrary case. Italy in 1922 was to all intents and purposes, ripe for Socialism. All that she needed was an Italian Lenin. But the man of the hour did not arrive and the opportunity slipped out of Socialist hands. It was immediately seized by the Fascist leader, Benito Mussolini. By his march to Rome and his seizure of power, Italian history took an altogether different turn and Italy ultimately went Fascist instead of going Socialist. Doubt and vacillation had seized the Italian leaders and so they failed. Mussolini had one supreme virtue which not only saved him but brought him the laurels of victory. He knew his mind and he was not afraid to act. That constituted the essence of leadership.

Today our leaders are wobbling and their vacillation has demoralized a section of Leftists as well. 'Unity', 'National Front', 'Discipline' — these have become cheap slogans which have no relation to reality. Befogged by such attractive slogans, they seem to have forgotten that the supreme need of the hour is a bold, uncompromising policy leading us on to a national struggle. Whatever strengthens us for this purpose is to be welcomed. Whatever weakens us is to be eschewed. Unity which ties us to the apron-strings of Rightist politicians is by no means a blessing. We might as well induce the Congress to effect unity with the Liberal Federation — if unity is to be desired under all conditions and circumstances.

In the present crisis, the most distressing phenomenon is the disruption within the ranks of those who were hitherto regarded as Leftists. The immediate future will prove to be the acid test of Leftism in India. Those who will be found wanting will be soon exposed as pseudo-Leftists. The members of the Forward Bloc, too, will have to demonstrate by their work and conduct that they are really forward and dynamic. It may be that in the ordeal that is ahead of us, some of those who are branded as Rightists today, will prove to be genuine Leftists — Leftists in action, I mean.

A word is necessary here in order to explain what we mean by Leftism. The present age is the anti-imperialist phase of our movement. Our main task in this age is to end Imperialism and win national Independence for the Indian people. When freedom comes, the age of national reconstruction will commence and that will be the Socialist phase of our movement. In the present phase of our movement, Leftists will be those who will wage an uncompromising fight with Imperialism. Those who waver and vacillate in their struggle against Imperialism — those who tend towards a compromise with it — cannot by any means be Leftists. In the next phase of our movement, Leftism will be synonymous with Socialism — but in the present phase, the words 'Leftist' and 'Anti-imperialist' should be interchangeable.

The problem of the hour is — 'Will India still remain under the thumb of the Rightists or will she swing to the Left, once for all?' The answer to this can be furnished only by the Leftists themselves. If they adopt a bold, uncompromising policy in their struggle with Imperialism, regardless of all dangers, difficulties and obstacles, then the Leftists will make history and India will go Left.

To those who may still be thinking of a compromise, the recent history of Ireland and the sequel to the Anglo-Irish Treaty should prove highly instructive and edifying.

A compromise with Imperialism will mean that an anti-imperialist national struggle will soon be converted into a civil war among the people themselves. Would this be desirable from any point of view?

In the event of a compromise being effected with Imperialism in this country, Indian Leftists will in future have to fight not only Imperialism, but its newfangled Indian allies as well. This will necessarily mean that the national struggle with Imperialism will be converted into a civil war among the Indians themselves.

Let us take time by the forelock and let us act while it is not too late. Swami Sahajanand Saraswati has sounded the clarion call. Let us respond to it with all the strength and courage that we possess. From this Conference let us send out a warning to both Imperialism and its Indian allies. The success of this Conference should mean the death-knell of compromise with Imperialism.

Before we part, let us also set up a permanent machinery for implementing the resolutions of this Conference and for waging an uncompromising war with Imperialism. Everybody now realizes that if the Working Committee of the Congress does not give the call for launching a national struggle, others will have to do so. It would, therefore, be in the fitness of things for this Conference to set up a permanent machinery for undertaking this responsibility — should the Working Committee fail us in this crisis. I hope and trust that the deliberations of this Conference will be a prelude to work and struggle on a nation-wide scale and on an All-India front.

'Inquilab Zindabad'

27
The Bengal Hindu Mahasabha

Signed editorial in the *Forward Bloc*, 30 March 1940

The annual All-India Conference of the Hindu Mahasabha was held in Calcutta towards the close of last year. As a conference it was a great success and it afforded considerable satisfaction to the Mahasabha leaders who began to hope that their organization would forge ahead in Bengal. At that time, it was whispered about that the conference was merely a preparation for the coming Municipal Election in Calcutta and subsequent events have not belied that report.

With a view to promoting the civic welfare and advancement of Calcutta and in order to avoid unnecessary friction and clash over the elections, the Bengal Provincial Congress Committee and the Bengal Hindu Mahasabha arrived at an understanding through their respective representatives. The terms of the understanding were duly published in the press. The basis of the understanding was that the elections would be run in the name of the joint Congress Corporation Election Board and that all those who would be elected would join the Congress Municipal Association. The Congress Corporation Election Board would co-opt six nominees of the Hindu Mahasabha and the Committee that would select candidates would have an equal number of representatives from both the organizations. But the elections would not be run separately by the Hindu Mahasabha nor would there be a separate Hindu Mahasabha Bloc in the Corporation. If any communal question came up before the Corporation in future, the Congress Municipal Association would not make it a party question but would allow liberty to the members to vote as they desired.

The aforementioned agreement did not last long. Differences arose over the selection of candidates and the agreement had to be abandoned.

Prior to the above understanding with the Hindu Mahasabha, I had made a public appeal to all organizations interested in the elections and particularly to the Hindu Mahasabha and the Muslim League, asking for their co-operation in the domain of civic affairs, in spite of any differences that might exist on other questions. I also addressed letters to several organizations in this connection. We naturally felt gratified when the Hindu Mahasabha responded in the above manner.

According to our reading of the situation, the temporary agreement was possible because of the pro-nationalist elements in the Hindu Mahasabha. The agreement fell through because the diehard communal elements in the Hindu Mahasabha, who were throughout opposed to any understanding with the Congress, ultimately got the upper hand.

There has been a country-wide propaganda against us because of our understanding with the Hindu Mahasabha over civic affairs. Much of this propaganda is mendacious, while some of it is based on misunderstanding. We are convinced that the basis of the understanding was a sound one and was fully consonant with Congress principles. If the understanding had been implemented in due course, the principles of nationalism would have triumphed and not those of communalism. Unfortunately, to some politicians and political agents we are the '*bete noire*' and any stick is good enough to beat us with. But we desire to assert even at this late hour that the basis on which we arrived at a temporary understanding with the Hindu Mahasabha is a basis on which a similar understanding could be arrived at with any other organization.

The New Calcutta Municipal Act, which is the result of the recent Amending Bill and according to which elections have just been held, has created a new situation for Calcutta which is fraught with danger. If the Indian members of the Corporation, both Hindu and Muslim, do not join hands, then the Corporation will pass into the hands of Britishers. A handful of Britishers will begin to dominate the Corporation as they have been dominating the Bengal Assembly.

We tried to avert this calamity by seeking the co-operation of the Hindu Mahasabha in civic affairs while adhering to Congress principles. We have been disappointed. Moreover, the tactics employed by some Hindu Mahasabha leaders for whom we had great personal regard, as also by some Hindu Mahasabha workers in connection with the elections, have caused us pain and sorrow. The Hindu Mahasabha did not fight a clean fight.

What is more, the Hindu Mahasabha candidates included men who had tried their level best to break the Congress Municipal Association and to that end had formed the United Party in the Corporation in co-operation with British and nominated groups of councillors. Some of them have been re-elected and one could easily anticipate how they would behave in future. The Hindu Mahasabha has given evidence of greater desire to do down the Congress than to save the Corporation from British domination.

It remains to be seen if any other Indian group in the Corporation will show more keenness to resist British domination than to fight the Congress.

The above action of the Hindu Mahasabha is the beginning of a new phase in its history. It has come forward to play a political role and to make a bid for the political leadership of Bengal, or at least of the Hindus of Bengal who have been the backbone of nationalism in this country. With a real Hindu Mahasabha, we have no quarrel and no conflict. But with a political Hindu Mahasabha that seeks to replace the Congress in the public life of Bengal and for that purpose has already taken the offensive against us, a fight is inevitable. This fight has just begun.

28
The Call of Ramgarh

Signed editorial in the *Forward Bloc*, 6 April 1940

In the last issue we published in full the resolutions passed at the All-India Anti-Compromise Conference which met at Ramgarh on the 19th and 20th March, at the time that the Indian National Congress assembled there. The Conference was organized in the teeth of opposition on the part of Right Wing Congressmen. Till the very last, unscrupulous methods were employed by them in order to frustrate our Conference. Nevertheless, the Conference proved to be an unqualified success. Not only was the attendance phenomenal, surpassing that of the Congress itself — but the Conference afforded a much-needed platform to all genuine anti-imperialists who gathered together from every corner of the country.

The main resolution passed at the Ramgarh Anti-Compromise Conference on the 20th March dealt with the question of our National Struggle. That resolution was passed unanimously, amid wild acclamation and frenzied enthusiasm. As soon as it was declared carried, the bugles were sounded and one hundred thousand people jumped to their feet, mad with joy and holy inspiration. It was a sight which human memory will never forget.

Ramgarh gave the call and we who were there at the Conference, responded to a man. Our fight has already begun. It is now for the nation to take it up.

On 6th April, will begin the annual observance of the National Week. That week is a week of humiliation in the recent history of India, for in 1919 the Jallianwala Bagh massacres took place at Amritsar in the Punjab. But it is often necessary to remind a subject nation of its humiliation in order to rouse it to a sense of self-respect and honour.

This year the National Week will have a unique significance, because the Anti-Compromise Conference has ordered that on 6th April, all local struggles should be intensified and a struggle should be commenced on an All-India basis and on an All-India front. Today we stand on the eve of the National Week with hearts pulsating with new life and inspiration.

Who knows what the future has in store for those who stand on the brink of a precipice? Will they win Swaraj or will they not?

Will they be able to overcome enemies abroad and croakers at home, both on the Right and on the Left?

They may win Swaraj or they may not. But one thing is certain. They will have the satisfaction of having done their duty when others failed. They will be upholding the honour of the Indian nation at home and abroad. And what is more, they will be ensuring the future of the Left Movement in this country. Whether Independence is won by one stroke or not, the grave of Rightism will be dug once for all and Leftism will be firmly rooted on Indian soil.

The bugle has been sounded. The die has been cast. Let nobody falter at this hour. We have to leap ahead and ever ahead. Out of the unborn future will spring the light that will bring us all that we have been striving for throughout the ages — Liberty and Equality; Peace and Bread; and above all, the Holy Grail of joy sublime.

29
The Caravan Marches

Signed editorial in the *Forward Bloc*, 13 April 1940

The political stalemate is now broken. The call of Ramgarh has borne fruit. The bugle that was sounded there was echoed and re-echoed all over the land and from the living hearts of the people has come the response. During the last week, one has been thrilled to read the papers from day to day. No longer are we merely criticizing and cogitating. No longer are we engaged in endless controversy and in hair-splitting arguments on Local Struggle vs. National Struggle. We are on the march. Annapurnaiah in Andhra, Senapati Bapat and ex-civilian Kamath in Bombay, kisan leader Bhuskute in Maharashtra, Professor Ranga in Madras, Ashrafuddin Chowdhury and Satya Ranjan Bakshi, Secretary of the Bengal Congress and of the Bengal Forward Bloc respectively and a host of comrades — belonging mostly to the Forward Bloc and the Kisan Sabha — are now in prison. They have gone forth first and theirs is the glory. All honour to them.

The problem now is — what are we to do? In 1930, when India was in the throes of a revolution, a body of croakers, then regarded as ultra-leftists, stood aloof from the movement and refused to join it on the ground that Congressmen were counter-revolutionaries. To call those men and women counter-revolutionaries who were defying alien 'law and order', braving the rigours of prison-life and facing the baton-charges of the police was a bit too much for even the gullible Indian. The movement grew from strength to strength and inspired the teeming millions of this country and the ultra-leftists were left high and dry and completely isolated from the revolutionary masses.

Today, the same ultra-leftists are in a similar situation. Like truly doctrinaire politicians and bookish revolutionaries, they are standing aloof from the struggle that has begun. By this policy, they will hurt nobody but themselves. The caravan will march on, despite their indifference and possible obstruction. This is the time for action — not for wordy warfare or hair splitting over the meaning of words.

Reports that have reached us from different parts of the country go to show that everywhere our functions have been an unqualified success. In some places, Gandhiites joined hands with Congress Socialists and 'National Fronters' in order to frustrate our work, but they met with miserable failure. There can be no doubt today that the masses are with us.

Is it not an irony of fate that the National Front Group are not coming forward to join the National Struggle? They could at least have come forward to intensify the local struggles and extend their scope, leaving it to others — to the Kisan Sabha and the Forward Bloc, to wit — to work as they liked. But their present policy appears to be almost like a 'dog in the manger' policy. They will neither join the struggle themselves, nor permit others to do so. In 1930, those who had gone in for a National Struggle were condemned as counter-revolutionaries: today they are being condemned as disruptors of unity. The ultra-leftists have yet to learn that that unity is real and is worth having which leads to action and struggle. Unity which paralyses action is meaningless and ineffective and can be described as the unity of the graveyard.

As the hours roll by, excitement and inspiration are on the increase. As if to help us in our mission, the Government struck on the first day and again on the last. The more they strike and the harder they strike, the stronger will be the reaction and the greater the response. The day has gone by when people would be cowed down by repression.

As we march on, many others have to follow, though rather tardily. The Rightists are setting up Satyagraha committees, War-councils and the like and the leaders are parading in shirts and shorts. This is all to the good. But how long will this prelude last? When will the real drama begin? If only it had begun at Ramgarh, we would have been behind the Rightists and not ahead of them. But destiny has forced us to act as the spearhead of the struggle and as the vanguard of the national army. This is a role which will do honour to anybody and no sacrifice is too great that may be necessary in order to fulfil it.

Let the drums beat and the bugles be blown. Let youthful hearts pulsate with life and the blood dance with joy. The hour of deliverance is at hand — we have only to do our duty and to pay the price. India has arisen from her age long slumber, reborn and rejuvenated. Her sons and daughters are going forth to fight the battle Royal. Let all join in sympathy and help.

The supreme test is taking place now. The chaff is separating from the grain, the Rightists from the Leftists. Out of this ordeal, Leftism will emerge triumphant. The overthrow of Rightism will mean the defeat of Moderatism, Reaction and Compromise. And when Leftism emerges triumphant, no power on earth can deny India any longer her birthright of liberty.

30
Swamiji's Message

Signed editorial in the *Forward Bloc*, 20 April 1940

The British Government, like any other imperialist government, are unsparing, ruthless and determined. They do not hesitate to strike whenever that is deemed necessary and they seldom respect persons. The tallest in the land have therefore to suffer when they happen to incur the wrath of the powers that be.

Swami Sahajanand Saraswati is, in this land of ours, a name to conjure with. The undisputed leader of the Peasant Movement in India, he is today the idol of the masses and the hero of millions. It was indeed a rare fortune to get him as the Chairman of the Reception Committee of the All-India Anti-Compromise Conference at Ramgarh. For the Forward Bloc it was a privilege and an honour to get him as one of the foremost leaders of the Left Movement and as a friend, philosopher and guide of the Forward Bloc itself. As a matter of fact, following Swamiji's lead, a large number of front-rank leaders of the Peasant Movement have been intimately associated with the Forward Bloc.

The Sword of Damocles at last fell on Swamiji and he was arrested this morning at Patna under the Defence of India Act. Yesterday he was in Calcutta and we spent long hours in conversation with him. Little did we know at the time that the warrant for his arrest was waiting for him at Patna. He left Calcutta last night and this morning at Patna he was placed in custody.

Before he left Calcutta, we issued a joint statement under our signatures appealing for a proper observation of May Day throughout the country. That statement will be found in this issue.

On hearing of his arrest, we immediately decided to observe 28th April as an All-India Swami Sahajanand Day for the purpose of protesting against his incarceration. We earnestly hope that that day will be observed in such a manner as to give a fitting reply to the British Government.

We congratulate Swamiji on the signal honour he has won through his arrest and incarceration. In fact, one feels like envying him for being able to force the Government to take action against him.

Swamiji's arrest is to be welcomed. It will inspire millions to break the stalemate and take the plunge. One can no longer continue sitting on the fence. The time for action has come and we must act.

Swamiji has disappeared behind the bars, but he has left behind a legacy. We have to learn from him the lesson of his life — the lesson of service and sacrifice, the sound political instinct, of radicalism and dynamic socialism. He is essentially a man of action and when arrested, he appealed to his countrymen not to delay and procrastinate — but to act at once.

Swamiji's arrest is nothing less than a challenge to New India. That challenge we have now to take up. Let this British Government see and note that the country stands solidly behind him.

With the sacred resolve 'Give me Liberty or give me Death', let us continue our march with redoubled vigour and renewed determination. All obstacles will then disappear and freedom will dawn on this benighted land.

31
The New Parade

Signed editorial in the *Forward Bloc*, 27 April 1940

London has spoken again. But the day is dead and gone when a prospective utterance of a Secretary of State for India used to whet the curiosity of the Indian public. That is why the announcement regarding Lord Zetland's speech as well as the actual text of it have fallen flat on our people. The speech has been brushed aside as one of the usual, unimaginative, bureaucratic utterances that emanate from the banks of the Thames.

Judged from the British point of view, the Indian situation may be described in one word as a stalemate. But who can end this stalemate and how? Can British Imperialism do it? Evidently, it lacks this dynamism because it has lost the sense of justice as well as the revolutionary mind that are needed if such a crisis has to be met and solved in a proper manner.

An old imperialist mind always works in a groove. It can never strike out a new path. That is why when decay once sets in, it is difficult to arrest the downfall of Imperialism. One is reminded here of the old Austro-Hungarian Empire which collapsed almost like a house of cards at the end of the Great War. Even after 1914 when the Great War began, the Empire could possibly have been saved if the rulers had taken a bold step and fulfilled the reasonable demands of suppressed nationalities like the Czechs, Serbs, Croats, Slovenes, etc. Imperialism — and particularly old Imperialism — is traditionally 'wooden and inelastic'.

But we need not regret this phenomenon. The very fact that the old Imperialisms lose their elasticity and their capacity to adjust themselves to the changing environment may in the long run be a blessing, though it may render our immediate task more difficult than it otherwise would be.

During the last four years and particularly during the last eight months, one has noticed that as compared with the old imperialist powers, a new imperialist power like Germany has shown far greater dynamism and mobility. Without this dynamism, a revolutionary and unheard-of step like the Soviet-German Pact would not have been possible. And without this mobility a swift attack on Scandinavia which has taken the whole world by surprise would never have been possible.

Dynamism is a sign of life and a sign of growth. But that dynamism is healthy, beneficial and good which is the expression of a progressive idea. The latter type of dynamism India badly needs today.

It is not Whitehall alone that is marking time today. Wardha, too, is doing the same. How the Congress Working Committee intends breaking through the mist of uncertainty and inaction that has enveloped us, we do not know. Nor, perhaps, do they know. The Gandhian Congress waits impatiently at the Mahatma's door-step for the 'inner light' to shine forth. But what if that light should fail us as it did at Rajkot the other day? When it failed at Rajkot, its substitute, the new light or the new technique, was neither welcomed nor accepted by the people. History may once again repeat itself, in connection with the present crisis.

After the All-India Anti-Compromise Conference which met at Ramgarh on the 19th and 20th March at the time of the Congress, there has been some activity in Congress headquarters. A Satyagraha pledge has been devised and members of all executive committees of all Congress organizations are obliged to take it on pain of disciplinary action. We cannot possibly take this pledge and for more reasons than one. Firstly, our struggle has already commenced. Secondly, there is no knowing if and when the Congress Working Committee will launch the struggle. Thirdly, by taking the pledge we shall place ourselves entirely under the discipline of the Congress Working Committee and it will no longer be possible for us to participate in a struggle launched by any other organization or agency. Nevertheless, we would welcome this move provided it does ultimately lead to a National Struggle.

We have had evidence of another form of activity in Congress headquarters. Leaders' camps are now being organized in several places and leaders are taking part in drill and parade. Pictures of this new parade have appeared in the press and they are interesting. No such parades took place in 1921 or 1930 or 1932 when the country had experience of a nation-wide struggle for Swaraj. The novelty of this new parade has proved attractive. This also has to be welcomed because it is an advance on the marking-time policy of the Congress Cabinet. But when will this 'field-parade' lead to action in the wider domain of mass satyagraha? This is what worries us now.

There is a widespread notion today that a very restricted form of Satyagraha may be started in the near future by the Congress Working Committee as a result of the pressure exerted by the anti-Compromise-wallahs. There is also a rumour that this restricted form of Satyagraha may take the form of hunger-strike or 'fast unto death' on the part of one or more leaders. But we should not be misled or carried away by such tactics. Neither Chauri Chaura, nor Delhi Pact nor Harijan Movement nor a new fast unto death should divert our attention from the path of uncompromising mass-struggle. We want freedom for the masses and freedom which will be won by the masses through their own effort, suffering and sacrifice. Only then shall we attain real Swaraj and lasting Swaraj.

32
Congress and Communal Organizations

Signed editorial in the *Forward Bloc*, 4 May 1940

There was a time, not long ago, when prominent leaders of the Congress could be members and leaders of communal organizations like the Hindu Mahasabha and the Muslim League. In those days the communalism of such communal organizations was of a subdued character. Hence Lala Lajpat Rai could be a leader of the Hindu Mahasabha and the Ali brothers could be leaders of Muslim League. In Bengal, an ex-President of the Bengal Provincial Congress Committee and of the Bengal Provincial Conference, like Moulana Akram Khan, could be a leader of the Muslim League. But in recent times, circumstances have changed. These communal organizations have become more communal than before. As a reaction to this, the Indian National Congress has put into its Constitution a clause to the effect that no member of a communal organization like the Hindu Mahasabha or the Muslim League can be a member of an elective Committee of the Congress.

Since the Congress imposed this ban, a tendency has developed among certain circles to regard these communal organizations as untouchable. While trying to discard social untouchability, we are, as it were, encouraging political untouchability. Consequently, whenever an attempt is made to bring these organizations nearer to the Congress, many people are scandalized. This happened in the case of the Bengal Provincial Congress Committee when it attempted an understanding with the Hindu Mahasabha and later on, with the Muslim League, in the domain of civic affairs.

Two attempts were made at a rapprochement with the Hindu Mahasabha. The first was made towards the end of February last, prior to the Calcutta Municipal elections. The second was made about the middle of April (last month), after the General election and on the eve of the Alderman election.

The basis of the first agreement was that the elections would be run in the name of the Congress alone and that after the elections, all the successful candidates would join the Congress Municipal Association. The election of candidates would be made by the representatives of the Hindu Mahasabha and the Congress jointly and the Congress Election Board would co-opt a member of representatives of the Hindu Mahasabha. This agreement broke down ultimately over the selection of candidates and in consequence thereof, the Congress and the Hindu Mahasabha fought a battle royal at the polls.

Judged in the light of Congress principles, the above understanding was unassailable. Nevertheless, a great deal of prejudice and resentment was in evidence not only among Muslims but also among orthodox Congressmen, including Gandhiites when the news was published. One can account for this only on the theory that of late we have been developing a species of political untouchability.

The second understanding with the Hindu Mahasabha broke down on the night of 16th April at about 10 p.m. over the selection of five candidates for the posts of Aldermen to be elected by the Councillors in a body. After this final breach, negotiations between the Congress and the Muslim League were started at 11 p.m. and they culminated in an agreement at about 2 a.m. in the morning.

The agreement took place over the question of Aldermen and Mayor. If all goes well, the agreement will be extended to other municipal problems. And with good luck, the scope and sphere of such an understanding may one day be enlarged so as to embrace much larger questions concerning the province and the country.

Thanks to the Hindu Mahasabha and to papers like '*The Amrita Bazar Patrika*' that have suddenly developed a rabid communalism, communal venom is being emitted from day to day, with a view to poisoning the minds of the Hindus in Bengal and elsewhere. But all attempts to mislead the Hindus have so far failed. Two mammoth meetings of the citizens of Calcutta were held at Shraddhananda Park and Deshbandhu Park recently, for obtaining the verdict of the Calcutta public on the above Congress-League

Pact. At the first meeting, at a modest estimate twenty thousand people were present and at the second meeting thirty thousand. At both meetings, a unanimous vote of confidence was given to us. Nevertheless, one cannot ignore the fact that a certain number of communally-minded Hindus are furious over the above understanding.

We, on our part, do not regard the communal organizations as untouchable. On the contrary, we hold that the Congress should try continuously to woo them over to its side. During the last three years, repeated attempts have been made to bring about a rapprochement between the Congress and the Muslim League. At a certain stage, the writer, then President of the Congress, met Mr Jinnah, the President of the Muslim League, and several interviews took place. At that time, the attempt failed, though the writer had been blessed by the Congress Working Committee and by Mahatma Gandhi. Those who had not objected to that attempt which failed ultimately, now strongly object to the present attempt, because it has succeeded. Can prejudice go any further?

We regard the present agreement with the Muslim League as a great achievement not in its actuality, but in its potentiality. During the last three years, we have been groping in the dark, but without success. Every time we have come up against a dead wall of communal prejudice and passion and we have been frustrated in our efforts. This time we have broken through the wall and through the fissure, a ray of light has poured in. There is now some hope that we may ultimately succeed in solving a problem which has proved well nigh insoluble to many. Great achievements are often born out of small beginnings.

33
Wake Up, India!

Signed editorial in the *Forward Bloc*, 11 May 1940

Events in Europe are rapidly heading towards a crisis. The Nazi invasion of Holland, news of which has reached us, is a sure indication of the determination and ruthlessness of the present-day rulers of Germany, as well as of the speed with which they can act. What has happened since the outbreak of war has not taken us by surprise, except perhaps the Scandinavian exploits of the Nazis. In fact, actual events have confirmed our prognostications to a very large extent.

In October 1938, we began to talk publicly about the impending war-crisis in Europe. The resolution passed unanimously at the Bengal Provincial Conference at Jalpaiguri in February 1939, gave expression to this thought and suggested the presentation of an ultimatum to the British Government on the issue of India's National Demand. The Jalpaiguri resolution was brought before the Tripuri Congress in March 1939, but it was unceremoniously rejected. If it had been adopted there, the ultimatum would have been presented to the Government, preparations for the national struggle would have begun in right earnest and on the expiry of the stipulated period of six months, the national struggle would have been launched. But nothing of the kind happened. On the contrary, the Congress Working Committee launched the offensive against the Left Wing. This drive has continued till today.

Six months after the Tripuri Congress, war broke out in Europe in September 1939. With the outbreak of war, hopes were raised in many quarters that there would be a closing-up of the ranks, preparatory to a commencement of the struggle for freedom. The resignation of Congress ministries in the Provinces intensified these hopes, but they were soon dashed to the ground. Various arguments were advanced with a view to evading a struggle with the British Government. We, on our part, consistently and continuously urged an immediate launching of the struggle — for more reasons than one. One of the major considerations lay in the fact that in the spring of 1940, the war would enter a critical phase and it was but natural that we should try to time our own movement accordingly. If we wanted a crisis in India in the spring of 1940, it was necessary for us to launch the campaign a few months earlier. But our argument and our appeal did not go home. It was contended against us that when the crisis in Europe would not come till April 1940, we should not be in a hurry to start our movement.

Our leaders talked and talked — argued and argued, as the months rolled by. Nothing effective was done and the spring of 1940 arrived. With the breath of spring, the military activities of the Germans assumed an aggressive form. One fine morning, Denmark was occupied and Norway was invaded. Germany struck with lightning speed. The Allies were surprised and out-manoeuvred.

Holland has now been invaded and will probably be overrun in no time. What more surprises are in store for us nobody can tell. People are talking of a Japanese attack on the Dutch East Indies. The Italian army seems to be getting ready for the fray — with the Duce making bellicose speeches from the balcony of Palazzo Venezia and the crowd outside shouting — 'Tunisia, Tunisia'. The Cabinet in London is tottering after the debacle in Norway.

But what is India doing? What is the Indian National Congress doing?

Hindus and Muslims are drifting apart. The Congress Right Wing is attacking the Forward Bloc and the Kisan Sabha. The Forward Bloc and the Kisan Sabha, on their part, are endeavouring to carry on without the help of the Congress High Command. The Congress High Command is undecided as to what should be done and its attitude of doubt and vacillation is proving contagious and demoralizing to a degree. The Muslim League is more concerned with communal than with national problems. The cumulative effect of all these is that India as a whole is in a morass today. In the absence of a dynamic leadership the people, as a whole, seem to have lost their dynamism.

How can we save our country from this political rut, utilize the international crisis to India's advantage and win freedom for ourselves? This is the supreme problem of the hour.

As every day passes, one feels like biting his fingers in helpless agony. Can nothing be done to save India even at this late hour? Will not the enslaved people of India cast off their lethargy, sink their petty differences and stand up as one man to demand liberty for this great and ancient land?

We are prepared to play our humble part at this critical juncture, so that we may yet be able to retrieve what we have lost and achieve our national liberation. Let the Supreme Executive of the Congress call upon the nation to resume the struggle. We shall then fall in line with them in that great and noble task. Unity within the Congress could be achieved on the basis of a dynamic programme of national struggle. And we can then make a desperate attempt to achieve Hindu-Muslim unity on a permanent and enduring basis.

When Europe is in the melting-pot, who can withstand the united demand of three hundred and fifty millions of Indians. Freedom is now almost within reach. We have only to seize it with our united strength. Shall we do so?

34
Act Quickly

Signed editorial in the *Forward Bloc*, 18 May 1940

In our last issue we referred to the present international crisis in our editorial columns and we appealed to our countrymen to rise to the occasion and face the situation boldly. We also addressed an appeal to the Congress High Command and implored them to unite all Congressmen on the basis of a dynamic programme of national struggle — adding that we were prepared to play our part in this urgent and all-important task. The fundamental issue on which we had to part company with the High Command was that of national struggle and if the latter satisfy us on that point, there is nothing to prevent our joining hands with them, regardless of all our past differences and disputes. If the different parties in Great Britain could forget their past antagonisms within twenty-four hours and form a 'national' cabinet, cannot Congressmen who profess to have the same political goal close up their ranks when menaced by an unprecedented crisis? If we all have a sense of honour and of patriotism we should be able to do so.

The programme of national struggle for which the Forward Bloc had stood right from its birth has by now justified itself. But for it, the Congress Working Committee would long ago have followed the path of Gandhiji and offered unconditional co-operation to the British Government. We have successfully resisted the policy of compromise and surrender and over and above that, we have launched a struggle with British Imperialism which is bound to gain in strength and volume as the days roll by.

As the crisis in Europe deepens, the Western Imperialist powers will be weakened more. In that proportion will our task become lighter and lighter. And if British Imperialism ultimately suffers a reverse, the problem of national struggle will lose its importance. Whom shall we fight if British Imperialism ceases to be a political and military force as a result of vicissitudes in war?

It is quite on the cards that owing to the new situation that is fast developing, the problem of fighting British Imperialism will slowly but steadily usher in a complementary problem, viz. that of internal unity and consolidation. Political power that we have been aspiring after for so many decades is now within sight. How shall we seize it? And how shall we retain it when we have won it?

There is today dark uncertainty before us as to our future fate. But all this will vanish in no time, if we can achieve two things — unity among Congressmen and a Hindu-Muslim settlement. We shall then be able to win Swaraj easily and also to retain the Swaraj that we shall win.

The time at our disposal is exceedingly short and we shall have to act quickly if we are to act at all. Events are taking place in Europe with lightning speed and if we are to keep pace with the march of events, we too must be equally prompt. Let us all bestir ourselves while yet there is time. Delays are always dangerous and more so today.

35
Forward, Bengal!

Signed editorial in the *Forward Bloc*, 1 June 1940

It is not generally known outside Bengal that, after the outbreak of war in Europe, Emergency Ordinances were promulgated in the province which virtually strangled public life there. In the matter of rigour and ruthlessness, the 'Ordinance Raj' introduced in other provinces administered by Congress ministries could not stand a moment's comparison with what obtained in Bengal. The Bengal Provincial Congress Committee waited for nearly five months to see if the Bengal Government would alter their ways, and the latter were actually advised by influential quarters to do so, but to no avail. During these five months, the Congress Working Committee had to be approached three times for permission to start Civil Disobedience as a protest against the Ordinances.

By the middle of January, the Bengal Provincial Congress Committee reached the limit of patience and it decided to start a campaign of Civil Disobedience before the month was out. The most obnoxious feature in the 'Ordinance Raj' was the banning of public meetings, demonstrations, etc. throughout the province of Bengal, whereby public activities were virtually brought to a standstill. The first public meeting in defiance of the Ordinance was convened by the writer on the 31st January at the Shradhananda Park in Calcutta. Politically-minded Bengal was bursting with excitement on that day in the expectation that wholesale arrests would be made and that the Government would endeavour to put down the movement by force.

Nothing of the sort happened. For inscrutable reasons, the Government surrendered and everything went off peacefully. From that date onward, the Ordinance was defied by the Provincial Congress Committee and its supporters all over Bengal. In consequence thereof, the 'status quo' prior to September was automatically restored and such civil liberty as existed in this enslaved land before the outbreak of war was recovered by the people. The magnitude of the B.P.C.C.'s success was unexpected and unprecedented. Arrests made by the above Ordinance were, however, comparatively few in number. But perhaps for that very reason, the success achieved by the B.P.C.C. though substantial, was not spectacular.

This is how the B.P.C.C. has behaved since January last. But what about the Gandhiites and the neo-Gandhiites, viz. our National Fronters? It is reported that the authorities banned a Gandhiite Conference in Arambagh sub-division in Hooghly district and the local Gandhiites did not think of violating that order. In Nadia district, the neo-Gandhiites wanted to hold a meeting. But when the authorities did not permit it, they demonstrated that discretion was the better part of valour and abandoned their project. On May Day, the Provincial Trade Union Congress held a rally in Calcutta with governmental permission, but the meeting and rally arranged by the B.P.C.C. on that very day, was done without any reference to the authorities.

In May, Bengal stood in need of a fresh spurt. The struggle for the restoration of civil liberty had proved successful. The attempt of reactionary elements like the Ad Hoc Committee (the creature of the Congress Working Committee), the Hindu Mahasabha and the treacherous newspapers like '*The Amrita Bazar Patrika*' and the '*Yugantar*' to do down the B.P.C.C. had failed miserably. People were looking forward eagerly for a further lead.

To furnish that lead, a special session of the Bengal Provincial Conference was held at Dacca on 25th and 26th May. It was indeed a brilliant idea to have convened that conference. The number of delegates who attended was considerable, viz. nearly 600 and they all came with great alacrity. Dacca gave a wild and tumultuous reception to the President-elect and the writer on the 25th May. The main conference drew a vast crowd of visitors and sideshows like the Students' Conference, Workers' Conference, Kisan Conference and

Women's Conference were also successful. Everybody returned from Dacca with hope, confidence and buoyant expectation.

What was it that inspired those who attended the Dacca conference? It was the bold and clear lead given there. The call of Dacca was a call for the intensification of the struggle and the widening of the fighting front. But it was not an appeal addressed to a subject race. The Indian scene having changed beyond recognition during the last few months, the clarion-call was sent out to a people who had regained their self-respect and self-confidence and had begun to think, feel and act in terms of an independent nation.

The conference, therefore, urged the people to cast off and demolish all emblems of political servitude which militated against the newly awakened consciousness of Free India. The Holwell Monument in Calcutta which advertises the slavery of the Bengalis in the very heart of the city must now go. So also must disappear another symbol of our subjection, viz. political prisoners in jail and in restraint. And all this as a prelude to wiping out from the face of Free and Fair India all the stain of the past two centuries.

The Dacca conference struck another much-needed note of warning to the Indian people. With kings and kingdoms toppling down overnight, power appeared to be within sight and within reach. To seize that power and to retain it for all time, national unity and national solidarity seemed essential and indispensable. An appeal was, therefore, made for the restoration of unity within the Congress and for a lasting solution of the Hindu-Muslim problem. In a word, the direction of the Provincial Conference was 'Struggle and Unite' — struggle against alien Imperialism and unite among yourselves — if you want to win freedom and preserve it.

All this great and noble endeavour has to be made under the rallying-cry of 'All power to the Indian people'. 'All or none' is to be our principle and there is no room for compromise or halfway halt.

36
Is It Fair?

Signed editorial in the *Forward Bloc*, 8 June 1940

If even the devil is entitled to its due, why not the Forward Bloc? Our friends of the Right and of the Left have been criticizing us incessantly for not doing this and for failing to achieve that. But do they ever stop to consider what tremendous odds we have had to contend against? Have they ever condescended to lend us a helping hand? Far from doing so, they have, on the contrary, done much to frustrate our activities. We would not be either wrong or guilty of exaggeration if we were to charge them with actual sabotage. In the arduous task of launching a national struggle and of intensifying it and widening its scope — no help, no sympathy has come either from the Gandhiites, or the Radical Leaguers or the Congress Socialists or the National Fronters. The Kisan Sabha of Swami Sahajanand and Prof. Ranga and the Forward Bloc have had to depend entirely on their own resources. If the above-mentioned parties of the Right and of the Left had at least chosen to remain neutral, we would have thanked our stars. But deliberate hostility is what we have met with in many quarters. Before we launched the struggle, we were often accused of criticizing the Congress High Command and not doing something off our own bat. When the struggle was initiated this accusation was turned into ridicule. The struggle was pooh-poohed and people were told that it would never be effective without the active participation of the Gandhiites. No attempt was, however, made to persuade the latter to fall in line with us.

Strangely enough, whenever our comrades were arrested and incarcerated, we were told that that was no mass-struggle. At best, it was a Gandhian form of struggle. When they were not arrested in large numbers, as in Bengal, we were told that everything was quiet and no fight was on. And on top of all this wonderful reasoning, there was banter and ridicule.

Let us, however, take stock of our achievements in a thoroughly cool and dispassionate manner. In the first place, we may perhaps claim that we have so far prevented a compromise with British Imperialism as well as co-operation with the British Government in the prosecution of the war. One can easily imagine where the High Command would have landed the country by now, but for our persistent anti-compromise campaign. Secondly, we may perhaps claim that we have been able to create an atmosphere of struggle in the country and particularly within the ranks of Congressmen. Despite the fact that during the last eighteen months, Mahatma Gandhi has been consistently opposed to the idea of launching a national struggle — despite the fact that as early as September 1939, he was in favour of offering co-operation to the

British in the prosecution of the war, we find that today the Congress Working Committee is ordering the Congress organizations to convert themselves into 'Satyagraha' committees and is instructing the 'leaders' in the different provinces to get into shirts and shorts and begin drilling. Would this strange metamorphosis have been possible if there had been no Forward Bloc in the country and if the Anti-Compromise Conference had not been held at Ramgarh in March 1940?

Last but not least, we may perhaps claim that we have actually launched a national struggle with such strength and resources as we command. Eight members of the All-India Working Committee of the Forward Bloc are in prison today. Innumerable friends and co-workers in different parts of the country are behind the bars. In Bihar and U.P. the campaign is in full swing. In Bengal, the first phase of the struggle over the issue of civil liberty has seen the virtual surrender of the Bengal Government. Many of the war ordinances have been nullified since our struggle was launched and in consequence thereof the status quo prior to September 1939, has been restored in a very large measure. The Bengal Provincial Congress Committee is now preparing for the second phase of the struggle, after the inspiring lead given by the Dacca session of the Provincial Conference held on 25th and 26th May last.

It always takes time to develop a non-violent mass struggle in a vast country like India and the effort needed is not a small one. But the task becomes a thousand times more difficult when there is deliberate hostility on the part, not only Rightists, but also of so-called Leftists. Then there are non-Congress and anti-Congress organizations whose opposition has also to be faced by us and overcome. And to crown all, there is the colossus of British Imperialism with its allies, both British and Indian, that we have to combat with. Considering the obstacles we have to overcome and the tremendous odds we have to contend against, we have not done badly at all. Despite hostility, banter and ridicule, our movement will gather strength and volume as the days roll by. Let those who will not help, have the kindness to at least remain neutral. Whatever results we may actually achieve or however unworthy we may be as individuals there can be no doubt whatsoever that our cause is sublime and our endeavour noble. If we win — if our object is fulfilled — it is the country that will gain, and not we as individuals. Soldiers on the march! If we cannot agree about our methods and tactics, can we not agree to differ? And can we not have charity enough to respect one another's motives and wish one another well?

37
A Provisional National Government

Full text of a statement issued from Kurseong on 8 June 1940

The recent statement of His Excellency the Viceroy, the utterance of the Commander-in-Chief and the moves of the Provincial Governors have made it perfectly clear that at long last the British Government are going to make a really serious effort to exploit India for Britain's war purposes and this effort will be made without satisfying India's demand for Independence.

Personally, I am of the opinion that the British Government have felt emboldened to adopt this new policy because of the recent utterances of Mahatma Gandhi wherein he has stated clearly and unambiguously that India should not embarrass Great Britain in her hour of danger. This view is endorsed not only by Gandhian leaders but also by Pandit Jawaharlal Nehru. It would, therefore, be not wrong to infer that the Congress Working Committee is indirectly responsible for the new policy of British Imperialism in India.

So far as I can judge, the British Government will not easily slacken their efforts in that direction. Consequently, for all those who stand by the War resolution of the Haripura Congress, a serious situation has arisen. I have no doubt that if the armed forces of Great Britain happen to suffer more reverses in future, the British will inevitably fall back on India more and more, regardless of what Indian public opinion may declare.

But what interest can we have in European affairs, so long as India remains enslaved? We want our Independence and that too without delay. Promises made by the Government to be fulfilled at some future date will fall flat on our people. We shall judge the British in the light of what we shall get here and now. We have had enough experience of political promises that are made only to be broken. Let not the Government try to bluff us once again with high-sounding pledges.

Short-sightedness has been the character of British foreign

policy in recent years. It is this, more than anything else, which has brought disaster to Great Britain. I am afraid that the same short-sightedness is still hanging to the coat-tails of British politicians. They are thinking of saving Britain now with the help of India. But how can an enslaved India save England, or any country for the matter of that?

India has first to save herself. And she can save herself only if the Hindus and Muslims put forward a joint demand for a Provisional National Government to whom all powers should be immediately transferred. This is the procedure followed in every revolutionary crisis in history. This Provisional National Government at the Centre can fit into the existing constitution with certain consequential changes made in the Government of India Act of 1935. But the Provisional National Government must have full sovereign power. After a time, when the present crisis flows over, the Provisional National Government, free from British control, will convene a Constituent Assembly for framing a detailed constitution of India in keeping with her new status of Independence.

The first task of the Provisional National Government will be to arm the Indian people as fully as possible and also to enter into alliances with friendly foreign powers, so that India's safety may be completely ensured under all circumstances. If these measures are adopted, we need not be afraid of internal chaos any more, nor should we be afraid of any untoward consequences accruing to India as a result of the military success of the Nazis in Europe. When India is free and strong enough to save herself, she can lend a helping hand to other friendly countries.

The immediate duty of Indians is, therefore, to stand up for the slogan — 'all power to the Indian people' — and make an immediate demand for a Provisional National Government vested with full sovereign powers. This demand can be made irresistible if it be a joint demand put forward by the Hindus and Muslims of India. Can the Congress and the Muslim League agree on this issue? If they can, then they will save India once for all.

If unfortunately, this demand is turned down, we shall have no other option but to invite the Indian masses to the path of struggle.

I respectfully warn the British Government not to seek to exploit India's resources while India remains enslaved. Let them be not led astray by the soothing words of Mahatma Gandhi or of any Gandhian leader or leaders. When these leaders talk of compromise and co-operation, they do not represent Indian public opinion or the Indian masses. The suggestion now being made in some quarters that because of Nazi success the present war has ceased to be an imperialist war, is a puerile one and will not deceive any intelligent person in this country.

In conclusion, I would request the British Government to coolly consider what consequences will follow if they endeavour to save Britain with the resources of an enslaved India. This path will not bring salvation to England — but it may bring further disaster to India. A free, strong and united India will not only save herself unaided from every conceivable danger — but may also bring succour to other friendly nations, including Britain. If British politicians still continue to be bankrupt, despite all our passionate appeals, we shall be no party to the new policy being adopted by the Government of India, regardless of what Mahatma Gandhi may say or do.

38
Long Live Deshbandhu

Signed editorial in the *Forward Bloc*, 15 June 1940

Fifteen long years have passed since Deshbandhu Chittaranjan Das left this world of ours. He did not live to see his dream of a free India fulfilled, but he did achieve success in some of his immediate plans. Just when people had begun expecting greater things from him, death laid its cruel hand on him. He had won the confidence of his countrymen in an unmeasured degree and they had enthroned him in their hearts. Hence the mourning over his death was as universal as it was sincere. But while grieving over his untimely demise, we should not forget that he died in a blaze of glory. He was not one of those unfortunate beings who outlive the period of their greatness and linger on until life begins to ebb away, turning them into reactionaries.

Today, on the eve of the anniversary of his death, there is one thought uppermost in our minds — 'Oh, friend of the Nation! in this hour of trial and tribulation, India hath need of thee'. We want more than ever before, that rare combination of Idealism and Realism which constitutes the essence of leadership and which was the secret of his greatness. We want that unbounded love which made him a friend of the people and which drew the Muslims and the backward classes so close to him.

We want that dynamism which would not let him rest and which drove him from struggle to struggle. We want, above all, that all-consuming passion for liberty which is the source of all inspiration and the mainspring of all activity.

Let us pay our annual tribute of respect and gratitude to his hallowed memory. Those who want to be great, have to begin life by worshipping greatness wherever they find it. Those who desire to become heroes should first learn to do hero-worship. Hence the annual function on the 16th of June is a much-needed one and all sections of the people should rally together on the occasion.

The writer was a devoted disciple of Deshbandhu and when speaking of the departed great, it is difficult for him to do so with restraint. The debt he owes him is one that cannot be repaid. In fact, Deshbandhu's teachings have become a part of his very being.

39
After Paris

Signed editorial in the *Forward Bloc*, 15 June 1940

When the Nazi hordes crossed the German frontier into Holland and Belgium only the other day with the cry of 'nach Paris' on their lips, who could have dreamt that they would reach their objective so soon? A miracle in military warfare has happened, as it were, before our eyes and for an analogy, one has to turn to the Napoleonic wars or to the catastrophe at Sedan in the Franco-Prussian war of 1870. Whatever the French High Command may say in the face of mechanized transport, innumerable tanks and dive-bombers, no resistance worth the name is possible after the capitulation of Paris. The days of trench warfare are over.

But what next? It is clear that Reynaud's Government will not make a separate peace treaty with Germany, leaving Great Britain in the lurch. But how long will he be able to retain the confidence of the French people? The fall of his cabinet, a tempting offer from Germany and Italy, a new cabinet ready to make peace on those terms — these are events not altogether beyond the domain of possibility. The British Premier, Mr Winston Churchill, made an ominous reference to this in his historic speech the other day.

And England? What is she likely to do, with or without France? The answer to this question could be furnished by that inexplicable factor — 'the public morale'. Unfortunately, the morale of the British people has been badly shaken and the speeches of the Premier and of other ministers give ample proof of it. Why should it be necessary to tell the British people that they should not go about with long faces as if they were at a funeral? Why should it be necessary to tell the world that even if Great Britain is overrun by the Nazis, the Empire will go on fighting and in God's good time, the New World will come to the rescue of the Old World? The British people are famous for their dogged pertinacity and their unflinching nerves. They are now confronted with what is perhaps the severest ordeal in their history. Let us see how they will acquit themselves.

The Nazis have performed a miracle with the help of a new military technique, invented by the younger generals and military strategists. The Allies have fallen back on their war-renowned, hoary-headed generals who have been found wanting however. Have the Nazi generals exhausted their new technique? Have the Allies any military secrets or any new technique up their sleeves? Much will depend on the answers to these two questions.

We used to hear much of the chemical preparations of the Reichswehr (German army). Have they really perfected a new technique of chemical warfare? If they have, then we shall get evidence of it in the days to come. And it will then be seen how men's nerves behave under those new conditions. Will they collapse as the nerves of the brave Abyssinians did when attacked by Italian aircraft? Or will the soul conquer matter?

Judged from the realistic point of view, it is difficult to realize how the war can continue, if Great Britain is overrun. The United States of America cannot go beyond a certain limit in helping the Allies, lest Japan should make trouble in the Far East. And there is no hope, whatsoever, that Sir Stafford Cripps will succeed in dividing Germany and Soviet Russia. It is more than possible that there is a definite agreement between Soviet Russia on the one side and Germany and Italy on the other. If I were to make a guess as to the terms of that agreement, I should hazard a statement of this sort:

1. Germany will have a free hand on the Continent minus the Balkans.

2. Italy will have a free hand in the Mediterranean region.
3. The Balkans and the Middle East will be the Russian sphere of influence.
4. The resources of Africa should be shared by all the Big Powers.

Since both Germany and Italy — and perhaps Soviet Russia now regard Great Britain as public enemy no. 1, it is also likely that they have a plan of carving up the British Empire. In this task they may invite Japanese help and co-operation, knowing that Japan has always cast longing eyes on the entire Archipelago from the Dutch Indies to Australia.

In this scheme of things, how and where does India stand? Let those who claim to be leaders of the Indian people answer this question.

40
Come to Nagpur

Signed editorial in the *Forward Bloc*, 15 June 1940

The second session of the All-India Conference of the Forward Bloc will meet at Nagpur on the 18th June, after or along with the meetings of the Working Committee of the Muslim League and of the Congress. Apart from the fact that it is time to hold the All-India Conference, the present crisis which is deepening and worsening from hour to hour, makes an early session imperative.

What will be the task of the conference? No doubt we shall have to do a lot of stock-taking and heart-searching after recapitulating the events of the last twelve months; we shall have to ratify our present policy and programme or modify it, if necessary. But more urgent than that, is the need to determine our policy and programme '*vis-à-vis*' the British Government. The struggle launched at Ramgarh in March will have to be intensified and widened in its scope. Simultaneously, we shall have to work for national unity and solidarity. Those two issues will naturally raise a host of questions which will have to be answered satisfactorily.

In this connection, the statement made by Mr Amery, the Secretary of State for India, to the London Correspondent of '*The Hindusthan Times*' is illuminating. It reveals once again that imperialists will never learn the lessons of history. This statement was made when the Germans were at the gates of Paris!

Confronted with danger at home, the British Government now want to fall back on India and her resources. As if an enslaved India, impoverished and exploited, can save imperialist England in the present crisis! With a leadership that is seized with mental and moral paralysis and is determined not to embarrass British Imperialism, the outlook for India is indeed gloomy.

But are we to throw up our hands in despair? Our comrades in prison are looking through the barred windows on the world outside. What shall we say to them?

The imperialist offensive against the Forward Bloc, in Bengal and outside, is becoming more and more ruthless. Simultaneously, War committees are being formed throughout the country for exploiting enslaved India for war-purposes. Confronted with such an unprecedented crisis in our own history, we say to our imperialist rulers with a full sense of responsibility: 'We have accepted your challenge. You may do your worst but you will not succeed in resisting our march to Liberty.'

41
The Nagpur Address

Presidential Address at the second session of the All-India Forward Bloc Conference held at Nagpur, 18 June 1940

Comrades,

Early in May 1939, the Forward Bloc of the Indian National Congress was inaugurated in Calcutta following a momentous session of the All-India Congress Committee. In the last week of June 1939, the first session of the All-India Conference of the Forward Bloc was held in Bombay and the constitution and programme of the Bloc were adopted there. Since then, a year has rolled by — a year which will be memorable not only in the history of India, but in the history of the whole world. We are, therefore, meeting at a most opportune moment and not a day too soon. We shall have to do a great deal of heart-searching as well as stock-taking. We shall then have to determine our course of action in the crisis which has overtaken India and the world — the crisis which is deepening and worsening, not only from day to day but also from hour to hour.

The first question which I shall pose before you is: 'Have our policy and line of action been a correct one? And have we acted in the best interests of the country by launching the Forward Bloc?' To that my reply is: 'Most certainly, yes.' I shall remind you that we were constrained to start the Forward Bloc in the light of four considerations. The Right Wing had definitely told us that they would not work in co-operation with the Leftists in future and they had rejected the proposal of a Composite Cabinet which was our demand. Secondly, Mahatma Gandhi and the Right Wing had told us that a national struggle in the near future was out of the question. Thirdly, the attempt to consolidate the anti-imperialist and radical elements in the Congress under the name of the Left Bloc had been given up by the Socialists and Communists. Consequently, a further attempt at Left-consolidation could be made only by us and for that the Forward Bloc had become indispensably necessary. Fourthly, the Gandhiites or Right Wingers had already consolidated themselves under the aegis of the Gandhi Seva Sangha and any further delay on our part would have meant the strangling of the Leftist elements in the Congress by the Rightists.

It was clear in 1939 that most of those who had entered the Congress as Leftists in 1920 and 1921 and had retained the leadership of the Congress in their hands for well-nigh two decades, had ceased to be revolutionary or even radical. Any further political progress under such circumstances presupposed a consolidation of all anti-imperialist, radical and progressive forces in the country and particularly in the Congress.

Towards the end of April 1939, when I was seriously considering the idea of resigning the Presidentship of the Congress and inaugurating the Forward Bloc, I had an interesting and important discussion with a very prominent Leftist leader of the Congress who has since then thrown himself into the arms of the Gandhiites. He advised me to refrain from either course and he added that since an international storm was brewing, we should avoid everything in the nature of a split within the Congress. I replied saying that since a war was inevitable in the near future, it was all the more necessary that the Leftists should be organized and prepared in advance, so that in the event of the Rightists developing cold feet in a war-situation, we at least could do something off our own bat. Differences had become so fundamental between the Right Wing and the Left

Wing that a split, whether permanent or temporary, had become inevitable. That being the case, it was desirable that the internal crisis should come and should be transcended before the external or international crisis overtook us. I added that if I accepted my friend's advice and lay low for the present, the consequences would be far worse for us when the international crisis appeared. In such a crisis, we would never agree with the Rightists. But many people would blame us for causing a split, if we attempted to act on our own at that time. Moreover, if we did want to act independently, then we would have no organization behind us to fall back on. Consequently, the argument of my friend only strengthened my case.

Looking back on the last twelve months, can we not claim that events have justified our policy and line of action? Barring the Kisan Sabha of Swami Sahajanand (and Prof. Ranga, Comrade Yajnik, etc.) and Forward Bloc, who is there to stand up to the Rightists today? The Left Consolidation Committee which came into existence in June 1939, after the formation of the Forward Bloc, has disintegrated by now. The Royists (or Radical Leaguers), the Congress Socialists and the Communists (or National Fronters) have in turn deserted the Left Consolidation Committee and only the Kisan Sabha and the Forward Bloc have been functioning as the spearhead of the Left Movement in this country. This was evident when we held the All-India Anti-Compromise Conference at Ramgarh in March 1940. There we found that the Royists, Congress Socialists and National Fronters boycotted that Conference and threw in their lot with the Gandhites.

There can be little doubt today that if there had been no Forward Bloc and no Kisan Sabha, no voice would have been raised against the policy and line of action pursued by the Gandhiites during the last twelve months.

We shall consider another question: 'What has been our actual achievement during the past year?'

In the first place, we can claim to have successfully resisted the tendency towards Constitutionalism and compromise within the ranks of the Congress. Thanks to our efforts, the Congress ministries had to vacate office as a protest against the policy of the British Government. If they had not done so, they would have been carrying out the War policy of the Government of India, as agents of British Imperialism. In spite of all efforts made hitherto, no compromise has yet been made with the British Government and for this, we can legitimately claim some credit.

Secondly, we have so far frustrated all attempts to secure the co-operation of the Congress in the prosecution of the War. Friends will remember that in September 1939, when His Excellency the Viceroy invited Mahatma Gandhi for a talk at Simla on the War situation, the latter gave out that he was of the view that India should give unconditional help to Great Britain during the present war. This was reiterated by Mahatmaji in a press statement issued soon after the above interview. Nevertheless, until now, the Congress Working Committee, which usually follows Gandhiji blindly, has ignored his views on such an all-important issue. Would the same thing have happened if there had been no Kisan Sabha and no Forward Bloc?

Thirdly, we can perhaps claim that we have succeeded in creating an atmosphere of struggle. Today, we find Congress leaders drilling in shirts and shorts and Congress committees being converted into 'Satyagraha' Committees. Moreover, the Rightist leaders have been constantly talking of a struggle. Would all these have taken place, if there had been no Forward Bloc and if the Anti-Compromise Conference at Ramgarh had not shown which way the wind of public opinion was blowing? There is no doubt that today the talk of a struggle is everywhere in the air and the more our people talk of it, the more will they move away from a compromise.

Lastly, we can claim that at Ramgarh we launched our struggle with such strength and resources as we possessed. During the last three months, a large number of our fellow-workers, including men of outstanding influence in the country, have been arrested and incarcerated. Nine members of the All-India Working Committee of the Forward Bloc are at present in prison or internment. In addition to them, leaders of the Kisan Sabha headed by Swami Sahajanand Saraswati, Prof. Ranga and others, are behind the bars.

The National Struggle we launched at Ramgarh has been steadily gaining in strength and volume. The campaign has made considerable headway in Bihar and the United Provinces. In Bengal, the struggle was launched as early as January 1940, over the question of civil liberty, which had been violated by the drastic ordinances promulgated by the Government in September 1939. Thanks to the Civil Disobedience movement launched by Bengal Congress, we have restored in a large measure the 'status quo' which existed prior to September 1939. The special Session of the Bengal Provincial Political Conference which met at Dacca on 25th and 26th

May 1940, took stock of the situation in the province and formulated a plan for intensifying the struggle and widening its scope. The Bengal Provincial Congress Committee will give effect to this plan.

Before I proceed to deal with the international situation, I shall refer to one or two criticisms which are constantly levelled at us. We are told, for instance, that we have created a split in the Congress. The fact, however, is that it is the Gandhiites who have created a split by refusing to co-operate with the Leftists. We have all along been strongly in favour of joint action and a Composite Cabinet for ensuring such action.

We are also told that we have brought disruption within the ranks of the Leftists. But it is not we who have caused disruption or disunity. The Royists, the Congress Socialists and the National Fronters (or Communists) — have, one after another, deserted the Left Consolidation Committee. We stand today exactly where we did twelve months ago. During these months, we have passed through an ordeal. Suffering, persecution, banter, ridicule — such has been our lot. But we have gone ahead along the path of uncompromising struggle in a most unflinching manner. Numerous fellow-workers of ours have been persecuted by the Congress High Command and in the province of Bengal, owing to the disaffiliation of the Provincial Congress Committee, all Congressmen of our way of thinking have been virtually thrown out of the Congress.

The question which will naturally arise at this stage is: 'Why have the Royists and others deserted us?' So far as I can judge, they are afraid of being expelled from the Congress and they feel perhaps, that once outside the Congress, they will be completely lost. What amuses me, however, is that these comrades had been hoping to fight the Rightists and had not anticipated that before being defeated by the Leftists, the Rightists would do their worst and would do all in their power to maintain their supremacy in the Congress. The backbone, the stamina and the toughness that are needed in order to fight the Rightists successfully — these Leftists (or shall I say pseudo-Leftists?) comrades do not possess. We are now passing through a phase of our struggle when history itself will put all of us to the test and declare to the world as to who the genuine Leftists in India are.

We are also told that without the help of the Gandhiites, the struggle we have launched will prove to be a failure. To this allegation, our answer is as follows. It is too early to say whether our struggle will be successful or not. That will depend on whether the masses will join it or not. It always takes some time to get the masses to rally round the banner of a non-violent struggle. Let us, therefore, hold ourselves in patience yet a while.

But, supposing for argument's sake that the struggle will fail, does that mean that it should not have been launched? Could we not argue, on the opposite side, that the campaigns of 1921, 1930 and 1932 should not have been launched because they had not brought us Swaraj? Failures are often the pillars of success. So what does it matter if we fail for the fourth time! Not to try at all is more dishonourable than making the attempt and failing to achieve success. The whole world is watching us today. What will the free nations of the world think of us if we miss the golden opportunity that has now come — an opportunity that is rare in the lifetime of every nation? But nobody will think ill of us if we fight and then fail.

There is another point which we should not overlook either. Shall we not consider what posterity will think of us twenty or fifty years hence, if we do not acquit ourselves manfully today? What do people today think of the leaders who mismanaged the affairs of the country between 1914 and 1919? I, therefore, make bold to say that if we do not rise to the occasion and join the struggle without delay, neither history nor posterity will ever pardon us.

Twelve months ago when the Forward Bloc was formed we were obsessed, as it were, with the idea of the coming struggle and how to prepare for it in advance. At that time we did not know how far, if at all, outside events and international developments would aid us in our efforts to win Purna Swaraj. Consequently, we had to make 'self-reliance' our motto in life and action. Today, the situation has altered to some extent. In the war between rival imperialisms, the old ones have been faring very badly indeed. During the last few weeks the Germans have carried on the campaign with lightning rapidity. Kings and kingdoms have toppled down in the course of a few days and the German army — the Reichswehr — has proceeded to the gates of Paris and occupied that queen of cities in a way which appears to the layman as a miracle in military warfare. What has been happening in Europe in a kaleidoscopic manner has had its inevitable repercussion on India. With every blow that she receives in Europe, the imperialist might of Britain is bound to loosen its grip on India and other dependencies. The wheels of history are grinding on, quite regardless of what we may be doing in India. Even a child should, therefore, understand that in order to win Purna Swaraj under the altered conditions of today, we need much less effort and sacrifice that we did twelve months ago. But in order to fully utilize the opportunity which international events have presented to us, we must have sufficient unity and solidarity among ourselves. If India could speak with one voice today, our demand would indeed be well-nigh irresistible. It follows, as a consequence, that while we should think of intensifying the national struggle and widening its scope, we should at the same time try to develop national unity and solidarity to the maximum limit. But a struggle is needed in any case. Without it, our rulers may not easily bend. We know from experience that imperialists never learn the lessons of history. Further, our own leaders may be induced to go in for a compromise with British Imperialism if the Leftist pressure, exerted through a national struggle, is withdrawn. You will, therefore, have to consider what steps you should immediately take in order to intensify and widen the struggle and simultaneously to develop national unity and solidarity. National unity will presuppose unity within the Congress on the basis of a dynamic programme of struggle and at the same time unity between the Congress and other organizations like the Muslim League.

If we can develop sufficient unity and solidarity among ourselves in good time, we may very well hope that even if the country passes through a struggle and even if catastrophic events take place in Europe, the transference of power from the hands of British Imperialism to those of the Indian people will take place in a peaceful manner. It is not necessary that the Indian revolution should be a bloody one or that it should pass through a period of chaos. On the contrary, it is desirable that it should be as peaceful as possible and peaceful transition can be ensured if the people are united and are determined to have their freedom.

My own suggestion to you is that we should immediately go out into the country with the rallying cry — 'All power to the Indian people'. This will galvanize the masses in a moment. In order to put forward this demand in an effective and irresistible manner, we should leave no stone unturned in our effort to attain national unity. This effort will necessitate the setting up of a machinery which will preserve harmony and goodwill among the people under all circumstances. Such a machinery will be provided by a Citizens' Defence Corps organized on an all-party basis. But such a Corps should be quite independent of the Government and will not work for the safeguarding of an enslaved India. Our Citizens' Defence Corps will only aim at preserving internal peace, harmony and goodwill. The question of defending the country militarily from any other force or power is one which should concern the Government only and not the people, so long as India remains subjugated. What interest can we have in fighting for the perpetuation of our slavery, for that is exactly what is implied in fighting to defend an enslaved India.

Before coming to the epilogue of this address, which will be a consideration of the international situation of today and tomorrow, I should like to remind you of the historical role of the Forward Bloc. The Bloc has come into being as the result of historical necessity. It is not the creation of an individual or of a group of individuals. So long as it will serve a historical purpose, it will live and thrive — despite all obstacles, internal or external. We should also bear in mind that the Forward Bloc will have a role to play in the post-struggle phase of our history. It will have to preserve liberty after winning it and it will have to build up a new India and a happy India on the basis of the eternal principles of Liberty, Democracy and Socialism. Let us not commit the fatal mistake of thinking that our mission will be over, once we win our freedom. The organization or party that wins freedom must undertake the responsibilities of post-war reconstruction. Only in this manner will continuity of progress be maintained.

Let us now proceed to consider the international situation as we find it today and as it will probably be tomorrow. After reading the outspoken statements of Messrs. Winston Churchill and Paul Reynaud we cannot blink the prime facts of the situation as they emerge from the quick tempo of war. Everyday makes it more clear that M. Paul Reynaud's summing up of the situation in the Chamber of Deputies (that victory of the Allies could only be brought about by a miracle) was a true measure of the military conditions then obtaining. Dark as was the picture then, it has grown darker since. The prospect today is positively bleak. And when one remembers this is a totalitarian war, it dawns on us how impossible is the situation in which the losing side is placed.

We may also concede that Monsieur Reynaud's ringing resolution 'to intensify the struggle . . . and not to give up' is brave and resolute, and his words not empty heroics. For all that, he fails to convince when he says: 'We will shut ourselves into one of our

Provinces and if we are driven out we will go to North Africa and if necessary into our possessions in America.'

That is hardly the way to carry a war through to victory. If the Allies lose their foothold in Europe, they may conceivably fight on in Africa, in Asia, even in America; but it is for the ultimate aim of victory, useless.

Today we have every right to examine the stark realities of the War as it has developed until we see them in the white light of clarity. The leaders of the French and British peoples have been frank. We should also be frank with ourselves.

The cause of the Allies' continuous defeat seems today lodged somewhere in their system. It was a system which Mr Clement Attlee said had failed to meet the needs of the crisis. It was the fundamental weakness of a system in which slavery and freedom existed side by side that had resulted in Britain being 'decisively beaten' on the propaganda front. This was what the '*Daily Mail*' said was happening. Propaganda radiocasts from the Reich, it wrote at the end of March, were 'influencing not only the civilian population of Britain, but also our armed forces . . . ' 'Goebbels', it asserted, 'has had a walk-over.'

But we are not so much interested in a particular method as in the basic principles of action. And we are not to be dissuaded from pressing home our demand for the admission of our fundamental rights by a clouding of the issues and cry of 'saboteur'! We have too long been taken in by the cleverest imperialist propaganda.

We cannot but ask ourselves where we stand in this international flux. Following the sombre thoughts of Allied statesmen and strategists, we cannot but ask ourselves what we should do if British resistance collapses. This is by no means impossible. In fact, the Premier, Mr Churchill has already talked in terms of defeat for Britain. He talked much earlier in the strain in which Premier Reynaud has now talked — of dispersing to the far ends of the Empire to carry on the struggle. Some of our statesmen, it seems, have been possessed with the dream of India being converted into a bastion of democratic resistance against the dictators' hordes. What a grotesque picture!

Almost the whole of the English Channel coast on the French side is in the hands of the Germans, making ordinary communications difficult and hazardous and the transport of troops all but impossible. Some of the best industrial regions of France are in the hands of the invaders. Paris, the heart of France, has ceased to throb.

In the Champagne region a powerful German drive is developing to isolate the Maginot Line from the rest of France. In the South-East the powerful and fresh Italian legions are pressing, and everywhere the retreating French forces are harried by the admittedly superior air-arm of the admittedly superior Reichswehr. Such is the gloomy picture of the Allied position in Europe. From the Northern Arctic regions to the Atlantic, the Nazi eagle has spread its wings in an unbroken line. It is not surprising we should be told that there is no cause for optimism.

When the Nazi hordes crossed the German frontier into Holland and Belgium only the other day with the cry of 'nach Paris' on their lips, who could have dreamt that they would reach their objective so soon? A miracle in military warfare has happened, as it were, before our eyes and for an analogy, one has to turn to the Napoleonic wars or to the catastrophe at Sedan in the Franco-Prussian war of 1870. Whatever the French High Command may say, in the face of mechanized transport, innumerable tanks and dive-bombers, no resistance worth the name is possible after the capitulation of Paris. The days of trench warfare are over.

But what next? It is clear that Reynaud's Government will not make a separate peace with Germany, leaving Great Britain in the lurch. But how long will he be able to retain the confidence of the French people? The fall of his cabinet, a tempting offer from Germany and Italy, a new cabinet ready to make peace on those terms — these are events not altogether beyond the domain of possibility. The British Premier, Mr Winston Churchill, made an ominous reference to this in his historic speech the other day.

And England? What is she likely to do, with or without France? The answer to this question could be furnished by that inexplicable factor 'the public morale'. Unfortunately, the morale of the British people has been badly shaken and the speeches of the Premier and of other ministers give ample proof of it. Why should it be necessary to tell the British people that they should not go about with long faces as if they were at a funeral? Why should it be necessary to tell the world that even if Great Britain is overrun by the Nazis, the Empire will go on fighting and in God's good time, the New World will come to the rescue of the Old World? The British people are famous for their dogged pertinacity and their unflinching nerves. They are now confronted with what is perhaps the severest ordeal in their history. Let us see how they will acquit themselves.

The Nazis have performed a miracle with the help of a new

military technique, invented by the younger generals and military strategists. The Allies have fallen back on their war-renowned, hoary-headed generals who have been found wanting, however. Have the Nazi generals exhausted their new technique? Have the Allies any military secrets or any new technique up their sleeves? Much will depend on the answers to these two questions.

We used to hear much of the chemical preparations of the Reichswehr (German army). Have they really perfected a new technique of chemical warfare? If they have, then we shall get evidence of it in the days to come. And it will then be seen how men's nerves behave under those new conditions. Will they collapse as the nerves of the brave Abyssinians did when attacked by Italian aircraft? Or will the soul conquer matter?

Judged from the realistic point of view, it is difficult to realize how the war can continue, if Great Britain is overrun. The United States of America cannot go beyond a certain limit in helping the Allies, lest Japan should make trouble in the Far East. And there is no hope, whatsoever, that Sir Stafford Crips will succeed in dividing Germany and Soviet Russia. It is more than probable that there is a definite agreement between Soviet Russia on one side and Germany and Italy on the other. If I were to make a guess as to the terms of that agreement, I should hazard a statement of this sort:

1. Germany will have a free hand on the Continent minus the Balkans.
2. Italy will have a free hand in the Mediterranean region.
3. The Balkans and the Middle East will be the Russian sphere of influence.
4. The resources of Africa should be shared by all the Big Powers.

Since both Germany and Italy — and perhaps Soviet Russia — now regard Great Britain as public enemy no.1, it is also likely that they have a plan of carving up the British Empire. In this task they may invite Japanese help and co-operation, knowing that Japan has always cast longing eyes on the entire Archipelago, from the Dutch Indies right up to Australia.

Such being the situation, if Britain cannot save herself and her Empire from the German-Italian attack, it would be idle to expect, like Mr Churchill, that the Empire would save itself and Britain on top of it. Let us therefore, cease talking of saving Britain with the Empire's help or with India's help. India must in this grave crisis think of herself first. If she can win freedom now and then save herself, she will best serve the cause of humanity. It is for the Indian people to make an immediate demand for the transference of power to them through a Provisional National Government. No constitutional difficulties can be put forward by the British Government with a view to resisting this demand, because legislation for this purpose can be put through Parliament in twenty-four hours. When things settle down in India and abroad, the Provisional National Government will convene a Constituent Assembly for framing a full-fledged Constitution for this country.

Friends, these are some of my thoughts and suggestions today. I hope and trust that you will give them due consideration. In any case, I appeal to you not to leave Nagpur till you have in your pockets a concrete plan of action for winning Purna Swaraj in the immediate future.

Let us proclaim once again — 'All power to the Indian people, here and now'.

42
Task Before the Country

The following statement was published in the *Forward Bloc*, 29 June 1940

The world situation is in such a state of flux that one can notice a tendency in some quarters to stop thinking and to drift with the tide of events. But we should not forget that what has happened or is happening is not fortuitous in character but is the result of careful planning and preparation. For us, it would be a fatal mistake to suppose that simply because the situation is favourable for the attainment of our political goal, Swaraj will drop into our hands like a ripe fruit.

Since I left Calcutta ten days ago, I have met a number of India's foremost politicians and leaders, besides representatives of the Forward Bloc from different provinces. I have endeavoured in my talks to put forward the policy and programme of the Forward Bloc and to obtain light for myself in return. Though I cannot claim to have discovered an all-round agreement, I have certainly found to my pleasant surprise many points of agreement. As a result thereof, I have returned with a clearer perception of the task that is ahead of us.

In the first place, we should lose no time in putting forward a joint demand before the British Government for the immediate transference of power to the Indian people through a Provisional National Government. This demand is bound to be irresistible if the Indian people speak with one voice on this occasion. We should not be lured by promises or even by a partial transference of power now, because our slogan clearly is — 'All power to the Indian People'.

A National Cabinet at the Centre should be accompanied by National Cabinets in the provinces. The latter will naturally owe allegiance to the former. Moreover, they will ensure internal peace and harmony during the transitional period and will pave the way to a lasting Hindu-Muslim settlement. I feel convinced that the Hindu-Muslim problem is not insoluble. But its solution will come if we begin to concentrate on practical, concrete issues and if we do not waste our time or energy over issues that are theoretical or abstract in character. Co-operation between Hindus and Muslims wherever that is immediately possible will inevitably widen the sphere of such co-operation in future.

A moot point in this connection is as to whether we should try the experiment of National Cabinets in the provinces even if we cannot set up a National Cabinet at the Centre just now. To this query, my answer is 'Yes'. In the present dynamic situation, National Cabinets in the provinces will be a great help not only in maintaining internal harmony, not only in establishing Hindu-Muslim unity — but also in winning power at the Centre — should there be obstacles in the path of attaining Swaraj.

We should also push on with our scheme of a Citizens' Defence Corps. But it is necessary to explain to the public that this Corps will be quite independent of the British Government. Its task will be merely to help in maintaining internal peace, harmony and goodwill, so that Indians may not quarrel or fight among themselves at the time when they should concentrate on winning freedom for India.

In this connection, I should emphasize our conviction that we should not slacken in any way the struggle that we launched at Ramgarh. We do not believe that Swaraj will come automatically and without a struggle. The moment the struggle is abandoned, the atmosphere will be vitiated and the tendency towards compromise with Imperialism will again rear its head. We have, therefore, resolved to intensify the struggle we have commenced and to widen its scope.

In this fateful hour, when history is being created before our very eyes, what is needed most of all is that we should think of India and India alone — and not of parties or sectarian interests. No sacrifice on the part of any individual or party should be regarded as too great if only it serves the cause of India's emancipation.

43
Holwell Monument

An article in *Forward Bloc*, 29 June 1940

There has been unavoidable delay in bringing out this issue. In fact, we have been forced to miss one week, thanks to the kind attention of the Government of Bengal. Our office was searched and our security was forfeited. Fresh security to the tune of Rs 2000 had to be deposited before we could bring out the next issue.

This has been all for the good. It has put our back up. We have therefore, to push on with our plan of work and put more zest and more zeal into it. The campaign against the Holwell monument, which was the mandate of the Bengal Provincial Conference, has to be taken up at once. The third of July 1940, is going to be observed in Bengal as the Sirajuddowla Day — in honour of the last independent king of Bengal. The Holwell Monument is not merely an unwarranted stain on the memory of the Nawab, but has stood in the heart of Calcutta for the last 150 years or more as the symbol of our slavery and humiliation. That monument must now go.

On the 3rd of July next will commence the campaign against that monument and the writer has decided to march at the head of the first batch of volunteers on that day.

The second session of the All-India Conference of the Forward Bloc met at Nagpur on the 18th and 19th June. The Conference was a great success and a number of important resolutions were passed. The proceedings of the Conference have influenced public opinion throughout the country, including the mind of the Congress Working Committee, which was meeting simultaneously. Nagpur has virtually repeated the call of Dacca. The decisions at Nagpur may be summarized in the following manner.

1. Intensify the struggle and widen its scope under the slogan — 'All power to the Indian people'.

2. Demand from the British Government immediate transference of full power to the Indian people through a Provisional National Government.
3. Work simultaneously for national unity and particularly for Hindu-Muslim unity.
4. Organize Citizens' Defence Corps on a non-party basis with a view to preserving internal unity and solidarity during the transitional period.

Subsequent to and in furtherance of the Nagpur decisions, the writer has in a recent statement advocated the setting up of a National Cabinet at the Centre, accompanied by National Cabinets in the provinces.

The situation today is dynamic and in order to handle it properly, a dynamic policy is needed. History has put us to the test. Let us not be found wanting. It is for us now to make our country's future or to mar it.

44
Forward Bloc in Perspective

This incomplete article in his own hand was found among Netaji's personal papers of his last imprisonment in Presidency Jail, Calcutta, from July to December 1940. It has a striking resemblance to his Kabul thesis 'Forward Bloc — its justification' which he wrote in March 1941 while in Afghanistan during his escape from India. It is thus clear that he had decided to write the thesis and started it in jail. Ultimately he wrote and completed it in Kabul. In the process he changed the title and also made alterations in the text. The final complete thesis has been published in *The Essential Writings of Netaji Subhas Chandra Bose* (Calcutta and Delhi, 1997). — Ed.

The growth of a movement may be likened to that of a living tree. Neither growth is unilinear. There are inner upheavals and contradictions corresponding to breaks and bifurcations. But one of the essential conditions of development is continuity. Because of this continuity, an organic branch is different from a parasite. Every part of a living tree is organically connected with the roots which go deep into the soil, but this cannot be said of a parasite.

It is from this standpoint of organic evolution that the history of the Indian National Congress should be analysed and studied.

An inner upheaval or revolt usually appears when there is stagnation — or an attempt to strangle a movement. After I joined the Congress in 1921, the first sign of revolt appeared within the Congress as early as 1922, following the suspension of Civil Disobedience at Bardoli by Mahatma Gandhi. This revolt ultimately assumed shape and form a year later under the name of the Swaraj Party.

The Swaraj Party was composed of variegated elements, not all of which were revolutionary or radical in outlook or character. But the 'greatest common measure' which bound them together was a rational outlook on politics and a desire for a change. Hence the official Congress Party which adhered to undiluted Gandhism was called the 'No-change Party'. It will be remembered even at this distant date that the bone of contention was entry into the legislatures, to which the 'Non-changers', or orthodox Gandhiites, were dead opposed.

After a period of revolt there was reconciliation and synthesis. This began in 1924, during the lifetime of Deshbandhu C.R. Das, when the Gandhi-Das-Nehru Pact was concluded. After Deshbandhu's death, virtual fusion of the Congress and the Swaraj Party took place. The Congress adopted the Swarajists programme at the Cawnpore session in 1925 and Swarajists assumed full control over the Congress. This continued till the Lahore session of the Congress in December 1929. In 1929, Mahatma Gandhi's choice made Pandit Jawaharlal Nehru the President of the Lahore Congress. At that juncture, the then Swarajist generalissimo, Pandit Motilal Nehru, recanted and the Swarajist programme was scrapped, so that the 'No-changers' had their day after six long years. But withdrawal from the Legislatures was altogether uncalled for in 1930. It was quite unnecessary to make that a condition precedent to the starting of Civil Disobedience.

Under normal conditions of development one would have expected the next inner upheaval to appear from within the Swaraj Party — that is, from among the progressive elements in that Party — Let us see, however, what actually happened.

With a view to bringing the Congress round to the acceptance of the goal of complete Independence — the Independence League was launched at Lucknow in 1928, Pandit Jawaharlal Nehru, the writer and some others taking the lead in the matter. In December of the same year, when the annual session of the Congress met in Calcutta under the Presidentship of Pandit Motilal Nehru, a clash took place between the official party led by Mahatma Gandhi and the Independence Leaguers. The main resolution was moved by Mahatmaji, to which an amendment was tabled by the writer to the effect that 'Complete Independence' should be declared explicitly as the goal of the Congress. The amendment was lost, but the voting showed that the minority was strong and influential.

Gandhiji probably took the hint, for when the Congress met at its annual session a year later at Lahore with Pandit Jawaharlal Nehru in the chair, he (Gandhiji) himself moved the resolution on Independence which he had opposed and defeated at the Calcutta Congress. The resolution was adopted unanimously, but that did not mean that there was no tussle at Lahore within the ranks of the Congress. A Left Wing had emerged conspicuously for the first time at the Calcutta Congress in 1928 and a tug-of-war had taken place there over the question of the ideal or goal. At the Lahore Congress there was a clash over the question of the method, or plan of action, for achieving independence. The official plan submitted by the Working Committee, at Mahatma Gandhi's insistence, was thrown out by the Subjects Committee. That Committee also rejected the alternative plan moved by the writer on behalf of the Left Wing. The result was that though the Congress unanimously adopted Independence as its goal, it dispersed without deciding on any plan of action. From the temper of the house it was clear, however, that the general body of Congressmen wanted a militant programme of action.

At Lahore, Gandhiji undoubtedly gave evidence of superb diplomacy. Calcutta had shown that the Left Wing was no longer a negligible factor in Congress politics but a year later, the Mahatma administered what appeared to many as a knock-out blow. Pandit Jawaharlal was won over before the Congress met and at that Congress, Gandhiji well-nigh took the wind out of the sails of the extremists by moving the resolution on Independence. Nevertheless, though numerically weaker than at Calcutta, the Left-Wingers were more mature and determined when they met at Lahore and the Mahatma did not fail to notice it. Though he had an utterly blank mind as to his future plans when he was at Lahore, within a few months he launched the Civil Disobedience campaign in April 1930. This campaign represented the peak of his influence and popularity as a political leader, but it is extremely doubtful, at least to the writer, if the campaign would have taken place at all, but for the pressure continuously exerted by the Left-Wingers during a period of two years and particularly at the time of the Lahore Congress.

Though the main clash between the official party and the Left Wing was over the question of the future plan of action, minor skirmishes also took place, which revealed unmistakably that at Lahore authoritarianism had appeared in the upper ranks of Congress leadership. During one of these skirmishes, the writer and his fellow-delegates from Bengal were forced to walk out as a protest against the 'platform's' autocracy. They were joined at once by Left-Wingers from other provinces, led by Sjt. Srinivasa Iyengar, ex-President, Dr Alam, Swami Govindanand, etc. It was then decided to crystallize the amorphous Left Wing into a party, that being the only means whereby the autocracy of the 'platform' could be checked. The party was called the Congress Democratic Party and office-bearers of this newly formed Party were duly elected at Lahore.

We must stop here for a moment, for a retrospect is necessary. It should be clear by now that after the death of Deshbandhu Das, the upper ranks of Swarajist leadership began to suffer from a lack of dynamism. When further overtures were made from the Gandhian side in 1928 and after, a complete rapprochement with the Swarajist leadership took place. This was cemented by Mahatma Gandhi espousing the candidature of Pandit Jawaharlal for the Presidentship of the Lahore Congress. All those elements that were not uncompromisingly radical or revolutionary thereupon fell in line with the new Gandhian-cum-Swarajist-cum-Jawahar leadership. Even some Left Wing elements did the same, being drawn by the personal influence of Pandit Jawaharlal, who had begun to sail with the new Congress leadership, having practically disowned his own creation, the Independence League, after his election to the presidential chair.

The Swaraj Party was thus liquidated by its own generalissimo and its programme was scrapped. Likewise, the Independence League was given a stab in the back by one of its principal founders. Arrayed against the solid phalanx of Gandhiites, Jawaharites and a large number of Swarajists — the radical and progressive elements in the Congress, the majority of whom were to be found within the Swaraj Party, stood completely isolated. Nevertheless, the Left Wing would have forged ahead, but for two serious obstacles. Firstly, the Congress Democratic Party which was meant to be a rallying-ground for all Left Wing elements died a premature death. Secondly, the new Congress leadership played a Left Wing role by launching a major campaign of Civil Disobedience in April 1930.

Immediately after the Lahore Congress, the writer was sent to prison for sedition. Owing to differences with Gandhiji, Sjt. Srinivasa Iyengar retired from the Congress altogether. Dr Alam gradually drifted towards the official Congress leadership. And then in April 1930, when the mass Civil Disobedience campaign began, Left Wing elements plunged into the movement. As long as that movement went on, nobody could think of organizing a new party. In such circumstances, the Congress Democratic Party could not survive.

The campaign of 1930 culminated in the Gandhi-Irwin Pact of March 1931. That Pact demonstrated that the Congress leadership would not play a genuinely Left Wing role. Consequently, judged from one point of view, the time was ripe for resuming Left Wing activity. But on the other hand, after the Pact, Gandhiji's influence among the masses was at its zenith. Moreover, everybody expected a resumption of Civil Disobedience when the second Round Table Conference in London concluded its sittings. The period between March 1931 and January 1932 could not therefore be made use of for organizing the Left Wing. During this interval, individual Left-Wingers spent all their energy in preparing the public mind for the resumption of Civil Disobedience.

The campaign of 1932 was in reality a continuation of the campaign of 1930 — but it is doubtful if it would have taken place, but for the activities of Left-Wingers in the Frontier Province, United Provinces and Bengal. Those activities were directed not towards organizing a new party, but towards preparing the country for the revival of Civil Disobedience.

As long as the Congress was engaged in a life-and-death struggle and the leadership was on the whole dynamic, internal differences were submerged and a crystallization of the Left Wing was impossible. With the first signs of backsliding, however, an inner revolt began to rear its head again. Towards the end of 1932, the Harijan Movement was launched by Gandhiji while he was still in prison. This movement was not a novel phenomenon — being in reality a revival or strengthening of the movement for the eradication of untouchability among the Hindus. But by launching this movement afresh when the country was in the midst of the throes of a political struggle, Gandhiji served to sidetrack the main political issue. The Harijan Movement was the sequel to Mahatmaji's fast, protesting against the original Communal Award, in so far as it separated the depressed classes, or scheduled castes, from the main body of Hindus. That fast had also served to divert public attention from the Civil Disobedience Movement and had automatically weakened it. From the fast and its sequel, the Harijan Movement, shrewd political observers suspected that Gandhiji had begun to own defeat in his own mind and was trying to strike out a new line which would enable him to retain his hold over the masses through some kind of sideshow like the Harijan Movement.

They were not far wrong. In May 1933, Mahatma Gandhi announced the suspension of the Civil Disobedience Movement. This was the signal for a swing to the Right and a revolt from the Left. The clarification of issues brought about by the suspension was immediately followed by a sharpening of the conflict between the two wings. The spokesmen of the Right Wing were the neo-Parliamentarians, Mr Bhulabhai Desai and Dr Ansari and the old Swarajists Dr B.C. Roy and Mr Asaf Ali. After the suspension of Civil Disobedience, the Congress remained for some time in a state of suspended animation. According to the Parliamentarians, the best way to end that stalemate was to return to parliamentary methods which had been discarded in January 1930, prior to the launching of Civil Disobedience. Since Gandhiji had no alternative plan, he yielded to the pressure of the Parliamentarians and at that juncture it looked as if the Congress would become a purely constitutionalist body.

To save the soul of the Congress, a Left Wing revolt was a crying necessity. At a psychological moment in 1934, this revolt appeared under the name and guise of the Congress Socialist Party. Now, what was the composition of this party like? Did Independence Leaguers of 1928 and the Congress Democrats of 1929 swell its ranks?

The Congress Socialist Party, when it was first launched, had a very wide appeal and it drew the sympathy and support of all Left-Wingers, active or potential. Those Independence Leaguers and Congress Democrats who had not by then retired or drifted away, naturally joined it But in addition, a large number of influential erstwhile Gandhiites were found within its ranks. The latest phase of Gandhism had brought considerable disillusionment, both as a theory and also as a method. The Congress Socialist Party had an ambitious ideal, viz. to give the country a new theory and a new method as a substitute for Gandhism which was regarded as having failed in its purpose.

The future of the Congress Socialist Party depended on the answer it would furnish to two questions. Firstly, would it be able to give the country a new theory as well as a new method and would it be able to clarify its immediate and its ultimate roles? Secondly, would the erstwhile Gandhiites in the newly formed party work in harmony with those elements that had been playing a Left Wing role from a much earlier period?

Whatever its ultimate future, the Congress Socialist Party began well. It was not a parasitic growth on the Congress organization, nor was it a graft imported from abroad. It was undoubtedly a growth from within and in its composition were to be found people who had been through the previous phases of the Congress movement and had been enriched by it. But the principal rock that menaced its future advance from the very beginning was the possible influence of Gandhism as well as of certain prominent and influential leaders like Pandit Jawaharlal Nehru. It is an open secret that though Pandit Nehru did not join the party, he gave it a lot of inspiration, strength and encouragement through his personal hold over certain prominent leaders of that party. If the Congress Socialist Party did not overcome that menace, it would not be able to clarify its immediate and ultimate roles, nor would it be able to justify its emergence in Indian politics as the exponent of a new theory as well as of a new method.

The writer was in Europe when the party was inaugurated in 1934. In his book — '*The Indian Struggle 1920–34*' — which was completed in November 1934 and was published from London, he gave his warmest support to that Party. This was reinforced in his Presidential speech at the Haripura Congress in February 1938.

On analysis, we find that the Congress Socialist Party did not really give the country something altogether novel. Its socialism had been already preached by Left-Wingers like Pandit Nehru, the writer and others since 1928. Its anti-imperialist leftism had already manifested itself in Indian politics through other individuals and groups. Nevertheless, the C.S.P. served a very useful purpose. It sounded a clarion-call for the consolidation of all Left Wing elements and it was born at a psychological moment in the history of Indian politics. The chances appeared very bright that it would succeed in its mission, where others had failed before. As early as 1928, the writer had realized the growing menace of the Right Wing, the official Congress party, and the urgent need of organizing a Left Wing Party. Half consciously and half unconsciously, he along with mar others, had worked towards that end but had not succeeded. When a more hopeful effort was put forward by the Congress Socialists in 1934, it was naturally to be acclaimed with enthusiasm.

The writer was in prison or in virtual exile from January 1932 to March, 1937. By the time he was free to re-enter public life in 1937, the Congress Socialist Party had attained a certain degree of maturity. From personal observations made in 1937 and in 1938 it appeared that the C.S.P. had of late ceased to make any headway. This was alarming, since the loss of dynamic urge meant the beginning of decay. Immediately after the Haripura Congress in February 1938, the writer had serious talks with prominent members of the C.S.P., including members of the National Front group who were also members of the former party. It was suggested — and after mature deliberation it was generally agreed — that there was something defective in the work of the party and something lacking in its immediate plan of work, which should be rectified without delay. A large number of radicals in the Congress who did not belong to the official party had not been roped in, though it was essential to enlist them.

Till then, C.S.P. had done a lot of socialist propaganda, which was all to the good. It had also made its presence felt in meetings of Congress Committee and its members had moved extremist resolutions and amendments wherever and whenever possible. This was also beneficial, since Congressmen did need gingering up. But there were some outstanding shortcomings. Firstly, the C.S.P. did not have a mass-membership. It was more like a party of select individuals, on the lines of the Socialist League and similar organizations in Great Britain. Secondly, it did not lay sufficient stress on organizational work among the masses — namely, the peasants and workers. Perhaps, at the time of its inception different ideas were at work, which were discarded subsequently. Be that as it may, by 1937 and 1938, the C.S.P. had adopted a definite line of development which had obvious defects and which ultimately proved to be a mistaken one. These defects were probably due to want of clarification with regard to the aims and objects of the party and confusion and misunderstanding with regard to its role, both immediate and ultimate.

As long as the C.S.P. stood for a new theory and a new method, its birth and existence had a *raison d'etre.* Gandhism, despite its failures or shortcomings, had furnished a theory and a method. Consequently, if it was subsequently found to be inadequate or unsuccessful, what was needed was nothing less than a new theory and a new method. The writer has reason to believe that this idea prevailed in the minds of many people when the C.S.P. was first launched. But those who were called upon to build up the party gave it a totally wrong direction. Today, in the eyes of the man in the street, the C.S.P. has completely surrendered to the Gandhiites and perhaps it has in reality no more ambition than to ginger up the Congress machinery to a certain degree. But the Congress Socialist Party was created for doing something much more than merely gingering up the Congress and if it does not fulfil that larger function, some other organization will have to do it. The wheels of progress can on no account remain clogged for any length of time.

Analysing the Congress one finds that there has been, and there is, a definite party with a leader and an organization of its own. It may be called the official party or the Gandhi party or the Right Wing. It has commendable discipline within its own ranks and a mass-following which has been, and is being, carefully cultivated. It has numerous funds at its disposal and various subsidiary organizations, besides the Congress organization, through which it functions. The consolidation of this party has gone on for years and has been accentuated since Provincial Ministries were formed by its members in 1937. The taste of power has made this party more authoritarian and vindictive than ever before and more power-loving as well.

Now, do we believe that this party will be able to fulfil the task of making a new India? If we do, then we should give it our fullest allegiance and the only hostile action that may be permitted is the offering of 'friendly' criticism. But what if we do not? In that event, a new party will be needed — a party that will furnish an alternative theory and a new method. Such a party will have two roles to play — one role for the immediate and the other for the distant future. In order to fulfil these roles, the new party must have a mass-following and a larger following than what the Gandhiites can claim today. This mass-following will be possible only if the party undertakes propaganda among the masses and builds up a mass-membership. An organization like the Socialist League of Great Britain or the present-day C.S.P. of India can never be the organ or the exponent of a mass-movement. It will remain a thing in the air, as it were, without any roots in the soil.

There is considerable confusion with regard to the role of

such a party. As a matter of fact, the party will have to fulfil two roles — one immediate and the other ultimate. The immediate role is that of uncompromising, anti-imperialist struggle. The ultimate role refers to the post-struggle period. In that period of national reconstruction, the role will be a socialist one. During the period of struggle, socialist propaganda may and should be carried on, but the role of the party will be — not a socialist one, but an uncompromisingly anti-imperialist one. Many of the C.S.P. leaders have entertained the wrong notion that the present task of the party is merely to carry on socialist propaganda and at the same time, endeavour to ginger up the Congress machinery. This is one of the principal reasons why the party has suffered shipwreck.

For those who do not have implicit faith in Gandhism, the task is clear. That task is to build up a genuine Left Wing party, with all the elaborate paraphernalia which a modern political party possesses. There should be no doubt in anybody's mind that the moment this attempt is made, the wrath of the Congress High Command will descend. What is more, mean, unscrupulous and vindictive methods will be resorted to in order to crush the rising party. No surprise should be expressed at this, for such is the game of politics. The events of the last eighteen months have demonstrated that many prominent Left-Wingers did not anticipate a Rightist onslaught of this character. Let not this mistake be repeated in future and let everybody be wiser today in the light of past experience.

Readers will remember that between members of the C.S.P. and supporters of the Congress High Command (or Gandhian leadership) friction began at a very early stage. Pandit Jawaharlal also got into hot water by lending his support to the Congress Socialists. While he was Congress President in 1936 and 1937, he was anything but happy and he had to establish more amicable relations with the Gandhiites by toning down his support to the C.S.P. The Congress Socialists, on their part, when they felt the wrath of the High Command, did not stand up to it boldly — but began to drift, either consciously or unconsciously, to a position that would be less objectionable to the big folks in the Gandhian camp. This was noticed by the latter who accordingly continued their drive against the Left Wing with increasing vigour.

On behalf of the C.S.P. no statements or utterances were made which could be interpreted to mean that that party constituted a threat to the future of the Congress High Command. The latter was considerably reassured and thereafter one could notice individual Gandhiites praising individual Congress Socialists. These praises, coming sometimes from the highest quarters, further paved the way to their political doom. To afford a rational justification for shifting their ground, the slogan, of 'unity' was discovered and propagated by the Congress Socialists — but it was in reality nothing else than manoeuvring for safety. This new interpretation of unity ultimately brought the C.S.P. to a position where it did not venture to assume even the mild role of a parliamentary opposition — for even a parliamentary opposition has on occasions to dislodge the Government of the day and step into its shoes. In its last phase, the C.S.P. began to curry favour with the High Command so openly that if it said one word in criticism of the latter, it uttered a hundred in support of it and further affirmed its confidence and faith in Mahatma Gandhi in unmeasured terms.

It should be noted at this stage that Pandit Jawaharlal Nehru has always exerted a potent influence on the C.S.P. He was largely responsible for the birth of the party in 1934 and ever since, has guided the destinies of the party to a large extent. With his gradual return to the Gandhian fold since 1937, the C.S.P. has moved with him. We find in effect that the influence of Pandit Nehru and of the erstwhile Gandhiites in the C.S.P. has been so great that today one feels tempted to say that the C.S.P. is but a subsidiary organization of the Gandhiites.

The C.S.P. affords an illustration as to how bad leadership can ruin the future of a great party. Though the influence of theories or 'isms' on political affairs should not be minimized, one should not ignore the importance of the human factor either. What would have happened to the modern political parties in Europe, bereft of the personality of their outstanding leaders, I wonder.

In future, let no one think of playing a Left Wing role or of organizing a Left Wing party if he is not prepared for the worst attacks of the Congress High Command. The latter will go to any length in its attempt to crush all opposition that constitutes a future menace to its life and safety. And it will make use of the slogan 'Discipline' — just as the C.S.P. worked under the cloak of 'Unity'.

The same impulse to manoeuvre for safety was responsible for the moves of Comrade M.N. Roy and his Radical League since 9th July 1939.

45
My Personal Testament

(This piece of philosophical writing was found among Netaji's prison papers of 1940 and is being published for the first time. It was marked 'Not sent' evidently to mean that it was not forwarded to Government. It is clear that he wrote it on 29 November 1940, the day he commenced his fast unto death in the Presidency Jail, Calcutta, in protest against his illegal detention without trial. — Eds.)

The die is cast. I have crossed the Rubicon and my fast has begun this morning. I have already addressed a letter to the Bengal Government which contains my political testament. Herein I want to communicate what may be called my personal testament. When I am no more, I would like this to be conveyed to those who are interested in the deeper problems of life — and particularly to my dear boy who has already had an inkling of my philosophical notions.

I believe I was originally fashioned by Nature to be — first and foremost — a thinker, but circumstances have forced me into a life of hectic political activity with the result that I have not been able to make my contribution to the thought — life of India and of the world. But I have certain definite ideas on philosophic, social, economic and political problems and should like them to be amplified and worked out by the generation that follows ours. I have this much to claim for myself that my ideas do not float in the air. They are intimately related to reality as we know it and have sprung out of a life of ceaseless activity — a life that is not oblivious of the earth.

The next stage of world-evolution demands a new Philosophy, a new ethical conception and a new economic & political system. What contribution have we to make in this behalf?

New Philosophy — During the last few decades, England has made little contribution to philosophical thought which may be called original. America has contributed Pragmatism, France has produced Henri Bergson and Germany has given Hegel. The quintessence of Modern Philosophy is Hegelianism. Communism is built on one aspect of Hegelianism — i.e. Dialectics — but it has rejected Hegel's conception of Reality. Naziism has no philosophy, so far as I am aware. Gandhiism is based on wrong ethics and its philosophy is vague and mystical. If we want a new India, we must have a new Philosophy.

The two main philosophical problems are — (1) what is the nature of Reality in the absolute and (2) what is the nature of Reality as we know it (i.e. of the world of phenomena) and how does it evolve. (A sound view of evolution is essential to the adoption of a correct notion of Ethics, Economics and Politics).

The Vedanta is quite correct when it says that Reality in the absolute is unknown and unknowable. But that is no reason why we should not attempt to 'photograph' the Absolute through our mind, senses etc. This attempt has in fact been made from time immemorial — giving rise to different schools of philosophy which have often fought among themselves. It would be wrong to condemn any single 'photograph' as false — though one 'photograph' may have a greater degree of accuracy than another.

Ramkrishna–Vivekananda did not condemn any school of philosophy. They said, 'Man proceeds not from error to truth — but from truth to higher truth.' In my view they were right in thinking that every system of philosophy contains some element of truth.

The Absolute has been variously described as 'Thought' or 'Idea' (Hegel), 'Will' (von Hartmann), 'Elan Vital' or Vital Impulse (Bergson), 'Chit' or Consciousness (Vedanta), 'Ananda' or Bliss (Vedanta), 'Energy' or Power (Tantra), Love (several philosophies — Eastern & Western) etc. These conceptions are all true, though only partly so — but in my view 'Chit', 'Elan' and 'Love' give a truer description of the nature of the Absolute Reality than any others. In spite of our human limitations we cannot help trying to 'photograph' the Absolute — partly because of our irrepressible philosophical instinct and partly because a system of Ethics, Economics and Politics demands a definite notion of the nature of the Absolute. Without such a notion as our ultimate background we shall be liable to err. And whatever social order we may endeavour to set up should accord with our conception of the Absolute Reality.

The second philosophical problem is — 'what is the nature of the world and of the evolutionary process?' This problem relates to the world of phenomena and not the Absolute Reality which underlies it. The two facets of the problem are inseparably linked up; nevertheless the second has more practical importance than the first.

Perhaps the earliest scientific attempt to solve the problem was made by the Sankhya Philosophy. That Philosophy contained a conception of evolution which is highly interesting, though today it may appear to many as crude. Apart from the Eastern thinkers, the philosophers of Ancient Greece also tried to tackle this question. And the effort has gone on throughout the ages.

What is the nature of the world? Is it Matter or Energy or Mind? And what is Matter? A bundle of sensations? Or a conglomeration of atoms? Or energy in a static form? Does matter when analysed retain its material character or is it resolved into Energy or force? Are atoms particles of matter or centres of energy? These are interesting questions and the researches of science are daily throwing more light on them. Perhaps posterity will be more wise on this point than we are today. But an answer to the question concerning the nature of the world of phenomena is not of such great theoretical value because its validity will be only of a relative character and the Absolute will still remain unknown and unknowable. Nevertheless, it will have some practical value.

Of more practical value will be our notion regarding the nature of the evolutionary process. Beginning from the ancient times, we find today several conceptions of Evolution — the Sankhya conception, the Spencerian conception, the Bergsonian conception, the Hegelian conception and so on. Here again there is an element of truth in each conception, though in my view, the Hegelian conception approximates much more to the truth than the others.

According to Hegel, the evolutionary process is dialectical in character (thesis, antithesis, synthesis) and both thought and reality follow the same dialectical process. Now, Dialectics undoubtedly explains and accounts for much that we perceive — but not all. Actually, the evolutionary process is not as uniform or monotonous as Dialectics would have us believe. For instance, there is something explosive, accidental, inexplicable in actual evolution which impels us to hold that there is some truth in Bergson's conception of Creative Evolution. Moreover, in connection with the biological sphere it may be urged that Spencer's notion of evolution from simple to complex is not devoid of substance and that biological evolution cannot be explained simply in terms of thesis, antithesis and synthesis. Therefore, the safer and wiser course would be to hold that while other conceptions do contain some element of validity, the Hegelian conception approximates much more to the truth than the others.

To sum up, on the question as to the nature of the world of

phenomena, we better keep an open mind while making note of all that science has revealed to us so far. More light is bound to come, as science makes further advance. Meanwhile, we should bear in mind that the old conception of materialism has broken down completely. It has been under a cross-fire, being attacked by scientific research on one side and by philosophical reasoning and speculation on the other.

46
My Conscience is My Own

Report of an interview, 9 December 1940.

While convalescing after his release from detention following a hungerstrike, Netaji was asked to comment on a telegram received by a friend from Mahatma Gandhi on the question of withdrawal of disciplinary measures against the Bose brothers in order to effect unity in Bengal Congress ranks. Gandhiji's telegram was in the following terms:

Wardhaganj, 28/11/40.

> REGRET INABILITY EVEN UNWILLINGNESS TO INTERFERE NOTWITHSTANDING MY REGARD AND FRIENDSHIP FOR THE BROTHERS. FEEL BANS CANNOT BE LIFTED WITHOUT THEIR APOLOGISING FOR INDISCIPLINE.

Netaji's comment was a follows: 'I learnt the lesson from my political "Guru", Deshbandhu Chittaranjan Das, who is now no more, that personal relations should, as far as humanly possible, be kept above political differences. I have therefore been able to cherish deep personal regard and love for Mahatma Gandhi, despite all that I have suffered and am suffering at the hands of Gandhiites.

'At school I once read a poem on William Tell, the greatest hero of Switzerland —

> My knee shall bend, he calmly said,
> To God and God alone,
> My life is in the Austrians' hands,
> My conscience is my own.

'I am not aware of any wrong that I have committed in my political career. Consequently, my reply to the Mahatma will be on the above lines with a few verbal changes.'

47
On the Bengal Congress Tangle

Between the 10th and 24th December, 1940, Netaji issued a number of public statements on Bengal Congress affairs. A fresh crisis had just then been created in the Congress legislative front by disciplinary action announced against Mr Sarat Chandra Bose, Leader of the Bengal Congress Parliamentary Party, by Maulana Abul Kalam Azad acting in the name of the All-India Parliamentary Sub-committee of the Congress. The statements have been combined and some of the details of the dispute excluded to produce the following presentation reflecting Netaji's point of view.

During the last few days, I have had little peace of mind owing to a number of thoughts continually surging up within me. I believe that by unburdening myself of those thoughts, I shall have more peace of mind than at present and this will be conducive to my progress and recovery. I have, therefore, craved the indulgence of my doctors for issuing a few statements at leisure. Some of these statements are already with me in the form of incomplete letters written while I was in jail.

I shall first deal with the issue which is now convulsing Congress circles in Bengal, viz., the ukase of Maulana Abul Kalam Azad regarding Sj. Sarat Chandra Bose. It passes my comprehension how such a step could be taken by the Maulana when the country is passing through a crisis of this magnitude and the Congress leaders themselves have been making repeated appeals for unity. I need hardly say that we on our part desire national unity from the bottom of our hearts and we are fully prepared for an honourable solution of all outstanding differences and problems. But we cannot accept the position which some Congress leaders have taken up, namely, that no offer of honourable compromise can be made to the friends and colleagues of the Left. Consequently, if any attempt is made to insult or humiliate or discredit us in the public eye, we shall be in the painful necessity of not only resisting such an attack, but of counter-attacking, wherever we find it possible to do so. The fact that we are preoccupied with larger issues should not induce the Maulana and his friends to think that we shall ignore the attack from the Right on our 'home-front.'

The attack on Sj. Sarat Chandra Bose is but another phase of the attack on the Bengal Provincial Congress Committee which has been going on since July, 1939. Consequently, the B.P.C.C. cannot but be vitally concerned in this question. When a division has been forcibly created by the Maulana within the Bengal Congress Parliamentary Party, the B.P.C.C. would like to know who are for it and who are against it. It does not matter whether we shall have a majority within that Party or not. Majority or minority, our friends and supporters in the Bengal Legislature will continue to function under the name and style of the Congress Parliamentary Party. The *Ad Hocite*[1] members of the Legislature cannot claim to be the Congress Parliamentary Party, since they do not owe allegiance to the only valid Bengal Provincial Congress Committee.

It goes without saying that those who do not stand by the B.P.C.C. in this hour will forfeit all claim to renomination at the next general election. It does not require much intelligence to guess how many votes the Maulana's ticket will secure in general elections in Bengal and how many votes the B.P.C.C.'s ticket will.

And let me declare here and now that if the Congress High Command persist in their present policy, there will be parallel elections not only in Bengal but throughout India at the next general election. The Rightists will not be permitted to ride into office over the shoulders of the Left-wingers as they did last time.

The ultimate court of appeal on every public issue is the public. Let me therefore suggest a solution of the present parliamentary tangle in Bengal. Maulana Abul Kalam Azad has censured Sj. Sarat Chandra Bose and sought to expel him. Others have the fullest confidence in him. But what do the public of Bengal say? Let all the Congress members of the Assembly resign and seek re-election on this issue. It is no use fighting with smaller men, so let Mahatma Gandhi himself set up the Working Committee's candidates with his blessings and support. Against them, we shall set up the candidates

[1] An Ad Hoc Committee was set up in Bengal by the Congress High Command after the revolt of the majority of the elected Congress Committee against its policies.

on behalf of the Bengal Provincial Congress Committee. We shall then await the verdict of our electorate with the greatest confidence and composure. Will the Mahatma agree?

For carrying out the Party's mandate, the Maulana has sought to expel the Leader from the Party and from the Assembly. The Maulana's decision was arrived at in great secrecy behind the back of the Parliamentary Party and nearly six months after the incident had taken place.

This attack is in reality an onslaught on the Bengal Provincial Congress Committee and on its legislative front. Who does not know that we have a strong out-post in the Bengal Legislature? This out-post the Maulana has endeavoured to demolish and destroy, but he has failed.

I shall in this connection give the Maulana one piece of advice. He has completely set at naught the Bengal Provincial Congress Committee and the Parliamentary Party by issuing such a fiat over their head. But he has neither the position nor the following in this province which might have made it possible for the people to tolerate his authoritarianism. In future let him not therefore forget himself when he plays the Dictator's role.

. . . I think I have been able to prove that Maulana's charges against Sj. Sarat Chandra Bose have no legs to stand on. Maulana too is not altogether oblivious of the weakness of his position. That is why in private and in public he has to fall back on his one stock argument, viz., breach of discipline. Now let us examine the real implications of discipline.

Discipline in an autocratic organisation means obeying the orders of one's superior officer or officers. In a democratic organisation, it means abiding by the will of the majority. The Maulana and Congressmen of his way of thinking demand that since they are in a majority in the All-India Congress Committee, the Leftist minority should implicitly obey the majority's will and on their failing to do so, they should be punished. The same principle of rule by majority should naturally be applied to the Provincial Congress Committees as well, but it is not done. Here in Bengal the Rightist minority want to defy the Leftist majority with impunity and when they do so, they are always supported by the Rightist High Command. Now, one cannot have it both ways. You cannot have a rule by majority in the All-India Congress

Committee and a rule by minority in the Bengal Provincial Congress Committee. Consequently, the argument of 'discipline at any cost', which Maulana advances day in and day out — cannot hold water.

It may be urged that the High Command being the supreme Executive of the Congress, all Congressmen and Congress organisations should loyally obey its dictates. But this type of discipline is possible only in an authoritarian organisation. As I have already said, in a democratic organisation, discipline can only mean 'rule by the majority.' It cannot possibly mean obedience to a superior officer under all circumstances.

In the present case, the Maulana completely ignored the Bengal Congress Parliamentary Party and behind the back of the Party, he would penalise the Leader for giving effect to a resolution of the Party, viz. that the Leader should issue the whip for the indirect election to the Upper House.

If it be argued that the principle of rule by majority should apply to the All-India Congress Committee alone and all other Congress organisations have no independent existence of their own and should blindly obey the mandate of the High Command, which is the Working Committee of the All-India Congress Committee — then I should like to refer to the Congress Constitution. That Constitution clearly states in Article II that local organisations like the Provincial Congress Committees are as integral parts of the Congress as the All-India Congress Committee and do not owe their origin to the latter. The principle that should guide the All-India Congress Committee should therefore guide the Provincial Congress Committees.

Moreover, authoritarianism on the part of a dictator or a group may be tolerated if either of them has the necessary following and position in a particular area. In the case of Bengal, neither the Maulana nor even Mahatma Gandhi should be unaware of the real position.

In the last analysis, if the Congress is a national organisation as we all claim, the justification for that claim will depend on the degree of public confidence it can command. Since the Ad Hoc Committee does not command public confidence in Bengal, no fiats from Ballygunge Circular Road or from Wardha can infuse life into it and convert it into a Provincial Congress Committee. On the other hand, no ukase from either place can kill the valid Bengal Provincial Congress Committee. That is why even after the so-called suspension, we have continued to function under the Bengal Provincial Congress Committee and shall continue to do so in future.

It follows from this that only those members of the Bengal Legislature who owe allegiance to the valid Provincial Congress Committee will be entitled to work and function under the name of the Bengal Congress Parliamentary Party. If the adherents of the Ad Hoc Committee so desire they may form an *Ad Hoc* Party in the Legislature, but they cannot usurp the name of the Congress Parliamentary Party.

Along with the argument of discipline, another allied argument which is often trotted out is that the members of the Assembly accepted a certain pledge at the time of the General Election and they should remain true to it. This argument is too superficial to stand analysis.

Times, circumstances, conditions, etc., have completely changed since that pledge was taken. That Working Committee which commanded the confidence of the Bengal Provincial Congress Committee and which, in its turn, respected the latter — no longer exists. Today the Working Committee no longer commands the confidence of the majority of Bengal Congressmen. It certainly does not command the confidence of the B.P.C.C. and in its turn, it does not respect the latter. The old pledge has therefore automatically become null and void. Give us the old Working Committee and the old conditions and circumstances — and you will find that the old pledge will in that case stand — otherwise not.

I know that it will be argued that in every organisation and administration there is such a thing as 'continuity of policy'. But 'continuity of policy' is not possible when a revolutionary change takes place.

The B.P.C.C. is not the only organisation which has suffered at the hands of the High Command. Other Provincial Congress Committees like those of Delhi, Kerala, etc., have also suffered. But these organisations cannot be killed by waving the magic wand of the Congress Dictators. These organisations do not owe their birth to the High Command and the latter cannot therefore annihilate them by a stroke of the pen. So long as the public have confidence in these organisations, they will continue to function as Congress Committees. There can be no question of going out of the Congress, because we are Congressmen and our organisations are Congress organisations. If in future we have to fight the High Command in the elections throughout the country as we have fought in the extra-parliamentary sphere, we shall do so in the name of the Congress and not by going out of the Congress. The Congress is ours, as much as it is anybody else's.

I am told that the Maulana has told people that he is more than a Bengali. If so, let him follow the traditions of Bengal and follow in the footsteps of our great leader, Deshbandhu C.R. Das. Let him give up his policy of vendetta and through toleration and love unite the people of this province. It was through toleration and love that the Deshbandhu was able to convert foes into friends and present a united Bengal. No other gospel will appeal to this province.

Maulana Abul Kalam Azad and his satellites tried to save themselves from an overwhelming defeat by an eleventh-hour postponement of the meeting of the Bengal Congress Parliamentary Party. But if the Maulana had any knowledge of constitutional procedure, he should have realised that neither he nor the General Secretary of the Bengal Congress Parliamentary Party had power or authority to cancel the meeting of the Party after it had been duly convened.

Not being content with acting in an arbitrary and high-handed manner by ordering the cancellation of the above meeting, the Maulana has now come out with a whip to chastise those who did not feel cowed down before his imperial and impudent ukase. The Maulana has always claimed to be more than a Bengali. But he is entirely ignorant of the manners, courtesy and hospitality prevalent in this corner of the world. When the members of the Parliamentary Party assembled at his house at the instance and on the invitation of the General Secretary, the Maulana did not have the elementary courtesy to welcome them or to offer them seats. In fact, he did not even show his face as long as they were in his house.

It is high time that the great Maulana realised that it was no use trying to play the role of the Grand Moghul. In endeavouring to do so, he is only making himself ridiculous. With the scanty following and influence that he has in Bengal, he cannot drive a steamroller over the heart of this Province.

I am sure that the members of the Bengal Congress Parliamentary Party will treat his latest threat with the contempt it deserves. I would advise the Maulana to cease his efforts at creating further dissensions in this Province and turn his energy and attention to the larger issues that are now agitating the people of India.

One word more before I close. I would like to tell the Maulana that even under the Constitution and resolutions of the Congress, the All-India Parliamentary Sub-Committee is not as all-powerful as he thinks it is. The All-India Parliamentary Sub-Committee has to work in co-operation with the Provincial Congress Committees and so far as Bengal is concerned, who does not know which is the valid Provincial Congress Committee? Once again I may remind the Maulana that the Provincial Congress Committee in Bengal will run the Provincial elections whenever they take place and we shall then see how his offspring, the Ad Hoc Committee, fares at the polls.

The Grand Moghul of the Congress is fast becoming a comic figure. He is suffering from the delusion that from his room in Ballygunge Circular Road he can rule Bengal by hurling his disciplinary thunderbolts from time to time. It is of no concern to him that what he is doing is *ultra vires* of the Congress Constitution itself. And it is of no consequence to him that through his penal measures he may soon be expelling the entire public from the Congress.

He reminds me of the last Moghul Emperors who, because they were still surrounded with regal pomp and splendour, were entirely oblivious of the fact that the ground had slipped off their feet and that the empire had already passed out of their hands. I wonder who can restore sense to our modern Alanascar.

The Working Committee handed over all its powers to Mahatma Gandhi and most of its members walked into prison. Maulana Abul Kalam Azad has, therefore, no power left in his hands, but he persists in thinking like the great French Emperor — 'I am the State'. If today any single individual has authority to speak in the name of the Congress, it is Mahatma Gandhi and not Maulana Abul Kalam Azad.

Even when the Working Committee was functioning, neither the President nor the All-India Parliamentary Sub-Committee had power to take disciplinary action. Whenever disciplinary action had to be taken, the Working Committee had always to meet and decide.

If the Maulana has any doubt on this point, I would request him to refer to the terms of the resolution of the Working Committee appointing the Parliamentary Sub-Committee.

The Maulana's stock-in-trade is his argument regarding pledge and discipline. It never strikes him that because of a revolutionary crisis within the Congress since that pledge was given, that argument cannot hold water. The Working Committee does not command public confidence. In the case of Bengal, the Working Committee has forfeited the confidence of the valid Provincial Congress Committee. Consequently, the pledge has automatically become null and void. Restore the Working Committee of 1936–1937 with conditions prevailing then, and the pledge will still hold good. The argument that the present Working Committee is the heir of the Committee of 1936–1937 is also futile because when a revolutionary crisis occurs, old loyalties and pledges invariably snap.

The Maulana perhaps thinks that his word is law, no matter what the Congress Constitution or Constitutional Law may say. That is why in his ignorance of law and procedure, he mustered sufficient impudence to order the cancellation of the annual meeting of the Bengal Congress Parliamentary Party which had been duly convened by its General Secretary. And that is why he exhibited similar impudence when he ordered the Punjab Congress Parliamentary Party to elect a particular individual as Leader.

Unfortunately for the Maulana that Party elected Sardar Sampuran Singh as leader, despite his mandate, but ever since Sardarji's election as Leader, the Maulana has been after him. The Grand Moghul has now ordered the expulsion of Sardar Sampuran Singh from the Congress Party and it remains to be seen whether that Party will sacrifice its Leader or stand by him as it has done in Bengal.

Whatever happens, there is no doubt that by forcing out of the Congress Master Tara Singh and Sardar Sampuran Singh, the outstanding leaders of the Sikh community, the Congress High Command is virtually threatening to drive the Sikhs out of the Congress. One can only hope that the Sikhs will not meekly submit to this authoritarianism, because the Congress is a national institution and not the property of any individual or group.

The way our Grand Moghul has been bungling everywhere should cause concern to every right-thinking man. In the recent case of Sardar Sampuran Singh, the matter should have been dealt with by Mahatma Gandhi as the Congress Dictator, but the Maulana could not refrain from butting in.

It is now evident that he has been messing up things in Sind also. When the Congress Coalition Ministry was formed in Assam, despite the Maulana's violent opposition, he predicted that it would crash in no time. But true to my prediction, that Ministry stood like a rock against all onslaughts. The Maulana had his revenge when the war broke out and he then handed over that province to the political opponents of the Congress party there.

In the case of Sind, when the then Premier, Khan Bahadur Allah Bux, was dying for a coalition with the other parties, including the Congress Party, and I as Congress President strongly pleaded for it, the Maulana set his face against it. The result was steady deterioration culminating in a chaotic state of affairs in Sind.

After a long stay in Sind only the other day, the Maulana promised us a stable Ministry and communal concord there, but it now appears that all his arrangements are going to be torpedoed.

In conclusion, I would appeal to the Maulana once again to refrain from playing the Dictator's role in local and provincial affairs. In Bengal he has had numerous rebuffs in municipal, provincial assembly, provincial council and Central Assembly elections and it is high time he realised what little influence or popularity he has in this province. He would be doing a great service to the country if he gave up his present suicidal policy and concentrated on the larger issues which are now agitating the whole country.

Letters

Major Political Correspondence

Bose–Gandhi Correspondence 1940–41

38/2 Elgin Road,
Calcutta,
23.12.1940

My dear Mahatmaji,

When Mahadevbhai saw me in Presidency Jail, I took the opportunity of conveying a message to you. I requested him to tell you that if you launched a movement, then our services would be entirely at your disposal for what they were worth. I also wanted him to request you to take the initiative in settling the dispute in Bengal, so that the province could throw its whole weight into the movement. Since you had been appointed Dictator, you could easily take up this matter on behalf of the Congress. So I thought.

At the time, my fond expectation was that you would launch a mass movement, as you had done in 1921, 1930 and 1932 — though Mahadevbhai told me that you had been thinking of individual Civil Disobedience. Today it is clear that the movement launched by you is not on the issue of our national demand for Independence. Nor is this movement a mass struggle. If the Government were to permit antiwar speeches, it appears to me that the movement would come to an end. Nevertheless, we would like to cooperate with such a movement, despite its restricted scope and form, so far as it lies in our power, consistently with our political stand. We would like to know if you would accept our cooperation for what it is worth — and if so, what you would like us to do in pursuance of this offer of cooperation. This proffered cooperation is unconditional in the sense that whatever grievances we may have against the Congress High

Command will not stand in our way. If and when the High Command deal with us unfairly and unjustly, we shall have to react accordingly. We may have to fight them as we are forced to fight the arbitrary and highhanded action of Moulana Abul Kalam Azad at the present time. But this can never blind us to the larger issues before the country and there you can have our fullest cooperation, consistent with our political stand. I beg you to accept our offer of cooperation.

Regarding the Bengal situation I had told Mahadevbhai that if you desired unity you could have it for the mere asking and all that was necessary was a talk between you and my brother, Sarat Babu. Since then the situation has deteriorated. You have chosen to remain silent and indifferent. The Moulana has been rushing headlong along the mad path of what he calls disciplinary action. I am not bothered about it because if he wills it and seeks it — we are ready to meet him on his own ground. He cannot affect our public position in the least and he has only been making himself ridiculous before the public of this province and thereby dragging the name of the Congress to the dust. I may say in all humility that we are more than a match for him. Since Moulana's action seems to have your tacit approval, I am not seeking your intervention in this matter. All that I desire is that despite this unfortunate sideshow which has been forced on us, we should cooperate where larger issues are concerned and so far as we are concerned, we are anxious to cooperate. In all sincerity I am offering you our cooperation.

I am sending this letter through a relative who is going to Nagpur. I am asking him to wait for a reply.

How is your health? The papers again give disquieting news. I am progressing, but slowly.

With respectful pranams,

Yours affectionately,

Subhas Chandra Bose

Mahatma Gandhi,
Wardha.

✉

Sewagram,
Wardha,
29.12.1940

My dear Subhas,

You are irrepressible whether ill or well. Do get well before going in for fireworks.

I have not been in consultation with Maulana Saheb. But when I read in the papers about the decision I could not help approving of it. I am surprised that you won't distinguish between discipline and indiscipline.

But I quite agree with you either of you is more than a match for the Maulana Saheb as far as popularity is concerned. But a man has to put conscience before popularity. I know that in Bengal it is difficult to function effectively without you two. I know too that you can carry on even without the Congress. But the Congress has to manage some how under the severe handicap.

Suresh wrote to me that Sarat was coming. I have been waiting. He can come anytime he chooses and so can you too. You know you will be well looked after here.

As for your Bloc joining C.D. I think with the fundamental differences between you and me, it is not possible. Till one of us is converted to the other's view, we must sail in different boats though their destination may appear but only appear to be the same.

Meanwhile let us love one another remaining members of the same family that we are.

Yours
Bapu

38/2, Elgin Road,
Calcutta,
10.1.1941

My dear Mahatmaji,

I am glad to receive your letter of 29th Dec. — not so much for the contents, as for the clarification of your views which it contained.

On this side, it is not merely my personal desire to offer hearty and sincere cooperation, but it is the desire of many who stand with me. For doing this it is neither necessary nor desirable to surrender or abandon our political principles and convictions. As you are aware, in the previous struggles, many worked shoulder to shoulder with ardent Gandhiites while differing from them on several important questions. Why should not this happen again? I beg you to reconsider your decision.

There is one sentence in your letter the significance of which I am not sure that I have grasped correctly. You have said — 'Till one of us is converted to the other's view, we must sail in different boats, though their destination "may appear but only appear to be the same". Does this mean that in your view our political goals are different? How could that be? Kindly tell me what exactly you mean.

There are so many people who are anxious to know our views on the subject under correspondence and some among them expect an agreement between us. Here I have your permission to show them the correspondence and if necessary to publish it? So far, I have shown it to a couple of friends only.

I hope you are keeping well. I am better on the whole — but some of the complaints are obstinate.

With respectful pranams,

Yours affectionately,

Subhas

Mahatma Gandhi
Sevagram

Bose–Nehru Correspondence

From Jawaharlal Nehru

Anand Bhawan,
Allahabad.
July 11, 1939.

Shri Subhas Chandra Bose
Bombay.

My dear Subhas,

I have just received your letter of 8th July. I am afraid we differ on this subject as apparently we do on many others. It would serve no useful purpose to have an argument about it. My own view was this that Kamath had taken up a wrong position in this matter. You have attributed a particular motive to me which is neither fair to me nor to yourself. It was totally immaterial for me what views Kamath had in regard to Congress or other politics so long as his views were not aggressively expressed so as to come in the way of the work he was doing in the Planning Committee. I had taken exception early in January I think to a statement of his on planning. I did not object to that statement in the least but to the fact that he made it. It seemed to me that he was far more attracted by the publicity side of public life than by the side represented by the Planning Committee. If that was his desire, which he was perfectly entitled to have, then the Planning Committee did not afford any scope for him.

You refer to A.K. Shaha and suggest that he might have been appointed a Joint Secretary. Shaha as a member of the Planning Committee might have been appointed an honorary General Secretary but he could not be appointed a paid Joint Secretary unless he resigned his membership of the Planning Committee. We did not want him to resign this membership as we wanted to profit by his special experience in the sub-committees of which he is a member. He could not have been a member of a sub-committee if he became a Joint Secretary. I did not think that it was possible to make him General Secretary as this required not technical knowledge but a wide acquaintance with Indian economic conditions and people in India. I have been trying hard to get a suitable place for him in some provincial government.

I am sorry you find it difficult to understand me. Perhaps it is not worth trying.

Yours affectionately
Jawaharlal Nehru

Bose–Tagore Correspondence

To Rabindra Nath Tagore

Burdwan Station
11.12.39

Revered Sir,

For a long time I have been thinking of coming to you. There are lots of things to talk about — I need your advice. If I had known in time that you would be waiting for me in Calcutta, I would certainly have returned quickly from East Bengal. When I returned to Calcutta, I heard that you had gone back to Santiniketan after waiting for me in Calcutta. I am now returning from U.P. — I am not feeling so well. I hope I shall be better in two or three days. Before coming, I shall take your permission by telegram. Please accept my respectful pranams.

Yours humbly,
Subhas Chandra Bose

To Secretary to Rabindra Nath Tagore

Telegram

Calcutta 12 December 1939

SECRETARY RABINDRANATH TAGORE SANTINIKETAN
IS POET COMING CALCUTTA FIFTEENTH

SUBHASBOSE

Letters to Sarat Chandra Bose from Prison

CENSORED AND PASSED
Illegible, 28/10
For D.C.S.B.

Passed
Illegible
30/10/40
Lt. Col., I.M.S.

Presidency Jail,
Calcutta,
24.10.1940

My dear Mejdada,

I sent you my Vijaya pranams the other day to your Dehradun address. You must have received that letter by now.

All these days I have been thinking of Moulana Abul Kalam's letter to you and incidentally of the mutual admiration indulged in by Maulana Abul Kalam and Sardar Vallabhai in connection with the late Mr V.J. Patel's will.

I do not know your reaction to the first, but I am giving you mine for what it is worth. Since the next session is at hand, I do not think you should resign from the Bengal Assembly. But you may resign at a convenient time and challenge the Congress High

Command to put up their best man in opposition and have a test-election. A convenient time would be the last day of the ensuing session — provided there be time for re-election to take place before the next session. The announcement regarding your resignation at a convenient time may perhaps be made at an early date.

This is, however, a small matter, comparatively speaking. What is really important is the question as to whither we are drifting — I mean the Congress. One by one, people — sometimes, important people who have served and suffered and sacrificed — are leaving the Congress in disgust. Nothing has been done to compensate this loss by effecting alliances with other bodies, nor does there appear to be any such chance in the near future. And I do not find any new men joining the Congress.

Mahatma Gandhi probably realized that this process of disintegration would have tragic results for his party and sought to buttress himself and his followers by recanting his original attitude of unconditional co-operation and launching selective individual Civil Disobedience instead. But is not this an eyewash? It is neither co-operation nor mass-struggle. It pleases nobody and will lead us nowhere. And this campaign has nothing to do with Swaraj. It can only bluff a certain section of our countrymen who are gullible into thinking that something effective is being done by Gandhiji.

One can understand co-operation. One can also understand Royism, despite its inconsistencies. One can also understand mass-struggle. But what is this? Neither fish, nor flesh, nor red-herring.

This latest phase of Gandhism with its sanctimonious hypocrisy (the Patel Will affair), its outrage on democracy and its queer and ununderstandable formulae for political ills (advice to Hyderabad State subjects) — is sickening to a degree. One is forced to wonder which is a greater menace to India's political future — the British bureaucracy or the Gandhian hierarchy. Idealism that is devoid of Realism and whose only content is a frothy sentimentalism of a sanctimonious character can never be fruitful of results.

This game of bluff will deceive nobody — neither the Government nor the people — because the world at large is not as foolish as our brown hierarchy may think. We have to carry on with calm determination. The day is not far off when this brand of Gandhism will stand unmasked. I am glad that you have treated the Moulana's fiat with the contempt it deserves.

Hope all of you are improving there and particularly Mejbowdidi. When are you returning? You need not be in a hurry, for you must get well first. I find that the press people have been at you there. Are the Forward Bloc people also after you? We have very good public support in those parts.

I have been pressed to stand for the Central Assembly and I have agreed. So long.

Yours v. affly.

Subhas

P.S. Some time ago I sent a telegram to Moulana at Wardha thanking him for his Vijaya present. SCB.

Sarat C. Bose Esq.,
Royal Hotel,
Dehradun, U.P.

CENSORED AND PASSED
Illegible 4/11
For D.C.S.B.

Passed
Illegible
Lt. Col., I.M.S.
Supdt.

Presidency Jail,
Calcutta,
31.10.40

My dear Mejdada,

You must have received my Vijaya letter and the other one which followed it. I wonder how Dehradun has benefited Mejbowdidi and yourself. I hope it has.

You must have read in the papers about my election to the Central Assembly. I hope the Congress High Command will not fail to draw the necessary moral from it.

The more I think of Congress Politics, the more convinced I feel that in future we should devote more energy and time to fighting the High Command. If power goes into the hands of such mean, vindictive and unscrupulous persons when Swaraj is won, what will happen to the country? If we don't fight them now, we shall not be able to prevent power passing into their hands. Another reason why we should fight them now is that they have no idea of national reconstruction. Gandhism will land free India in a ditch — if free India is sought to be rebuilt on Gandhian, non-violent principles. India will then be offering a standing invitation to all predatory powers. We should concentrate on fighting the Congress High Command now and to that end, we should make alliances with other political parties wherever and whenever possible.

I have not been well during the last week owing to a pain in the abdominal region near the colon and appendix. The pain is however less now. I am addressing this to Woodburn Park because I don't know when you will be back. With pranams,

Yours v. affly.

Subhas

To
Sarat C. Bose Esq.,
Calcutta

CENSORED AND PASSED
Illegible 26/11
For D.C.S.B.

Presidency Jail,
Calcutta,
15.11.40.

My dear Mejdada,

I am writing to Amiya today by airmail giving him a brief account of my case and the illegality and injustice involved in it. I would like you to write him a detailed letter on the same subject by airmail. I want Amiya to pass the information on to my friends in Parliament and outside. This could be easily done through friends in the Indian Conciliation Group, India League, etc., like Miss Agatha Harrison, Krishna Menon and others.

Any number of people would be interested greatly — if only they had the information. Take, for instance, Mr Thurtle, M.P., Lansbury's son-in-law, who was your guest in Calcutta — or Mr Greenwood, M.P., who is now in the Cabinet and who presided at the public reception I had in London in 1938 — or Mr Vernon Bartlett, M.P., of the 'News Chronicle', whom I first met at Sir Walter Layton's luncheon at Chronicle House and who later had tea with me in Calcutta — or Mr Sorensen, M.P., the indefatigable questioner on Indian topics, with whom I got acquainted in London.

I do not know how long it takes airmail letters to reach London nowadays. In case delay appears more or less certain, please send a long cable instead.

I am telling Amiya that all that he has to do is to pass on my letter to 2 or 3 friends who will do the rest. It is not necessary for Amiya to bother about this matter any further.

Yours v. affly.

Subhas

Sarat C. Bose Esq.,
1, Woodburn Park,
Calcutta

CENSORED AND PASSED
Illegible 20/11
For D.C.S.B.

Presidency Jail,
Calcutta,
17.11.40.

Urgent

My dear Mejdada,

Both of my senior Advocates have fallen ill — I mean Barada Babu and Santosh Babu. I do hope they will get well soon. My case at Alipore comes up on the 23rd inst — Barada Babu appears there. If Barada Babu is not quite well by the 23rd inst, please make some arrangement for that day.

I hope you have by now received my letters of 24/10 and 31/10. Now the second scene in the Wardha farce has begun.

I have had a pain in the waist region for the last 2 or 3 days of a sciatica type. I can still walk about freely and there is nothing to worry about so far. Hope you are all well. How is mother?

Yours v. affly,

Subhas

Sarat C. Bose Esq.,
1, Woodburn Park,
Calcutta

Passed
Illegible
Lt. Col., I.M.S.
Superintendent
Presidency Jail

Jayaprakash Narayan's Secret Letter to Netaji 1940

While he was preparing for his escape from India, Netaji received the following secret letter from Jayaprakash Narayan, who was then in prison, through a special messenger. The undated letter was in Jayaprakash's own hand and written in ink. The writer did not sign the letter obviously for reasons of safety. Jayaprakash identified the original letter to be his own during one of his visits to Netaji Bhawan, Calcutta. The letter is preserved in the archives of Netaji Research Bureau. Editors.

Dear Comrade,

I am writing this letter not without considerable anxiety. Anxiety, because I am not sure how you will receive it. I did not know if you will take me seriously when I say that at no time did I bear any personal ill-will against you. There were political differences, which I did not try to hide. But anything more than that there never was. On the other hand, I have always admired your courage and steadfastness. And now, when it has been driven home to me, I admire your prescience and foresight.

Here I have been turning things in my mind. Recent events have led me to reorient my entire thinking. I admit that the Anti-Compromise Conference and the stand that you and Swamiji took have been completely vindicated. I shall say so publicly at the first opportunity I get.

I am writing to make an extremely important suggestion which I request you earnestly to consider. The suggestion concerns the whole course of our future action and the development of the revolutionary movement in India. I have discussed it here with Swamiji, who is favourably inclined. We have yet to discuss it in greater detail, the results of which I shall communicate in due time.

I have already sent the suggestion to C.S.P. friends outside. Possibly some of them will see you in this connection as also the Anushilan friends.

Before coming to the suggestion itself I should like to give briefly an idea of how I look at the present situation and the immediate future.

To my mind our basic task today is to chalk out a line of action that is fundamentally independent of the Congress. This task shall lose none of its importance or immediacy in the event of the Congress launching upon civil disobedience. There is not an iota of doubt left that civil disobedience if started would be for no greater purpose than that of forcing concessions out of imperialism. The Delhi resolution is by no means dead and buried as Jawaharlal suggests. It will be resurrected immediately as the British Government shows any willingness to compromise. At all events therefore the certain prospect before us is that of a Congress reconciled with imperialism at a price — high or low, depending upon the exigencies on both sides.

Hitherto the basic assumption of our work in the present had been that the Congress was the chief instrument of political action — a multi-class front (with the workers and the national bourgeoisie constituting the extreme ends) against imperialism. Our work henceforth must proceed on the opposite assumption entirely: that the Congress is no longer the main basis for political action. I am not suggesting that the Congress has lost its hold over the masses (though the opposite is more true today than at any time in the last few years: the masses have lost what hold they had over the Congress), or that it has exhausted its role of offering opposition to imperialism. Indeed the present situation makes such an opposition appear most likely. But its object would be the achievement of something as demanded by the Delhi resolution. Nor is there any chance whatever of our influencing the Congress in the present circumstances.

Here it is necessary to note the change that has taken place in the Congress. It indeed remains a broad-based mass organization, but its leadership is more then ever concentrated in the hands of a coterie that is anti-masses (anti-labour, anti-peasant, even anti-democratic to an extent), and completely bourgeois in ideology and sympathy. The peasant, labour and left national influences have been isolated. In these circumstances it would be a great folly to look to the Congress for a mass revolutionary action. Also we cannot vaguely expect to give a 'revolutionary turn' to the Congress struggle if and when it starts. We must rule out every possibility of it.

There is a further consideration why we must endeavour in the present to lay down a basis for political mass action independent of the Congress. The task of the Congress was the achievement of national independence. This task could have normally been fulfilled in a revolutionary manner only; and the Congress was expected to tread the revolutionary path (with its vacillations) up to a considerable distance. In the present circumstances, however, there is every likelihood of this task being fulfilled to the extent desired by the Congress (as at present constituted) through a compromise with imperialism. Doubtless pressure is required for compromise and doubtless Congress would continue to exert pressure (even going to the length of some form of direct action). The power however which Mr Rajagopalachari hopes to 'capture' by offering the blood and sweat of millions of the Indian people cannot be complete independence. It would be just as much of independence as Mr Rajagopalachari and his 'Congress' would dare to have consistent with their desire to retain British military and economic tutelage (in order to protect their 'independence' from aggression from without and 'disorder' within, and to safeguard and preserve the economic status quo). It is not too much to expect that this sort of arrangement would not be repugnant to the British ruling class under certain circumstances that may arise sooner rather than later.

This leads us to the conclusion that we have reached the end of a stage. The united offensive of the Indian people (national bourgeoisie, urban middle class, peasantry, workers) against imperialism is at an end. The national bourgeoisie and a section of the middle classes (the upper strata) are deserting the struggle (in the name of national defence, etc.) They will have seized a certain amount of power from imperialism, but they cannot be expected to fight on till every vestige of imperialism is destroyed. The task of destroying what would remain of imperialism and of carrying forward the democratic revolution devolves on the workers, peasants and the lower middle classes. Thus in the second stage in a country like India the role of the peasantry must be predominant and this stage is mainly the stage of the agrarian revolution. This means that the period of the bourgeois revolution (an agrarian revolution is also a part of it) is not over and the stage of the proletarian or socialist revolution has not yet arrived. But the first part of the bourgeois democratic revolution (the period of united front struggle against imperialism) is over, and the second and last part, that of the agrarian revolution, begins.

Here again I am not suggesting that the agrarian revolution has actually begun in the sense that the peasants have taken the initiative with themselves of seizing the lands of the Zamindars, of driving them out of the villages, of taking possession of large holdings and distributing them among themselves. This indeed has not begun as it did in China in 1927. But what I wish to point out is that the preceding stage of the Indian revolution has reached its end, and now we must positively and clearly prepare and work to usher in the next stage.

There is also some talk in certain quarters of establishing soviets immediately. This is 'leaping to defeat' in Stalin's words — leaping over a whole stage. Unquestionably it is the Kisan Sabhas that exist and that will arise everywhere that will play the predominant part in the present and be the organic precursors of real peasant soviets. (We need not borrow the word soviet. Kisan Sabha is a good enough easily understood name with a revolutionary tradition).

The foregoing implies that we have to direct our chief attention from the Congress to the Kisan Sabhas. The fact that the Kisan Sabhas are not to be found in large numbers and their organization is not as widespread as that of the Congress need not deter us. Given the proper approach and the appropriate slogans, they can be made to rise up like mushrooms.

My emphasis on the Kisan Sabhas should not be taken to mean that we are to neglect our other activities and our work side by side for the proletarian revolution. The working class movement must continue to receive our utmost attention.

Some people get exercised over the question if we should leave or remain in the Congress. To me the question is of secondary importance. The main thing is that for us the Congress no longer remains an instrument for revolutionary action and that therefore we must prepare an independent basis for such action. We may continue in the Congress as long as it serves any useful purpose. But we cannot continue to ask the masses to look to the Congress for their economic and political emancipation. To keep the masses tied up to the Congress is to do them the greatest disservice and to sabotage the revolution. It is our clear duty to remove the dependence of the masses upon the Congress. For this we need not ask the masses to turn against the Congress. We must, however, do two things: one positive and the other negative. We must explain the character of the present Congress leadership in plain terms to the masses (negative). We must build up their own instruments of struggle and teach them to depend solely upon those.

Such being our tasks as I conceive them, the first thing that has to be done is to build up a revolutionary ideology, i.e. a revolutionary socialist party. As far as my own party, the C.S.P. is concerned its framework has become too inadequate for the task before us. The present is a golden opportunity to bring together all revolutionary elements into a revolutionary party. The fact that we shall start on clear slate should make it possible to unite the several revolutionary strands in the country. And here is my suggestion.

Let us form a new revolutionary party out of the C.S.P., the Anushilan, the Forward Block, the Kirti, the Labour Party and other such groups or elements. A party based squarely on Marxism-Leninism, independent of all other political organizations and parties. I think this is eminently possible if you only wish it. The C.S.P. may or may not be kept going merely as a cover and platform for the new party and particularly to function within the Congress as long as we consider it feasible to do so.

I have not mentioned the C.P. among the elements from which the new party has to be built, because the C.P. by its very constitution and the constitution of the C.I. cannot merge its identity in another socialist party. Even if they profess to do so that would be merely to get an opportunity of entering the other party and capturing (i.e. disrupting) it. The new party thus should be distinct from the C.P. but there should be a working alliance between the two.

This does not mean that I conceive the new party as being anti-C.I. We should indeed have contacts with Moscow and seek the aid of the Soviet in our revolution. It must, however, be free to follow its own policies without dictation from Moscow.

I conceive the new party as an entirely underground party of whole-time revolutionaries. Its activities must include (I cannot complete the sentence. You will understand).

This is in short my proposal. I am in deadly earnest about it. And I request you to consider it in all seriousness. I expect to be out by the end of next month. I shall try to meet you during your trial. In the meanwhile kindly discuss the matter with friends there, particularly the Anushilan friends. You may send me your tentative advice through Swamiji. If we are able to carry out this plan we shall be able to do something on a big scale in India.

Apart from the party, we need mass organs of struggle and for seizure of power. I see these in the Kisan and Mazdoor sabhas chiefly. These will have to be united in a mighty union of peasants' and workers' unions (Congress of Peasants' and Workers' Soviets). The formation of this union should be one of our objectives in the immediate future.

I hope you are keeping good health and are having your well-deserved rest. We are quite well here.

With best wishes,

Your Comrade

Letters to Lord Linlithgow

38/2 Elgin Road,
Calcutta,
29th December, 1940.

Your Excellency,

After considerable hesitation, I have decided to address Your Excellency on the situation in Bengal, though I am still confined to bed. The matter is one of extreme urgency and does not brook delay. Moreover, Your Excellency is, fortunately, now in Bengal and it should be easy to study the situation on the spot and verify at once the accuracy of what I am going to say. The opportunity is a rare one and in the public interest I should not miss it. That is my excuse for encroaching on Your Excellency's time and attention.

2. Under the Government of India Act 1935, despite the scheme of provincial autonomy, the Governor General-in-Council has certain responsibilities in the provincial sphere as well. But this constitutional provision would not, by itself, afford a sufficient 'raison d'etre' for expecting Your Excellency to look into a provincial affair. The War has, however, brought about constitutional changes in India in the direction of centralization and the Government of India have assumed direct responsibility for the administration of the whole of British India.

3. I shall now come straight to the issue which I desire to place before Your Excellency. Since April 1937, Bengal has been ruled by a Ministry which is predominantly communal in outlook and purpose. Behind this rule, stands an alliance — perhaps an unwritten alliance — between some Muslim M.L.A.s on the one side and the British Government and the British mercantile community on the other. On communal questions, the Muslims are given a free hand, while on political issues the will of the Governor and the British mercantile community is allowed to prevail. Those who belong to neither side have had no place in the administrative picture of Bengal since 1937. But their exclusion would not have been of much consequence if the administration had been carried on with reasonable efficiency, purity and impartiality. But such is unfortunately not the case. Rank communalism seems to be the basic

principle of the administration, the other features of which are inefficiency and corruption.

4. I should hasten to remark at this stage that in criticizing the Bengal Ministry in the above manner, I have nothing in common with the mental attitude of the Hindu Mahasabha. People like myself are prepared to concede to the Muslims, gladly and voluntarily, their legitimate share in everything which interests them. We have already proved our bona fides in this matter by our action in the past — action which at times has made us unpopular with the section of the Hindus which is communally-minded. Today we represent perhaps the only party in India that can still hope to bridge the gulf between the two major communities and can still claim to possess the goodwill of a large section of Indian Muslims.

5. Nobody will deny that Bengal has been the cradle of Indian Nationalism since the dawn of British rule in this country. Hindu Bengal, in particular, has throughout these decades thought and striven in terms of nationalism, with the result that the Hindu Mahasabha movement has never had a strong foothold here. But today a wave of communalism is spreading over Hindu Bengal, as an inevitable reaction to Muslim communalism. In the face of this communal vortex with its unending eddies, those who believe in nationalism are looking on helplessly.

6. One may say that it is of no direct concern to the British Government, or to the British mercantile community or to the Muslims in general that the Hindus of Bengal have been suffering since 1937 or that communalism has been gaining ground among them or that administration is characterized by communalism, inefficiency and corruption. But this is only superficially true. My proposition is that though today the Hindus of Bengal may find themselves in trouble and jeopardy — the situation is developing in such a manner that very soon it will affect all the other communities as well. To use different language, the Muslim Ministry in Bengal has been using a boomerang which will before long recoil on all the other communities. And when the Sindh crisis is reproduced in Bengal, the situation will be beyond repair.

7. I desire to draw Your Excellency's attention to the serious potentialities of the situation in Bengal, not because the Hindus have been having a bad time, but because the peace of the whole province may be upset in future if an immediate remedy is not found and applied.

8. One of the possible remedies and perhaps the best remedy under the existing circumstances is to have a Government that will command the confidence of both the major communities and will work for the welfare of the province as a whole. An administration based on justice, purity and efficiency would be the ideal solution. At present though we have ministers who call themselves Hindus, they have no following worth the name, with the result that the Hindu community as a whole has no confidence in the present Government. In the case of scheduled castes, the majority of their representatives in the Bengal Legislative Assembly sit on the opposition benches, and the two scheduled caste ministers have not been able to break the scheduled caste opposition in the Assembly, though they are in a position to distribute patronage liberally. So far as the Muslims are concerned, it would be only fair to say that an influential section among them is strongly dissatisfied with the present reactionary administration. As a proof thereof, the Krishak-Proja Party, with a following that is not negligible, has been consistently siding with the Opposition.

9. Your Excellency has a great responsibility in the matter — both direct and indirect. The direct responsibility emanates from constitutional sources. The indirect responsibility springs from the fact that the present ministry depends entirely on the support of the Governor and the British mercantile community for its existence.

10. If Your Excellency is satisfied with the situation in Bengal, whatever the reasons may be, I have nothing further to add and this letter may be ignored altogether. But we know it for a fact that the situation is pregnant with serious possibilities and both the British Government and the British mercantile community should, in their own interests, look into the matter. In the case of the Holwell Monument Satyagraha, the non-official British community took up a farsighted attitude, which was greatly appreciated. And it is just possible that that community may not be found wanting in political sagacity today.

11. Another remedy which strikes me is the suspension of the Constitution during the period of the war. But that is a remedy about which I would rather not say anything now, since another solution is available.

12. If the British Government and the British mercantile community continue to play the role that they have been playing in the public life of Bengal since 1937, the situation will steadily deteriorate until it reaches a stage which will be beyond repair. If that

development unfortunately takes place we shall at least have the satisfaction of having brought the matter to the notice of the highest governmental authority in the land in good time.

I am,
Yours faithfully,

Subhas Chandra Bose

38/2 Elgin Road,
Calcutta,
Dated 3rd January 1941

Your Excellency,

I am thankful for Your Excellency's message conveyed in Mr Laithwaite's letter of the 1st inst. There is one other point regarding the Bengal situation which I feel I should have brought to Your Excellency's notice.

2. About a couple of months ago, a fresh notification was issued by the Bengal Government banning all meetings, processions, demonstrations etc. which constitute an indispensable concomitant of public life. This order is more stringent than the one issued by the Bengal Government at the outbreak of the war in 1939.

3. The Government spokesmen, when questioned, usually say that the supposed ban is, in reality, no ban — since meetings etc. could be held by obtaining necessary permission from the authorities concerned. But people of my generation who have been in public life for twenty years have never applied for permits from the authorities for organizing meetings etc. and we shall not depart from that practice now. The Government, too, are not unaware of it. Consequently, the above notification has become in reality a ban on all public meetings etc.

4. Your Excellency may remember that last year I brought to the notice of the Central authorities the ban imposed by the Bengal Government early in September 1939. Thereafter, I approached both the Hon. Chief Minister and the Hon. Home Minister and appealed to them to withdraw that strange notification and thereby fall in line with other parts of British India. I pointed out how incongruous it was for me to be able to lecture all over the country

including Delhi, and to have to shut up as soon as I entered Bengal. I further pointed out that the Bengal Government, like other Governments, could take action in the case of seditious, anti-war speeches — and that it was not only unfair but unnecessary to impose a general ban on all meetings etc. My appeals fell flat and ultimately after waiting for five months, we began to defy the ban in sheer exasperation. Some of our men were arrested at first — but soon after, better counsels prevailed and the authorities did not subsequently interfere with our meetings. I do not think that the Bengal Government enhanced their prestige by such strange behaviour.

5. Exactly the same situation has arisen today and the Bengal Government by their incomprehensible policy are only inviting a Civil Disobedience Movement. I feel tempted to ask Your Excellency as to what a freedom-loving man could or should do in such circumstances, when he has failed to move the Local Government.

6. Our Government here have not neglected the Press either. In the first place, the daily censorship is much more rigid here than in other provinces, as will be borne out by a comparison of the newspapers of different provinces. But what is more important is that on the slightest pretext, a complete ban on certain news is imposed by the Government. At the time of the Holwell Monument Satyagraha, the Bengal Government, by notification, banned the publication of all news concerning that movement. What a contrast with the present policy of the Government of India regarding publication of news concerning the Gandhian Satyagraha!

7. About a month ago, when some political prisoners in Bengal Jails went on hungerstrike, the Bengal Government, by notification, banned the publication of all news, notices etc. concerning the hungerstrike. During my twenty years experience I have not known of a similar incident. The most regrettable feature of this incident is that it has occurred under the aegis of a 'popular' Ministry. No wonder that the people of this province do not feel enthusiastic over such a 'popular' Ministry.

8. When it suits their purpose, the Bengal Government talk of uniformity of practice. But when the practice elsewhere is in advance of what prevails in this province, the argument is conveniently forgotten.

9. My object in writing this is not to seek redress, but to keep

Your Excellency informed, so that the difficulties under which we have to live and work here may at least be appreciated.

I am,
Yours faithfully,

Subhas Chandra Bose

His Excellency the Viceroy and Governor General of India.

'My Political Testament' and Letters to the Government

To The Superintendent, Presidency Jail

The Superintendent
Presidency Jail

Dear Sir,

I have to bring to your notice a complaint of assault on a convict under the orders of a warder on duty in 'Forty-four Cells' this morning. The convict in question is my 'Phaltu' or attendant. The assault took place in the early morning about the time that the Jailor goes on his first round.

I have tried to ascertain the facts from my convict attendant and what I have gathered is briefly as follows.

He was slow in getting up when the Jailor passed along in front of his cell. He says that he did not hear the warder's 'word of caution' and that there was no deliberate neglect on his part. For this fault of his, the warder ordered the convict overseer, the parawalla and another convict to perform 'dholai' i.e. give him a good beating. The assault took place after the Jailor had left that ward (Forty-four cells).

I believed what the convict says, because he is really hard of hearing. I have often to shout myself in order to get myself heard. As a matter of fact, I was thinking of complaining about his deafness and getting him transferred but I did not do so because he is well-behaved and does his work well.

I had thought that in the year 1940 the 'dholai' system had ceased to exist. From what I gather, however, it appears that it is not an uncommon occurrence. But there is no provision in the Jail Code for it.

I request you to take official cognizance of this case.
Thanking you,

Yours faithfully,

Subhas C. Bose
15.7.40

To The Superintendent, Presidency Jail

To *17.7.40*
The Superintendent,
Presidency Jail

Dear Sir,
As a prevention against sore-throat, nasal trouble, influenza etc. I have been regularly using nasal spray with very good results. At present the medicine necessary for spraying is exhausted. It is an only stuff containing menthol etc. and was prescribed by my brother Dr Sunil C. Bose. I would like to get the prescription from him and I am sure it could be dispensed at the Jail Hospital. Could you kindly ask some member of your staff to ring up Dr Bose (Park 679) and ask him to send the prescription to you? This would bring you the prescription in one day. Otherwise there is no knowing when my letter will reach him. The letter I wrote home ten days ago has not yet been delivered, because the articles asked for have not come yet. Thanks.

Yours faithfully

Subhas C. Bose

Would you kindly see the last prescription, sent from your home. It is said that the prescription already sent contained the problem for the nasal spray too.

Sd. Illegible
17/7

The last prescription is sent herewith. It is the prescription for the digestive medicine, but not for the nasal spray. Please return the prescription after necessary inspection and use.

S.C. Bose
17/7

Seen & returned. Arranged for

Sd. Illegible
17/7

Interview petn rejected
(i). Miss Illa Bose — twice
(ii). Kalyan Bose
P.C. Rs 35–8–9 balance

Sd. Illegible
17/7

To
The Hon'ble Home Minister
Govt. of Bengal

Through the Supdt. Presidency Jail

Dear Sir,

I have just read in the Statesman of today's date report of your speech in the Bengal Legislative Assembly on the 18th inst on the adjournment motion moved by Mr J. Hashemy, over the ban imposed on newspapers etc. in connection with the Holwell Monument agitation. I do not know if the Statesman's report is correct. It is grossly inaccurate and consequently unfair to one who cannot speak in reply, because he happens to be behind the bars. Before I lodge my protest, however, it is only right that I shall have a true copy of your speech. I shall, therefore, request you to kindly let me have a true copy of your speech.

If I do not get it within a reasonable time, I shall have to address you on the basis of the Statesman's report.

Yours faithfully,
Subhas C. Bose

Presidency Jail
19.7.40

To The Superintendent, Presidency Jail

To
The Superintendent
Presidency Jail

Dear Sir,

On the 5th instant I addressed the Hon. Home Minister on the question of our status. Pending a definite reply from Government to that letter, there are a few points which may be settled by you and which appear to be within your jurisdiction.

1. *The question of Association*
I have been segregated and confined by myself since the 5th instant. I have already protested verbally to you more than once and on one occasion I wrote for permission to have association for an hour or so daily with the others detained under the same Section as myself. This sort of segregation which now seems to be a permanent arrangement is altogether unscientific and unhealthy and has never been imposed upon me so far, during the long periods I have spent in confinement.

2. *The question of daily exercise*
This ward has hardly any facilities for walking, being so small in area. I therefore, request you to permit me to have a walk in the evening after lock up within the Jail compound. There is not a single jail in India or Burma where this has been refused at any time. I am giving, as examples, the names of some of the jails:

1. Alipore Central Jail, Calcutta
2. Berhampur Jail, Bengal
3. Seoni Jail — C.P. (outside Jail walls)
4. Jubbulpore Central Jail — C.P.
5. Arthur Road Jail — Bombay
6. Mandalay Jail }
7. Rangoon Jail } Burma
8. Insein Jail }

3. *Interviews*
One of my applications for interviews has been refused. I am sure that some of my relatives have by now also applied for interviews and since they have not been allowed to interview me — I can presume that they too have been refused permission. I shall, therefore, feel obliged if you kindly enquire from the proper authorities as to who among my relatives are under the ban. Ours is a large family and I can easily ask for interviews with those who are not under any ban, so far as interviews are concerned.

The interview with my brother Mr Sarat Chandra Bose was a special one arranged direct through the Government in the Home Department.

If any of these points are at the present moment not entirely under your jurisdiction, please take them up with the proper authority.

Thanking you

Yours faithfully
Subhas C. Bose

Presidency Jail
23.7.40

To
The Superintendent
Presidency Jail

Dear Sir,

Reference the talk we have just had, I am jotting down in a hurry some of the points that I would request you to consider and sanction (of course, with the sanction of Government where that is necessary). I would beg you to kindly note that I am not making any extravagant demands. In fact, there is not one single new item which has not been allowed by previous Governments.

I. Diet and other allowances to be as during previous periods of detention (I think the diet allowance was Rs 6/10 per diem in 1924–27 and Rs 4/8 per diem in later periods of detention).

II. Same facilities as on previous occasions in the matter of supply of letter paper, exercise books, crockery including knife — other articles like suitcase, clothing etc. without being hindered by usual jail restrictions.

III. No ban on the supply of particular daily newspapers (e.g. in the last detention period — 1936–37 I was allowed all newspapers).

IV. All literature that is not banned or proscribed by Government to be allowed.

V. Liberal policy regarding the no. of letters I can write (e.g. as on the last occasion 1936–37) when it was 4 to 5 letters a week.

VI. Supply of gramophone at my expense. The hours of use will of course be so adjusted as not to interfere with the work in jail.

VII. I may be allowed to consult my Doctor brother — Dr Sunil C. Bose with the approval of the Superintendent from time to time.

VIII. The most important points now are regarding *exercise and interview.*

Regarding exercise, I may be allowed morning or evening walks on the river side the car expense being mine. This was allowed in 1937.

Regarding interview, I may be allowed to go home in the afternoon as in 1937. If this is objected to, then I may be allowed daily interviews. Those interviews may be permitted in the ward without any police officer being present (in December 1936 and early in 1937 I was allowed daily interviews in the Medical College Hospital where I was a state prisoner without anybody being present at the interview. Later on I was allowed to go home daily for interviews).

In the case of daily interviews in prison, it is desirable to have them in the ward, since it does not inconvenience either me or anybody else. As a detenu or state-prisoner, I have usually been allowed interviews in my own ward in jails where I happened to be confined at the time. I can furnish several instances of this if necessary. I may add further that in 1921 and 1922 Lt. Col Hamilton allowed daily interviews in this ward in this jail in the case of the late Mr C.R. Das and Major Salisbury allowed it in the Alipore Central Jail though he was under trial and later, was convicted.

I have made herein suggestions which can fit in with my present position, viz. jail confinement and I am writing this in great hurry. The underlying assumption is that I have the status of a state-prisoner. I shall only add that the most important points now are regarding exercise and interview. The present confinement has, I am sorry to say, begun to tell on my health and on my nerves.

To facilitate matters for Government, I may say that should the above facilities regarding exercise and interviews be given and should they trust my honour, I shall reciprocate that trust. But even H.E. Sir John Anderson's Government, which was known to be a 'strong' Government, never asked me for any cause for complaint when they allowed the above facilities for exercise and interview.

Thanking you,

Yours faithfully,

Subhas C. Bose

Presidency Jail
7.8.40

To
The Superintendent
Presidency Jail

Dear Sir,

After repeated protests against what virtually amounted to solitary confinement, Govt. have been pleased to order Sj. Amarendra N. Bose to shift from Ward . . . to this ward. I presume that this is for the purpose of affording me 'association'. If so, I may inform Govt. that this purpose has not been fulfilled by the above order. It will only enable Govt. to say that I am not in solitary confinement.

2) I had made only a simple request, viz. that I should be allowed to go over to the political prisoners Yard (I mean ward 17) for an hour or so every day, if I desired to have some company for a while. This has not been allowed for reasons that I cannot understand. Here in this ward there are undertrial prisoners charged with manslaughter, cheating etc. apparently they are good enough associates — but not people who have been detained without trial in Ward 17. (If I cannot leave this yard, then they may be permitted to come here in batches).

3) There is another thing which Govt. can easily sanction if they do not desire that I should go off my head under such conditions of restraint. They may allow me a radio at my expense — which I undertake to use in such a manner as not to disturb the normal work in jail. This will not harm anybody but may afford me relief and relaxation. Nowadays radios and cinema shows (talkies) are allowed in jails all over the civilized world. As a matter of fact, there was a talkie here inside the jail only the other day for the benefit of the ordinary prisoners. Unless Govt. intend placing us in a worse category than criminals, I think I may be allowed to have a radio for which I am hereby making a personal request.

Should this matter need the sanction of the higher authorities, I shall be greatly obliged if you please send this up for necessary orders.

Thanking you,

Yours faithfully

Subhas C. Bose

Presidency Jail
22.8.40

To
The Superintendent
Presidency Jail

Dear Sir,

I have seen your note in the Requisition Book re. my interview. I must once again protest against your disallowing the interview here. And you are disallowing interview at a time when one needs interviews more than at any other time.

2. It is a common thing in jail for a person to have interviews inside — whether in the jail hospital or in his cell — when he is ill. If interviews inside the jail are banned altogether, it will mean that as long as he is ill, he will not have any interviews. This is clearly an impossible position. In the present case, you should treat me as a patient in hospital, not only with regard to medical treatment but in other matters as well.

3. I have been seldom ill in the comparatively short periods I have spent in Bengal jails — but I know at first hand of any number of persons having interviews inside the jail. In this very ward (and also within the Alipore Central Jail when he was transferred here) the late Deshbandhu C.R. Das was allowed daily interviews with his family for several hours in the afternoon.

4. Whenever I have happened to be ill at interview time, I have received the same facilities and there has never been the slightest objection on the part of the jail authorities on the point — e.g. in Mandalay, Rangoon and Insein Jails in Burma — Seoni and Jubbulpore Jails in C.P.

I would therefore request you to reconsider the matter and let me have the interview here. To deprive me of interview this week amounts to punishment, particularly when I am quite alone once again. Should your answer be in the negative even after reconsideration, I shall be obliged if you kindly refer this matter to Government.

Yours faithfully,
Subhas C. Bose

Presidency Jail
30.8.40

To
The Superintendent
Presidency Jail

Dear Sir,

Re. the permission I have received from Govt. to consult my lawyers. I desire in the first place to interview my constituted attorney and decide my future line of action after discussing the matter with him.

I take it that this interview will follow the usual procedure and be a private one where no officer will be present.

My attorney is Mr Nripendra C. Mitra, of Messrs. Mitra & Mitra, Solicitors, 5 Hastings Street, Calcutta. The name of the firm Messrs. Mitra & Mitra is on the telephone list. Mr Mitra is in his office at about 11:30 a.m. every morning. His residence is also on the telephone list under name N.C. Mitra, 2B Abhoy Guha Road, Calcutta. As tomorrow is a holiday, I would like to have the interview this afternoon.

Thanking you,

Yours faithfully
Subhas C. Bose

Presidency Jail
31.8.40

To
The Superintendent
Presidency Jail

Dear Sir,

After writing one letter to you this morning, I find in the Hindusthan Standard that a warrant has been issued by the Chief Presidency Magistrate against me and that I have been charged under two heads. This makes it all the more imperative that I should consult my legal advisers at once. I shall therefore be obliged if the interview with my attorney Mr Nripendra C. Mitra is fixed up for this afternoon.

To avoid misunderstanding or unpleasantness at the time of the interview I shall be obliged by your leaving instructions that the interview, according to the usual procedures, will be a private one.

Thanking you,

Yours faithfully
Subhas C. Bose

Presidency Jail
31.8.40

To
The Superintendent
Presidency Jail

Dear Sir,

The P.W.D. representative showed me a note the other day saying that earth connection costing Rs 22 would be indispensably necessary for the radio set. I have consulted the radio supplier twice and they have assured me that earth connection as recommended by the P.W.D. is not necessary. I know also from personal experience that at home it was not necessary for my radio set. The radio suppliers are experts in their line and know their job. Moreover, they will incur loss if they bring about damage through wrong advice and defective fittings. In the circumstances, I do not feel like ignoring their expert advice. Will you kindly consider this matter and if necessary take the matter up with the P.W.D.?

Last but not least, my stay here is temporary and a permanent connection as recommended by the P.W.D. would appear unnecessary from that point of view.

Yours faithfully

20.9.40 Subhas C. Bose

To
The Superintendent
Presidency Jail

Dear Sir,

I have seen the note of the Dy. Jailor about the rules and restrictions regarding Durga Puja. They have come as a surprise to me.

The concessions re. Durga Puja followed the hunger strike of the Bengal detenues in Mandalay Jail in 1926. At that time we were given full facilities for performing the Puja and the Government sanctioned a Puja allowance as well. There was only one self- imposed restraint which we observed. Though we were allowed music, we saw to it that it was played with the minimum of noise possible.

The following points regarding the Durga Puja have to be noted:

(1) It is the great national festival among Hindus in this part of the country.

(2) It is a congregational worship. Hence it is called not merely 'Puja' but 'Utsav' also.

(3) Three priests are necessary for Durga Puja — including 'Chandi-Path' — the recital of Chandi. It is physically impossible to do with less than two — and that is possible only by saddling one of the priests with 'Chandi-Path', which they often refuse as involving too much strain.

(4) The hours of Puja are fixed by astronomical calculations. For instance, the most important ceremony is 'Sandhi Puja' which is held on the 8th day of the moon — and the Puja hour is often late at night (I do not know yet what the hours for 'Sandhi Puja' are this year).

Durga Puja in Jail will consequently be possible only if the following extra concessions are allowed:

(1) Since Durga Puja is congregational in character all Hindu prisoners who are so desirous should be permitted to participate. It may be remarked here that similar facilities are given to Muslim prisoners during Id and to Christian prisoners in Alipore Central Jail during Christian festivals. In any case there is no reason why all Hindu political prisoners should not be allowed to participate.

(2) At least two priests should be allowed.

(3) They should be allowed to perform the ceremony in the hours fixed by astronomical calculations, whatever those hours may be.

(4) Minimum music should be allowed. Music is essential for 'Arati' ceremony in particular. (The question of Puja allowance should be considered along with the general question of our status which is under consideration).

If these concessions are not allowed it will mean virtually that Govt. do not allow Durga Puja in Jail. This will be an unjustifiable cancellation of the concessions we gained after considerable suffering in Jail in the fifteen-day hunger strike in 1926. It will mean, further, that concessions allowed by the bureaucratic regime are being withdrawn by the popular ministry.

The consequences of such situation will naturally be serious for us. Kindly give the matter your close consideration and if necessary take the matter up with the higher authorities.

Thanking you,

Yours faithfully,

20.9.40 Subhas C. Bose

P.S. — Durga Puja begins on the 6th day of the moon and ends on the 10th day — but three days are more important among the five.

S.C.B.

To
The Hon'ble Home Minister
Govt. of Bengal

Dear Sir,

I have to bring to your notice the fact that in the two trials that are now going on concerning myself the public are not allowed free access to the Court, though the general public are given the impression that the trials are 'public' and not 'in camera'.

Unfortunately this fact was brought to my notice only yesterday when I had an interview with my people — otherwise I would have taken earlier steps to vindicate my rights as a citizen.

The Govt. have to do either of two things:

(1) Announce to the public that the trial will be in camera and then exclude the public. In this case, we shall know how to react.

(2) Hold a public trial and allow the public free access to the Court.

But the Govt. cannot make a show of public trial and, in fact, exclude the public. One cannot have the cake and eat it as well.

I know of a significant case in which a near relative of mine was trying a leader of eminence. The police wanted to exclude the public but he refused to allow it. The police then took up the plea that there was not enough room in Court. Thereupon the trying Magistrate went into the open and had the trial under a tree, allowing the public full liberty to watch the proceedings of a public trial. This is the spirit which should animate a public servant — whether high or low — for a public servant has to serve the public and not to take orders from the police.

I cannot disbelieve the report that the police do not allow the public free access to the Court — because I was myself twice insulted by a Police Sergeant in the Bankshall Court. He was ultimately brought to his senses because I flared up and sought the protection of the Court.

Owing to police interference, my relatives have the greatest difficulty in attending the trials. It is to me unbearable that members of the public including my relatives who wish to attend the trials should be insulted by petty police sergeants and men of that ilk.

Until the matter is settled to my satisfaction along the lines indicated above, I decline to attend the Court on the 3rd and 28th inst. (Bankshall Court and Alipore Court respectively). Things which we did not put up with under a bureaucratic regime, we shall not tolerate now — simply because there is a 'popular' ministry in office. I shall of course, face the consequences of this attitude however unpleasant or painful they may be for me.

The matter may be treated as urgent as the next date for appearing in Court is the 3rd Inst.

Yours faithfully,

Subhas C. Bose

Presidency Jail
1.10.40

To
The Trying Magistrate,
Alipore

Dear Sir,

On the 1st inst. I addressed a letter to the Hon. Home Minister on the question of interference on the part of the police with the public including my relatives — desiring to attend my trials at Alipore and Bankshall Courts. Since then I have received information from Govt. through the Superintendent of this Jail to the effect that instructions have been issued which will remove the cause of complaint. I hope that so far as it lies in your power you will kindly see to it that the policemen on duty at the time of my trial behave themselves properly.

Yours faithfully,

Subhas C. Bose

Presidency Jail
22.10.40

To
The Hon. Home Minister,
Government of Bengal,
Through the Superintendent, Presidency Jail

Dear Sir,

I have been in Jail for about four months under a section of the Defence of India Rules which does not necessitate a trial by a Court of Law. Over and above that, I have been an undertrial prisoner for the last two months. Detention without trial under one section and prosecution under another section of the above Rules — constitute a combination of executive fiat and judicial procedure which is not only unprecedented, but is manifestly illegal and unjust.

2. Further, when bail applications were made before the trying Magistrates, the Public Prosecutors opposed them, presumably under instructions from the Local Government, with the result that the applications were not granted. This is an evidence of undue governmental interference in the course of judicial proceedings. This interference is all the more objectionable because the Local Government are not giving effect to the instructions issued by the Government of India with regard to cases under the Defence of India Rules.

3. It is unfair, unjust and illegal to forcibly detain me in prison in this manner when I am being prosecuted. Once I have been produced before a Court on the charge of offending against the D.I. Rules, the law should be allowed to take its own course. How can I again be imprisoned without trial under the same D.I. Rules?

4. It is surprising and painful that all this is happening under the aegis of a 'popular' ministry. I have been watching how the self-same Ministry has been behaving in the case of citizens professing the Islamic faith — particularly when they happen to be members of the Muslim League. It is not necessary to furnish Government with the numerous relevant instances, culminating in the sudden release of the Maulvi of Murapara in Dacca District. Every single instance of this sort has been duly noted by me.

5. In view of these and numerous other considerations, Government should release me forthwith. My election to the Indian Legislative Assembly also demands that I should be permitted to attend its sittings which commence on 5th November — of course, health permitting. If the Burma Government could allow a convicted

prisoner to attend the Assembly sittings, should not the 'popular' ministry of Bengal allow the same facilities to one who is not a convicted prisoner?

6. Last but not least, my continued detention in the present state of my health is nothing short of a vindictive policy on the part of Government, which is altogether inexplicable to me.

This letter is written in all seriousness and I pray that it be given the consideration it deserves.

Yours faithfully,

Presidency Jail, Subhas Chandra Bose
30.10.40

To
The Superintendent,
Presidency Jail.

Dear Sir,

I have addressed the Hon. Home Minister today on the question of my continued detention in Jail. I desire that along with that letter, Government should be informed of the consequences, for me, of their refusal to withdraw the order of detention. I am therefore writing this to you with the request that you may kindly bring the contents to the notice of Government as confidentially as possible. I am sending it to your office under closed cover so that nobody else need see it. This letter is nor a threat and I hope it will not be treated as such. It is meant to be a frank communication regarding certain developments which may soon become unavoidable for me.

I do not expect that Government will be moved by the consideration mentioned or implied in my letter to the Hon. Home Minister. I have therefore been pondering for the last two months over the course of action that I should adopt. There is no other alternative for me but to register a moral protest against an unjust act and as a proof of that protest, to undertake a voluntary fast. This fast will have no effect on the 'popular' ministry, because I am neither the Maulvi of Murapara, Dacca nor a Muhammadan by faith. Consequently, the fast will, in my case, become a fast unto death. I know that even that will not move this Government and I have no illusions on this point. The 'popular' ministry, like all bureaucratic governments, will raise the question of official prestige and the familiar argument will be trotted out that Government cannot be coerced by a fast. I was in England when Terence Macswiney, Lord Mayor of Cork, was on hunger strike on a similar issue. The whole country was moved — all the political parties in Parliament and H.M. the King also were visibly affected, but Lloyd George's Government was adamant. As a consequence, the King had to declare publicly that because of the Cabinet's attitude, he could not exercise the Royal Prerogative. I am recounting all this just to convince you and the Government that I have examined the whole situation in the cold light of common sense and logic and that I have not been thinking light-heartedly.

Thus while I do not expect any tangible result to follow from the fast, I shall have the satisfaction of recording a moral protest against the iniquitous action of Government. Britishers and the British Government have been talking of upholding the sacred principles of freedom and democracy, but their policy nearer home belies these professions. They want our assistance to destroy Naziism, but they have been indulging in super-Naziism. My protest will serve to expose the hypocrisy underlying their policy in this unfortunate country — as also the policy of a Provincial Government that calls itself 'popular', but which, in reality, can be moved only when there is a Muhammadan in the picture. Incidentally, I shall have the further satisfaction that my fast and its sequel will have repercussions outside India, for I happen to be one of the Indians known outside the frontiers of the country.

The only other point to consider is as to whether the remedy suggested is not worse than the disease and I have taken long days and nights to ponder over it. My answer to the question is that life under existing conditions is hardly worth living. In this mortal world, everything perishes except principles. These principles can live only when individuals do not hesitate to die for them. When individuals perish for a sacred principle, that principle does not die — but incarnates itself in other individuals. And it is through vicarious suffering alone that a cause can flourish and prosper. Just as flesh begets flesh — so also does spirit beget kindred spirits. Consequently, if I have anything worthy in me, neither my country nor humanity will lose as a result of my death. On the contrary, God willing, they may be elevated to a higher moral plane — for, after all, the highest sacrifice that one can make is the voluntary sacrifice of one's life, without taking the life of another.

One word more before I finish. I have been in Jail for long periods and have also been on hunger strike before. I know all the steps that overzealous officials sometimes take in order to frustrate the object of hunger strike. Naturally, I shall be prepared for them in advance. Moreover, I shall not permit forced feeding. Nobody has any moral right to feed me by force. This point was thrashed out with the British Cabinet in the case of Terence Macsweeney and at a later period with the Government of India during our hunger strike of 1926. Any circulars of Jail Code provisions which may have come into existence since then will not have any binding effect on me.

I repeat that this letter, written on the sacred day of Kali Puja, should not be treated as a threat or ultimatum. It is merely an affirmation of one's faith, written in all humility. Hence it should be handled as confidential document to be communicated to Government confidentially. I only desire that Government should know how my mind has been working so that they may appreciate my motives as well as the consequences, for me, of their decision.

Thanking you for your uniform courtesy,

Yours faithfully,

Presidency Jail, Subhas Chandra Bose
30.10.1940

To The President
Indian Legislative Assembly

To
The Hon. President,
Indian Legislative Assembly
New Delhi

Sir,

I have just been elected unopposed to the Indian Legislative Assembly from the Dacca Division constituency. As you may be aware, I have been in Jail custody since 2nd July 1940, under Section 26 of the Defence of India Rules without trial. Over and above this detention without trial, I am being prosecuted under another Section of the D.I. Rules and have thus been an undertrial prisoner, for about two months. Bail applications made on my behalf before the Trying Magistrate were not granted because of Government spokesmen opposing them.

According to the provisions of Constitutional Law I claim immunity from arrest and detention when the Legislature is in session and I therefore request you to kindly take steps so that I may be able to attend the session commencing in the first week of November, 1940 at New Delhi.

It may be argued against my claim that in the Indian Statute there is no explicit provision for immunity as stated above. In that case, I beg to submit that this right is implicit in any Constitution and the Indian Constitution can be no exception to it.

You may be aware, Sir, that recently a convicted prisoner, who was member of the Burma Legislative Assembly, was allowed to attend the sittings of the body. Surely, I cannot claim anything less, when I am not a convicted prisoner.

I shall be obliged by your taking early steps in this matter.

Yours affly,
Subhas C. Bose

Presidency Jail
Calcutta
1.11.40

Copy to the Hon. Deputy President
Indian Legislative Assembly
New Delhi

The Superintendent,
Presidency Jail.

Dear Sir,

I hope you have duly forwarded to Government the confidential letter I wrote to you on 30th October last — the day of Kali Puja. This is in continuation of that letter and both the letters are to be read in conjunction with my letter to the Hon. Home Minister of the same date, viz. 30th October.

2. Since I wrote to you, the Government of India has made it clear in connection with the adjournment motion tabled by Pandit L.K. Maitra, M.L.A. (central), before the Indian Legislative Assembly that the responsibility for my arrest and imprisonment rests exclusively with the Government of Bengal which is claimed by its

supporters to be controlled and run by a 'popular' Ministry. It is also clear that the way I have been treated by this 'popular' Government is unique and unprecedented in this country and violates the instructions of the Government of India relating to D.I.R. cases. It pains me to find that a 'popular' Government is using the D.I. Rules not for defending India, but in order to shield a procedure that is at once illegal and unjust.

3. Yesterday, when application for bail was made by my lawyers, the trying Magistrate at Bankshall Court granted the application, but was constrained to remark that his order would remain infructuous because of the action of Government in detaining me without trial under Section 26 of the D.I. Rules. I cannot conceive of a more blatant example of interference in judicial procedure on the part of the Executive. Were the D.I. Rules enacted for defending of India or for defending illegality and injustice of this sort? I wonder.

4. I am sorry that this Government has perpetrated another wrong by supplying the Secretary of State for India with incorrect information about my arrest and detention. As is already known, in reply to Mr Sorensen's query, the Secretary of State announced in the House of Commons on the basis of the information received by him that I had been taken into custody in connection with the Holwell Monument affair. If the whole truth had been told, then one would have heard more on the subject in England, for I have friends there, both in Parliament and among the general public.

5. For vindication of what I consider to be a legitimate right, there is but one course open to me, viz. to content myself with recording a moral protest — since every other door has been banged on me by the 'popular' Government. Consequently, as already intimated to you on the 30th October and in accordance with the vow I have prayerfully taken on Kali Puja Day, I shall commence my fast very soon. I shall send a formal intimation to Government in due course mentioning the exact date, but that will be on the very eve of commencement of the fast. Since I wrote as far back as the 30th ultimo, Government has already had sufficient notice.

I shall be obliged if you treat this letter as confidential and kindly forward it to Government confidentially as early as possible.

Yours faithfully,

Subhas Chandra Bose

Presidency Jail,
14.11.1940

To
The Secretary
Govt. of Bengal
Political Department. *16.11.40*

Dear Sir,

I understand that a letter I wrote to Mr B.P. Pain M.L.A on 29th October has been withheld by the Special Branch. I would request you to look into the matter.

Yesterday I wrote 3 letters — to Mr Arthur Greenwood M.P., Mr Sarat Chandra Bose (Calcutta) and Mr A.N. Bose (London). If any of these is withheld, I shall appeal to the Bengal Government and in case the Bengal Govt. confirm the action of the Special Branch, I shall appeal to the Govt. of India.

Yours faithfully
Subhas C. Bose

'My Political Testament':

To
H.E. the Governor of Bengal,
The Hon. Chief Minister
and
The Council of Ministers,

Your Excellency and Gentlemen!

I am writing this in connection with my letter of 30th October 1940, addressed to the Hon. Minister (copy of which was forwarded to the Hon. Chief Minister) and my confidential letters to the Superintendent, Presidency Jail, dated 30th October and 14th November, which were forwarded to Government in due course. Herein I shall also put down in black and white the considerations that are impelling me to take the most fateful step in my life.

I have no longer any hope that I shall obtain redress at your hands. I shall, therefore, make but two requests, the second of which will be at the end of this letter. My first request is that this letter be carefully preserved in the archives of the Government, so that it may be available to those of my countrymen who will succeed you in office in future. It contains a message for my countrymen and is therefore my political testament.

I was arrested without any official explanation or justification on 2nd July 1940, as per orders of the Government of Bengal, under Section 129 of the Defence of India Rules. The first explanation subsequently emanating from official sources came from the Rt. Hon. Mr Amery, Secretary of State for India, who stated in the House of Commons quite categorically that the arrest was in connection with the movement for the demolition of the Holwell Monument in Calcutta.

The Hon. Chief Minister virtually confirmed this pronouncement at a sitting of the Bengal Legislative Assembly and stated that it was the Holwell Monument Satyagraha which stood in the way of my release. When the Government decided to remove the Monument, all those who had been detained without trial in connection therewith were set free with the exception of Mr Narendra Narayan Chakravarti, M.L.A., and myself. These releases took place towards the end of August 1940, and almost simultaneously an order for my permanent detention was served under Section 26 of the Defence of India Rules, in lieu of the original order under Section 129, which provided for temporary detention.

Strangely enough, with the new order under Section 26, came the news that prosecution was being launched against me under Section 38 of the D.I. Rules before two Magistrates — for three of my speeches and for a contributed article in the weekly journal '*Forward Bloc*', of which I had been the Editor. Two of these speeches had been delivered in February 1940, and the third one early in April. Thus the Government created a unique and unprecedented situation towards the end of August last by detaining me permanently without trial under one section of the Defence of India Rules and simultaneously prosecuting me before judicial tribunals under another section of the same Rules. I had not seen a similar combination of executive fiat and judicial procedure before this occurrence took place. Such a policy is manifestly illegal and unjust and smacks of vindictiveness, pure and simple.

One cannot fail to notice that the prosecution was launched long after the alleged offences had taken place. Nor can it be overlooked that for the relevant article in '*Forward Bloc*', the paper had already been penalized through forfeiture of the security of Rs 500 and deposit of a further security of Rs 2000. Moreover, the attack on the paper was made all of a sudden, after a long period during which no warning had been given to the paper in accordance with the practice of Government.

The attitude of the Bengal Government was further exposed when applications for my release on bail were made before the two trying Magistrates. Both these applications were stoutly opposed by the Government spokesmen. On the last occasion, one of the Magistrates, Mr Wali-ul-Islam granted the bail application, but was constrained to remark that this order would remain infructuous till the Government withdrew their order for my detention without trial under Section 26 of the D.I. Rules. It is thus as clear as daylight that the Government have been pursuing a policy which fetters the discretion of judicial tribunals and interferes with the administration of law. The action of the Local Government appears all the more objectionable when it is remembered that they have given the go-by to the instructions of the Government of India with regard to such cases.

Another interesting feature of the Government's policy is my simultaneous prosecution before two Magistrates. If the intention was to place more than one speech of mine before a Court of Law, that could very well have been fulfilled without resorting to two Magistrates, for I have delivered any number of speeches during the last twelve months within the limits of Calcutta proper. The man in the street is, therefore, forced to think that Government are so keen on seeing me convicted that they have provided for a second string to the legal bow.

Last but not least, Government's action appears to an impartial man to be altogether mala fide, because proceedings were instituted so long after the alleged prejudicial acts had been committed. If the acts in question were in fact prejudicial, then action should have been taken by Government long ago, i.e. at the time that the alleged offences were committed.

May I request you to compare for one moment your attitude towards people like myself and towards Muslims arrested and imprisoned under the Defence of India Rules? How many cases have occurred up till now in which Muslims apprehended under the D.I. Rules have been suddenly released without rhyme or reason? The latest example of the Maulvi of Murapara is too fresh in the public mind to need recounting. Are we to understand that under your rule there is one law for the Muslim and another law for the Hindu and that the D.I. Rules have a different meaning when a Muslim is involved? If so, the Government might as well make a pronouncement to that effect.

Lest it be argued or suggested for one moment that for my

incarceration, the Government of India and not the Local Government are responsible, I may remind you that in connection with an adjournment motion concerning myself, tabled by Pandit L.K. Maitra before the Indian Legislative Assembly only the other day, it was stated on behalf of the Government of India that the matter should not come before the Central Assembly, since I had been incarcerated by the Bengal Government. I believe a similar admission was made in the Bengal Legislative Assembly on behalf of the Ministry.

And we cannot forget that here in Bengal we live under the benign protection of a 'popular' ministry.

My recent election to the Indian Legislative Assembly has raised another issue — that of 'immunity' from imprisonment for members of the Legislature, while the Legislature is in session. This is a right inherent in every constitution, no matter whether it is explicitly provided in the statute or not and this right has been established after a protracted struggle. Quite recently, the Burma Government allowed a convicted prisoner to attend the sittings of the Burma Legislative Assembly, but though I am not a convicted prisoner, I have been denied that right by our 'popular' ministry.

If apologists attempt to invoke the precedent of Captain Ramsay M.P. in support of the Government, I may point out that Capt. Ramsay's case stands on a different footing altogether. Serious charges have been preferred against him, but all the facts not being known to us, it is difficult to argue either way. One may, however, urge that if Capt. Ramsay has been unjustly imprisoned and no redress will be ultimately forthcoming, it would lend substance to what Mr Kennedy (American Ambassador to Great Britain) and others are reported to have said — namely, that democracy is dead in England. In any case, Capt. Ramsay has had the opportunity of getting his case examined by a Committee of the House of Commons.

In dealing with my case generally, two broad issues have now to be considered. Firstly, have the Defence of India Rules any sanction — ethical or popular? Secondly, have the rules, as they stand, been properly applied in my case? The answers to both the questions are in the negative.

The D.I. Rules have no ethical sanction behind them because they constitute an infringement of the elementary rights and liberties of the people. Moreover, they are essentially a war-measure and, as is known to everybody, India was declared a belligerent power and was dragged into the war without the consent of the Indian people or the Indian Legislature. Further, these Rules militate against the claim so vociferously made in Britain that she is fighting the cause of freedom and democracy. And lastly, the Congress Party in the Central Assembly was not a party to the adoption of the Defence of India Act or the Defence of India Rules. In these circumstances, it would not be improper to ask whether the Defence of India Rules should not more appropriately be called the Suppression of India Rules or the Defence of Injustice Rules.

It may be urged on behalf of this Government that the Defence of India Act being an Act of the Central Legislature, all provincial Governments are obliged to administer the Rules framed there under. But enough has already been said above to justify the charge that the Rules, even as they stand, have not been properly applied in my case. There has been manifest illegality and injustice. Only one explanation can, to my mind, account for such a strange conduct, viz. that Government have been pursuing a frankly vindictive policy towards me for reasons that are quite inexplicable.

For more than two months, the question has been knocking at the door of my conscience over and over again as to what I should do in such a predicament. Should I submit to the pressure of circumstances and accept whatever comes my way — or should I protest against what to me is unfair, unjust and illegal? After the most mature deliberation I have come to the conclusion that surrender to circumstances is out of the question. It is a more heinous crime to submit to a wrong inflicted than to perpetrate that wrong. So, protest I must.

But all these days, protest has been going on and the ordinary methods of protest have all been exhausted. Agitation in the press and on the platform, representations to Government, demand in the Assembly, exploration of legal channels — have not all of these been already tried and found ineffective? Only one method remains — the last weapon in the hands of a prisoner, i.e. hunger strike or fast. In the cold light of logic I have examined the pros and cons of this step and have carefully weighed the loss and gain that will accrue from it. I have no illusions in the matter and I am fully conscious that the immediate, tangible gain will be nil, for I am sufficiently conversant with the behaviour of Governments and bureaucracies in such crises. The classic and immortal examples of Terence Macsweeney and Jatin Das are floating before my mind's eye at the moment. A system has no heart that could be moved, though it has a false sense of prestige to which it always clings.

Life under existing conditions is intolerable for me. To purchase one's continued existence by compromising with illegality and injustice goes against my very grain. I would throw up life itself, rather than pay this price. Government are determined to hold me in prison by brute force. I say in reply: 'Release me or I shall refuse to live — and it is for me to decide whether I choose to live or to die.'

Though there may be no immediate, tangible gain — no suffering, no sacrifice is ever futile. It is through suffering and sacrifice alone that a cause can flourish and prosper and in every age and clime, the eternal law prevails — 'the blood of the martyr is the seed of the church'.

In this mortal world, everything perishes and will perish — but ideas, ideals and dreams do not. One individual may die for an idea but that idea will, after his death, incarnate itself in a thousand lives. That is how the wheels of evolution move on and the ideas, ideals and dreams of one generation are bequeathed to the next. No idea has ever fulfilled itself in this world except through an ordeal of suffering and sacrifice.

What greater solace can there be than the feeling that one has lived and died for a principle? What higher satisfaction can a man possess than the knowledge that his spirit will beget kindred spirits to carry on his unfinished task? What better reward can a soul desire than the certainty that his message will be wafted over hills and dales and over the broad plains to every corner of his land and across the seas to distant lands? What higher consummation can life attain than peaceful self-immolation at the altar of one's cause?

Hence it is evident that nobody can lose through suffering and sacrifice. If he does lose anything of the earth earthy, he will gain much more in return by becoming the heir to a life immortal.

This is the technique of the soul. The individual must die, so that the nation may live. Today I must die, so that India may live and may win freedom and glory.

To my countrymen I say, 'Forget not that the greatest curse for a man is to remain a slave. Forget not that the grossest crime is to compromise with injustice and wrong. Remember the eternal law: You must give life, if you want to get it . And remember that the highest virtue is to battle against inequity, no matter what the cost may be.'

To the Government of the day I say, 'Cry halt to your mad

drive along the path of communalism and injustice. There is yet time to retrace your steps. Do not use a boomerang which will soon recoil on you. And do not make another Sindh of Bengal.'

I have finished. My second and last request to you is that you should not interfere forcibly with my fast, but should permit me to approach my end peacefully. In the case of Terence Macsweeney, of Jatin Das, of Mahatma Gandhi and in our own case in 1926 Government did decide not to interfere with the fast. I hope they will do the same this time — otherwise any attempt to feed me by force will be resisted with all my strength, though the consequences thereof may be even more drastic and disastrous than otherwise. I shall commence my fast of the 29th November 1940.

Yours faithfully,

Presidency Jail,
26.11.1940

Subhas Chandra Bose

P.S. As in my previous fasts, I shall take only water with salt. But I may discontinue this later on, if I feel called upon to do so.

S.C.B.

To
The Hon. Chief Minister
and
the Council of Ministers

Dear Sir,

This is my final appeal to you.

2. I have already written to Government requesting them not to resort to forcible feeding and informing them that if this is nevertheless attempted, I shall have to resist with all my strength, though the consequences thereof may be 'more drastic and disastrous than otherwise'. In my confidential letter to the Superintendent, Presidency Jail, dated 30th October and in my letter to Government, dated 26th November, I made my position perfectly clear. I was, therefore, surprised when I got hints from the Jail authorities that forcible feeding was still being contemplated in my case.

3. I shall not repeat all the arguments urged by me on this subject in the above two letters, but I desire to briefly recapitulate my position once again.

4. Firstly, Government have no moral right to feed me forcibly when they are responsible for making my life intolerable through injustice and illegality, strongly tinged with communalism.

5. Government have no legal authority either, to forcibly feed me in these circumstances. There is no law that I know of which empowers Government to use force in this matter. A departmental order of Government cannot take the place of law, particularly when it infringes the elementary rights and liberties of the individual.

6. If any attempt is made to forcibly feed me in spite of my repeated requests to the contrary, all those directly or indirectly responsible for it — will become civilly and criminally liable for any injury or pain, bodily or mental, that may be inflicted on me thereby.

7. Apart from the above points of principle, my physical condition, both before and after the commencement of fast, should render it impossible for forcible feeding to be attempted in my case. It should be quite clear that under such circumstances, forcible feeding will defeat its own purpose and instead of prolonging life, will hasten its end. Civil and criminal liability for the use of force will, owing to this consideration, be naturally aggravated.

8. I may inform you in this connection that in the event of forcible feeding being resorted to, I shall have no option but to take steps to relieve myself of the unbearable, protracted agony resulting from it. This could be done only by suicide and the responsibility for it will rest entirely with the Government. For a man who has turned his back on life, there are a hundred ways of reaching his end and no power on earth can prevent his death. I have chosen the most peaceful method and it would be sheer brutality to force me to adopt a less peaceful or more drastic remedy. The step that I have now taken is not an ordinary fast. It is the result of several months' mature deliberation, finally sealed by a vow prayerfully taken by me on the sacred day of Kali Puja.

9. I have been on hunger strike several times before, but this fast is of an unusual type, never resorted to by me previously.

10. Man does not live by bread alone. He needs moral and spiritual sustenance as well. When he is denied the latter, you cannot expect him to live — merely to further your plans or fit in with your scheme of things.

11. I have already said in my letter of 26th November, that I have but two requests to make of you — firstly, that my letter of 26th November, which is my political testament, be carefully

preserved in the archives of the Government and secondly, that I be allowed to approach my end peacefully. Is that asking too much of you?

Yours faithfully,
Subhas Chandra Bose

Presidency Jail,
2/5.12.1940

Letter to the Premier and the Council of Ministers:

38/2, Elgin Road,
Calcutta,
9.12.40.

To
The Hon'ble Premier
and
the Council of Ministers.
(Through the Additional Secretary,
Government of Bengal).

Dear Sirs,

On 5th December last at about 4.30 p.m. the Superintendent of the Presidency Jail came into my cell and after the usual greetings and enquiries said 'I have orders to send you home. The Ambulance is ready'. The meaning of this statement should be clear to the meanest intelligence.

The next morning I was surprised to learn that Government had only 'suspended' (not withdrawn) the order of detention under section 26 of the Defence of India Rules.

Even then it was presumed that the prosecution cases, at any rate, had been withdrawn. It now appears that that presumption also was wrong.

I only wish that I had been informed of all this while I was in Jail. However, I now request Government to kindly inform me —

(1) whether they will 'withdraw' the order under section 26 of the D.I. Rules;

(2) whether they will withdraw the two cases still pending against me.

On receipt of their reply, I shall decide whether I shall go back to jail and resume hunger strike after recovery or whether I shall do so forthwith.

It will be noted that the legal position concerning the two cases is extremely anomalous, because I am neither in police custody nor in jail custody.

In any case I desire to thank Government for the courtesy shown to me on the 5th instant.

Yours faithfully,
Subhas Chandra Bose

Copy forwarded to the Hon'ble Premier, Government of Bengal.

Other Letters

From M.N. Roy

3B Store Road
Ballygunge
Calcutta
June 12, 1939

My dear Subhas Babu,

Enclosed is the statement written according to your suggestion last night. I believe it meets the requirement. If that is so, you may release it to the press. Otherwise, please inform.

Yours sincerely,

M.N. Roy

Statement by M.N. Roy, Calcutta, June 12, 1939.

I have been invited by Mr K.F. Nariman to attend a conference of left-wing Congressmen which will take place on the eve of the meeting of the A.I.C.C. in Bombay to discuss the formation of the Forward Block. Since Sjt. Subhas Chandra Bose announced his intention to form the Forward Block as the rallying ground of all the left elements inside the Congress, there has been much controversy, and many demands for the various left groups and prominent leftists to define their attitude towards Sjt. Bose's proposal. Already, on more than one occasion, I have expressed my views on the matter. The attitude of the League of Radical Congressmen has also been publicly stated. The plan of creating a common platform for all the left elements in the Congress deserves the support and co-operation of all leftists who can place the general interest of the movement above the interest of any particular group. The generally desired co-operation for a common purpose can take place on the platform of the proposed Block, because Sjt. Bose does not want already existing left groups to merge themselves in the new organization. Therefore, the League of Radical Congressmen as well as myself personally welcome the movement started by Sjt. Bose with a laudable purpose. That being the case, we shall participate in the proposed conference with the object of promoting the mobilization of the radical forces, so that they could function more effectively and influence the future development of our struggle for freedom. I have stated publicly in the past, and I repeat it once again, that complete rejection of Gandhism and advocacy of other methods of struggle should be the main planks in the platform of the radical left wing, which must rise as the alternative leadership of the Congress. As far as I can judge from public pronouncements, the Forward Block has not taken up this position. We shall, of course, press our point of view. But our co-operation will not be conditional upon the acceptance by the Forward Block of what we consider to be the maximum programme of an effective left wing. We shall be ready to co-operate on a minimum programme which may be formulated by common consent in the proposed conference to be held in Bombay.

From M.N. Roy

13 Mohini Road
Dehradun
October 13, 1939

Dear Friend,

May I take the liberty of drawing your attention to a note in the Oct. 28 issue of the '*Forward Bloc*', referring to the telegraphic report of my opinion about the Working Committee's resolution regarding the resignation of Congress Ministries. From the original text of the document enclosed herewith, you will see that the remarks are not warranted, and will kindly do the needful for undoing the wrong done to me.

Yours sincerely,

M.N. Roy

To Sita Dharmavir

Train
12.11.39

My dear Sita,

I have not been able to write to you for some time past. I am now returning home after a nine-day tour in Assam and East Bengal. I am fairly well — can't hope to be better.

I hope all of you are doing well — Leila in particular. I am enclosing a few lines for Didi. I do not know if she is at Lahore or has shifted to Delhi by now with Leila.

With love to all of you.

Yours affly
Subhas

To Amiya Chakravarty
38/2 Elgin Road
Calcutta

Burdwan Station
11.12.39

Respectfully,

I was happy to get your letter. I've just returned today from U.P. Very soon I'm coming to Santiniketan. I hope you will stay there a few days longer. Is there any possibility of the Poet or yourself coming to Calcutta? My health is now poor. I feel as if I have influenza. I hope to recover in two to three days. Accept my heartfelt affectionate greetings.

As ever yours,
Subhas Chandra Bose.

From M. Annapurnaiah *Rajahmundry,*
15.1.40

My dear Subhas Babu,

I have been seriously thinking of the issues raised about the *struggle*

* Translated from the original Bengali.

and our bloc *going out of the Congress.* I have also consulted friends. I am seriously thinking of the contribution by *Andhradesa* to the struggle and my personal part in the matter. I have underlined the four points about which I will *give out my heart* fully in this letter.

1. It is my considered opinion that the call should be given at an early date by us.
2. My personal opinion is that one day or other, our going out seems to be inevitable. But one has to choose the most favourable and psychological moment to do so. Instead of allowing them to drive us out *at their convenience* it is better, we walk out *at our convenience.* But I would very strongly urge that these two matters should be thoroughly discussed in a meeting of our executive and then *only final decision* taken.
3. As regards the 3rd, the struggle in Andhra, I have already told you that we can start struggle on local issues at 4 places. And a general struggle has to be launched in the other districts. But our greatest handicap is *funds.* We most earnestly request you to give us Rs 1000 as *help for the struggle.*
4. As regards myself you know that I am prepared to do any thing for the bloc and for yourself. But I am also severely handicapped for want of money. As per your advice, I have definitely given up all insurance work. May I know if you can give me Rs 1000 only for *my family maintenance* till December 1940. I can give it to my wife and wander freely on the work of the bloc. A lot of time, worry and inconvenience will be saved and I can devote all my time and energy for the work of the party.

Thus I am requesting you for Rs 2000 only, half for party work and struggle and half for *my family maintenance.* If you can kindly arrange this amount, I can assure you that I will be in a position to give the party all my time, attention and energy and with *the possibilities in Andhra* I am sure that before the year 1940 closes the bloc will be very strong and influential *in the Telegu country.* This money will not really be sufficient for the work, but with this as nucleus, we will be able to raise further funds necessary for it. I know well that your greatest handicap is at present, funds. But in spite of that I request you to take the trouble of finding the money somehow.

I have nothing more to add than assuring you that I will always swim or sink with you. All sorts of opinion recall your tour is a great success here. I therefore request you to give us *ten days* in

February if you are out. Please give us positively *ten days as the minimum.* Please fix up the tour dates *by the end of the month.* Kindly let me know where and when you will fix a meeting of *our executive.*

If you send money, please wire *to me* to come and take it or please send a messenger to me from there. You can say that my house is only 50 yards from the Godavari station and any railway porter can bring the messenger to my house *or any Jetka wallah.*

If it is impossible for you to help me please let me know about it. I will in that case, go back to my residence work side by side with the political work. Please *do not keep me in suspense.* Lala Shankarlal also advised me to be a whole time worker for the party and told me that he could find me Rs 1000 which sum, he said, was not an unreasonable figure. I have not heard anything again from him.

Please therefore *reply me* promptly to the following address:

> Managing agents the National Chemical & Pharmaceutical Works, Rajahmundry. Have a cover inside and put it *in my name.*

I am really very sorry, that I had to raise my personal matter and trouble you. *But I could not help it.* Please excuse me for the same and oblige.

Yours sincerely,

M. Annapurnaiah

PS Summing up: (1) Please fix a meeting of our executive after the 26th. (2) Please give ten days for Andhra tour in February. (3) Please give Rs 1000 for struggle in Andhra and Rs 1000 for *my family maintenance.* The letter to be *kindly* kept *confidential* (4) Note the cover address given in the letter.

Please do reply promptly. I emphasize this because you are in your own words, 'a bad correspondent.'

MAP

From Dr Satyapal
B.A., M.B., M.L.A.
Physician & Dental Surgeon.

2, Abbot Road,
Lahore
23.1.1940

My dear Shrijut Subhas C. Bose

Messrs Habibulla & Fazal Hussain, representatives of the All Punjab Moslem Students' Federation are paying a visit to you to request you to visit Punjab at your very early convenience. I shall be very much obliged if you will please accept their request. You are very deeply interested in the student movement and I am confident that you will appreciate the sentiments of the members of the Federation and favour us all with your presence amidst us.

With best regards.

Yours sincerely

Satyapal

From Akbar Shah

Badrashi
Nowshera
19.2.40

Dear Comrade,

It is long since there is no letter from you. It appears you were on a long tour. I have already written one or two letters to you. I don't know whether or not you have received them.

Comrades from all around in this province are for struggle. I don't think we would be having any instructions to that effect from you before the end of the proposed Forward Bloc Conference at Ramgarh. At any rate please write to one something definite on this.

We are having about 13 delegates on Forward Bloc ticket to the Ramgarh session. We expected a majority in the house this time, but the rightist being in power were active enough either to reject our nomination papers or somehow or other manage our defeat. At any rate we are growing in strength; Our organization is spreading on all sides.

In Peshawar city we depended on the disorganized socialists who had joined the Forward Bloc, but it happens, that they have left us, though they have not organized any socialist party.

Some serious members of the right wing might join us in

Peshawar city. An ex-redshirt General gives us to understand that he is about to come over with a good number of the redshirts. Perhaps you know that in Peshawar city we have no redshirt volunteer with us so far. If we succeed in having him at the head of our volunteer corps, I am sure we would be very strong in the city.

Please instruct the manager of the weekly Forward Bloc to issue the paper in the name of the comrades on the paper enclosed here with.

Akbar Shah

From Prof. N.G. Ranga M.L.A.
Vice-President
All India Kisan Sabha
Nidubrolu (P.O.) S.I.

Madras Office:
South Indian Federation of
Peasants & Agricultural Workers,
57, Varada Muthiappan St.

G.T., Nidubrolu
20.2.40.

My dear Subhas Babu,

I am glad to say that the F.B. is progressing by leaps and bounds in the Andhra and Madras city. Thanks to the utterly wrong lead given by the C.S.P. & C.P. over the 26th and their foolish attacks upon both of us. All our Kisan Sabhaites are today determined to put a stop to this drift on the part of the leftists towards Rightism and so, have assured me to give their best effort to build up the F.B. They all know that I am behind all this Forward Drive towards the F.B. and so I feel confident that in a few weeks the F.B. will be the strongest leftist force in Andhra and Tamilnad.

By the way, we have at last decided to organize next session of the All India Kisan Sabha at Palasa, one nights journey from Calcutta on the B.N.R. The open session takes place on either the 25th or 26th and I am anxious that I shall come to give you special message. If possible we may invite you to perform the opening ceremony.

On 1st April or if necessary even on the 28th of March, we shall have the opening ceremony of our Andhra Peasants Institute in our village. I am keen on having you & open it, we are going to have a 100 students to be trained for developing our organization. Your stay in the school for two days will be of great use. So I request you to reserve that week i.e. 26th March–1st April for the Andhra.

I dare say comrade Annapurnayya has already written to you about Palasa.

I am going tomorrow to tour in Nellore Dist till the 26th and Salem on the 28th inst. I will be in Delhi on the 6th March and proceed then to Ramgarh where we shall meet.

With affection Ranga.

By the way Moulana Azad has given a good First Message. It strengthens us. So you were right after all about his leftism.

I have today issued a short statement welcoming his expressions in favour of the coming struggle.

I will be issuing another strengthening yours about the need for a great rally at Ramgarh against compromise.

But it is not enough. We not only want a fight but also a fight that will not be sabotaged. In short we will not be satisfied with any politics that will not fetch us complete Independence as a result of this war and our national effort. I do hope you will lead our national struggle. I do sincerely trust that you will see your way to get our Ramgarh conference committed to the assurance that we want independence in order to pave the way for the ultimate achievement of Socialist Republic i.e. Kisan Mazdoor Raj. Unless we secure such a pledge, there can be no genuine progress marking us as distinguished from others.

It is the C.P's opposition to our Madras F.B's 26th pledge incorporating our ideal of K.M. Raj that has brought it into serious trouble all over the South.

Anyhow as long as at least the F.B. & K. Sabhaites stick together the other leftists can be prevented from eventually to sink themselves in their self imposed one sided National consolidation.

From Indulal Yagnik

Prarthana Samaj
Astodia Road
Ahmedabad
20.2.40

Dear Subhas Babu

I was so glad to learn yesterday that you have agreed to inaugurate our Provincial Kisan Conference over which Swamiji will preside on April 20–21. We will endeavour to make this conference a landmark in the political history of Gujarat.

Now I want to know if you can possibly spare a few days, before or after the conference to make a hurried tour of Gujarat.

Is it necessary for me to attend the Ramgarh rally? Or can you spare me for my work over here? I have to attend the Kisan Conference in Andhra soon afterwards.

Your sincerely

Indulal Yagnik

From Carol Potee

Barnagore.
20th Feb. 1940

Dear Sir,

With a feeling of great delight and humble courtesy I approach you for a specimen of your message which will inspire me in future. I have collected many messages from many distinguished men and women of Hindusthan including Poet Rabindra Nath, Mahatma Gandhi, Pandit Jawaharlal, Sarojini Naidu etc, and yours will be a valuable addition to my collection.

I am an American girl of 14 years. I have come to Hindusthan about 6 months ago. I wish to meet you. But as you were making an extensive tour throughout India it was not possible for me to meet you. Perhaps this is due to my bad luck. I will leave India soon. I, therefore, request you to send the message at an earliest possible date.

One anna in stamps is attached herewith.

I am anxious about your health.

I remain,
Yours Obediently,
Carol Potee.

Subhas Ch. Bose. Esqr,
Calcutta

P.S. As I am staying with my friend Shri Bibhuti Bhusan Ghoshal. Please write in the care of his address. The address is given below.

Carol Potee
C/o Shri Bibhuti Bhusan Ghoshal
195, Pramanick Ghat Road
P.O. Barnagore,
Calcutta.

From Lala Shankar Lal

President: 'Forward Bloc'
Sjt. Subhas Chandra Bose

Genl. Secretary:
Lala Shankar Lal

Telegrams: 'TROIC'
Telephone No. 7286

Post Box No. 21,
New Delhi 21st Feb. 1940

Dear Bose,

I sent you a telegram on 16th instant reading as follows:

'PLEASE SEND CHEQUE FOR 5000 WORK AT RAMGARH MUST BE COMMENCED'

but unfortunately have received no reply. I know you must be busy and there must be some difficulties also, but the time is very short. Please arrange to remit the cheque at your earliest.

Yours sincerely,

Lala Shankar Lal

From M.N. Mukherjee
M.L.A.
Phone PARK 1203.

17 Haris Mukherji Road,
Calcutta
22nd February, 1940

My dear Subhas babu,

I duly received your letter from Patna desiring me to cast my vote as a member of the Bihar Legislative Assembly in favour of Mr Khalil Ahmed in the election to the Bihar Council. I had accordingly to write to another candidate, an old and esteemed friend, who sought my support that I must carry out your wishes even though I know nothing about Mr Khalil Ahmad. Since then I received a letter from Mr P.R. Das a copy of which is enclosed. Before I received your letter I had intended to vote for Rai Bahadur Shyam Nandan Sahay. I hope you have received Mr Das's letter and will not press me to vote for Mr Khalil Ahmad.

With kindest regards.

Yours sincerely,

Munindranath Mukherjee

Srijut Subhas Chandra Bose
38/2, Elgin Road,
Local.

From Swami Sahajanand Saraswati

THE ALL INDIA KISAN SABHA

General Secretary
Swami Sahjanand Saraswati
Camp Madhupur
E.I.R.

Shri Sitaramashram
P.O. & Tel. Bihta. E.I.R
Patna
Date 28.2.1940

No. . . . .

Dear Subhas Babu,

I am going to Giridih to begin my one week's tour in the Hazaribagh district which finishes on the 5.3.40.

You will be going to U.P. for your tour. I regret no tour of yours could be organized in some parts of Gaya and Monghyr districts during the last week of February. Sheelbhadraji sent a wire to you about it from Motihari. But no reply could be had there owing to perhaps your longer stay at Ramgarh. I am not aware what is being done at Ramgarh in connection with the Anti-Compromise Conference. Sheelbhadraji is again there and also Pt. Dhanraj Sharma.

You might have read in the press a statement of mine regarding the Anti-Compromise Conference. How do you like it? Are you convinced of its utility and opportuneness? Here in Behar all felt its necessity very much and they felt much relief when I issued it. Even our socialist friends appreciated it and they told me about its necessity. There was a wild propaganda of a very loose type going on against the conference and my statement has set all speculation and mischiefs at rest for the time being at least.

Will you not have some hundred volunteers for conference? I think it is most necessary to have them. And if so, what will be their uniforms? Have you thought over it? In my opinion if it is red it will serve in our Rally also. Will you get a few hundred such uniforms ready before we meet at Ramgarh? For our Rally my friends are managing for such uniforms numbering thousands. But I am not sure about the exact number of the same. Of course a few hundreds of yours will prove much helpful to us.

And what about the procedure etc. at our conference? Should there be a printed welcome address and also the presidential address? I think it is proper and necessary to get both the addresses previously prepared and printed. At such a critical moment extempore address will not do. If you agree I may prepare a short one. But where to get it printed? At Calcutta or Patna or elsewhere?

I doubt very much if this letter will reach you before you leave for U.P.

Sincerely yours

Swami Sahajanand Saraswati

From Mian Akbar Shah

Badrashi
Nowshera
29.2.40

Dear Comrade,

I am writing to you now & then in order to acquaint you with the conditions here. I have written to you how in an unbecoming way they managed my defeat.

I am trying my best to manage that some delegates may go from this province to Ramgarh, but I don't think more than a few would attend. We are holding a meeting of the Provincial Forward Bloc for the purpose.

I have sent you a new list a few days before & hope you might have instructed the manager of the Weekly *Forward Bloc* to issue the paper in their names.

Akbar Shah

From Indulal Yagnik

THE HINDUSTAN NEWSPAPERS LTD.
PROPRIETORS
THE ADVOCATE OF INDIA PRESS

Publications
HINDUSTAN & PRAJAMITRA.
Illustrated Gujarati Morning Daily
HIND-PRAJA.
Illustrated Gujarati Evening Daily
PRAJAMITRA-KESARI.
Illustrated Gujarati Weekly.

Telephone No 21172.
Telegrams 'HINDPRAJA',
Post Box No. 940,
21, Dalal Street, Fort,
Bombay.
March 2, 1940.

Dear Subash Babu,

I arrived here yesterday morning and hasten to reply to your telegram received on the 29th February at Ahmedabad. I received a call from Lala Shankarlal to hurry up to Ramgarh. But all my time is taken up today in placing the Gujarat movement on its feet and making intensive preparations for ensuring the success of the Provincial Kisan Conference that will meet in my District on 20th/21st April. And you have agreed to inaugurate the Conference.

If I attend Ramgarh Session I will have to leave Bombay by about 15th if not earlier and I will not be able to return to Gujarat till nearly the 1st of April, that would leave me only three weeks to organize the Provincial Conference.

Under the circumstances I beseech you with all the earnestness at my command to spare me from Ramgarh. Please explain the position fully and frankly to Lala Shankarlal and other friends so that they might not misunderstand my absence from Ramgarh.

Yours sincerely

Indulal Yagnik

To Sri Subash Chandra Bose Babuji, Calcutta

From Nanik G. Motwane

CONTRACTORS TO THE GOVT. OF INDIA, GOVT. OF BOMBAY, MILITARY, RAILWAYS, INDIAN STATES, MUNICIPALITIES, ETC.

CHICAGO TELEPHONE & RADIO CO., LTD.

TELEPHONE & RADIO ENGINEERS AND PUBLIC ADDRESS EXPERTS

TELEGRAMS:	HEAD OFFICE:	BRANCHES:	25, Chowringhee,
'CHIPHONE'	129 MAHATMA	Hazratganj,	CALCUTTA
	GANDHI ROAD,	LUCKNOW	Telephone:
	POST BOX 459,	The Mall,	CAL 1953
	FORT,	LAHORE	
	BOMBAY		

Your Ref. CALCUTTA,
Our Ref. NGM/GR/21/5498 *March 25, 1940*

Shree Subhas Chandra Bose,
38/2 Elgin Road,
Calcutta.

Respected Shree Subhas Chandra Bose:

I have written to you several letters from Bombay, but I have never received a reply from you.

This time, when I was coming to Calcutta from Ramgarh Congress, I was asked by Shree Nathalal Parekh, our mutual friend, to contact you and try and secure your patronage.

I had the pleasure of meeting you only for a few minutes at Ramgarh when you were passing in your triumphal procession and when I had the pleasure of filming you as I have done two of your previous processions, I had a smile from you and I had sympathetic looks from you. This has encouraged me to write to you again and hence this letter.

In every province, Congress supports me and my organization by giving us their all orders of Loudspeaker installations. On enquiry from my office here in Calcutta, I find that we are not blessed with this from you.

Whatever may be my organization's faults, you have to please overlook them and give us your patronage as every other Congress Province does. You will kindly pass instructions to your organizers to support us.

Our charges will be moderate and really reasonable. I trust, hereafter, we shall secure your patronage and you will find, as you know it, that our services will be satisfactory to you.

Trust, you will kindly look into this matter and please comply with my request,

I am, with best regards,

Yours sincerely,

Nanik G. Motwane

From Karim A. Chashma

TELEGRAMS: GARDEN CALCUTTA TELEPHONE: P.K. 1333

CHASHMA TEA COMPANY
TEA PLANTERS & DEALERS

LESSEE: KUCHILLA T.E.

CODES: BENTLEY'S & A.B.C. 5TH & 6TH EDITIONS

Ref. No. 40/68

17, Phulbagan Road, Entally,
Calcutta
Dated 9th April 1940

Chasma Brand
Sportsman,
Flavourous,
Md. Sporting,
Loose
All kinds

To
Mr Subhas Chandra Bose,
38/2 Elgin Road,
Calcutta.

Dear Sir,

Pardon my taking the liberty to write this letter to you which I hope will not be taken amiss.

It is my great desire that I should start a brand of tea of the very best quality in your name displaying your portrait on the cover of the package. This brand which I intend to name 'SUBHAS BOSE TEA' will be duly registered, samples of which will be offered for your goodself's use after everything in this respect is complete.

May I, therefore, request the favour of your kind permission to the above. I most fervently hope that this prayer of mine will not go in vain.

With apologies for troubling you and hoping to be excused for intruding upon your valuable time.

Yours faithfully,

Karim A. Chashma
Proprietor

From Gaganvihari L. Mehta

Gaganvihari L. Mehta. *Calcutta, 13th April, 1940.*

Dear Subhashbabu,

I received your personal letter of 11th April along with your formal letter which is undated. I am forwarding it to my Head Office at Bombay to look into the matter and issue necessary instructions to our Rangoon Agenda. I shall let you know when I hear from them.

I underwent an operation for appendicitis recently but have been recovering since then. I am expecting to go out for a change shortly.

Yours sincerely,

Gaganvihari L. Mehta

Sjt. Subhash Chandra Bose,
Calcutta.

✉

From Agatha Harrison

INDIA CONCILIATION GROUP

Chairman:	*at –*
Carl Heath	*2, Cranbourne Court,*
please reply to:	*Albert Bridge Road, S.W. 11*
Hon. Secretary:	*Battersea 2400*
Agatha Harrison	*April 20th 1940*

Dear Subhas Bose,

I think you and your brother will like to see the Order of Service used for the memorial for C.F. Andrews last week. His going is a great blow — for we heard he was 'Improving'. Working with him so closely over these past years, is a privilege I treasure. In airmail letters just to hand — I see you were at the service in Calcutta — and was glad.

Yours very sincerely,

Agatha Harrison

From Meghnad Saha

My dear Subhas Babu,

A few days ago you were kind enough to ask me for plans regarding the improvement of the city of Calcutta. I am giving my thought to the matter. In the meantime, world events are shaping in a way which we foresaw long ago.

I am enclosing copy of an application which will be sent through the Registrar to the Corporation of Calcutta. We are celebrating this year the Silver Jubilee of the Science College and we want to hold a Scientific and Industrial Exhibition. We have applied to the Corporation for a grant of Rs 25,000 as a contribution towards this object. The full details are given in the copy of the application which is enclosed. I shall be much obliged if you can kindly help us by extending to us your powerful patronage. We have already talked with Mr A.R. Siddiqui, the Mayor, and his attitude is not only very helpful but also very encouraging. If we can hold this exhibition in a proper way it will be a source of inspiration for the citizens of

Calcutta. We have included in our application the minimum sum which we want, and I hope the full amount may be given to us.

With kind regards,

Yours sincerely

M.N. Saha

Sj. Subhas Chandra Bose,
Alderman, Cal. Corporation,
38/2 Elgin Road,
Calcutta

SILVER JUBILEE
University College of Science and Technology
(foundation stone laid on 27th March, 1914)

Secretaries
Prof. M.N. Saha
Prof. B.C. Guha
92, Upper Circular Road
Telephone, Regent 159 and 160
Prof. K.P. Chattopadhyay
35, Ballygunge Circular Road
Telephone, Alipore 397

92, Upper Circular Road
Calcutta 1940

The Chief Executive Officer,
Corporation of Calcutta,
Calcutta.

Dear Sir,

On behalf of the Silver Jubilee Committee of the University College of Science, we beg to approach the Corporation for a grant of Rs 25,000 as their contribution towards the Scientific and Industrial Exhibition which it is proposed to be held in Calcutta during the Silver Jubilee Celebrations of the University College of Science and Technology in December, 1940. The Exhibition will be open for a period of at least three to four weeks, to which the public in general including the citizens of Calcutta will have access without any distinction whatsoever.

1. You may know that the University College of Science and Technology was founded on the 27th March, 1914, and last year it completed the 25th year of its existence. The University has appointed a Committee to celebrate the Silver Jubilee of the College in a befitting manner. The Committee has decided that one of the main items should be the holding of a Scientific and Industrial Exhibition, which in future is expected to be developed into a permanent Scientific and Industrial Museum for the City of Calcutta, which will be the first of its kind, not only in this City, but in the Province and even in the whole of India.

2. Science now plays far too dominant a role in national life to be ignored, and familiarity with science is needed not only by professional Scientists but also by the average citizen. To meet this demand, Western countries have been organizing science museums during the last 25 years. The best known are the Deutsches Museum in Munich, the Science Museum in South Kensington, London and the Science Museum of New York. In these museums representative experiments in each branch of science are exhibited in well-designed surroundings and visitors as well as students are allowed on payment of a small charge to inspect the museums and sometimes to carry on the experiments themselves. Frequently a scientific subject is explained to an audience by a recognized expert on the subject with the help of models and experiments which are always kept in readiness. These museums have become recognized centres of instruction and millions of people are found to attend them in course of a single year. For example, in the Deutsches Museum in Munich, the yearly attendance amounts to more than a million and it is a common sight to see batches of students from schools and colleges performing their own experiments according to directions laid on the table. After once the start has been helped, the Museums do not need to spend much. In fact, most of them have become self-supporting.

3. France was hitherto behind Germany and England and America in these respects, but in 1936 when the Popular Front Government came into power in Paris, they recognized the importance of science museums and at the instance of the famous Scientist Perrin, a large scale Exhibition was organized and demonstrated in a specially constructed Hall called the Palace of Discovery. This was attended by about three million people and brought to the Government Treasury an income of about 9 million francs. The exhibition has subsequently been converted into a permanent museum and is

now being used as a place of instruction not only for the young but also for the adult population.

4. It is a pity that the great City of Calcutta is without any such organization which can appeal to the man in the street and which will doubtless be a great place of scientific education for the general mass. The Silver Jubilee Committee, therefore, thought that they would give the lead in this matter by organizing a Scientific and Industrial Exhibition and they invited the co-operation of the scientists in Calcutta and outside. A large number of them have very kindly promised to co-operate in the matter. The University has sanctioned a grant of about Rs 12,000 and has placed its premises and grounds at 92, Upper Circular Road, at the disposal of the Organization. It is, however, felt that if the Exhibition is to be properly organized, a larger sum will be needed. In fact, our estimate runs up to Rs 50,000. As the exhibition is expected to prove a source of inspiration to the general public of Calcutta in matters of science, we wish to approach you for a grant of Rs 25,000 in order that the exhibition might prove to be a complete success. It might be mentioned in this connection that the City of Calcutta has deservedly won a high reputation as a centre of original Scientific research in the whole of India. The standards for scientific education and research work undertaken are fully comparable to the best obtainable elsewhere. Calcutta will further always be ranked as a centre of pioneer in science and technology. It is, therefore, only in the fitness of things that the first scientific museum in India will be started and located in Calcutta.

5. The grant which we seek is permissible under the special powers given to the Corporation under the Calcutta Municipal Act, 1923. Under Section 477 of this Act, it is within the competence of the Corporation (sub-section 13) not only to promote technical education, but also to contribute to the cost incurred on account of an exhibition for the purpose of spread of education (sub-sec. 15). From the legal point of view it is therefore abundantly clear that the grant which we seek is fully covered by the Statute.

We shall be glad if you will please place our application before the appropriate authority or authorities.

Yours faithfully,

To Kantilal Parekh *25.6.40*
26, Marine Drive,
Bombay

My dear Kantilal,

I hope you are all doing well. I have not heard from you for a long time. Your will perhaps remember the loan you took from me some time ago. I am now very urgently in need of money. Could you kindly let me have some money now? I shall be glad and shall feel a bit relieved if you can.

I am leaving for Calcutta latest tomorrow. You know my address — 38/2 Elgin Road, Calcutta. Love to all.

Yours affly
Subhas

To M.A.H. Ispahani

14.10.40

My dear Hasan,

Owing to my prolonged and enforced absence from public duty, I think I should resign the Aldermanship of the Calcutta Corporation. This will relieve me of a fretting conscience and enable the party to function as the members think best. I have referred the question to our party, through the Secretary, Sj. Indra Bhusan Boed and am awaiting their advice. Should the party endorse the idea, I hope you will not have any objection, since there is no better alternative.

Since I had undertaken a definite responsibility and since we had been working in collaboration, it is only fair that I should inform you and your party through you.

With kindest regards,

Yours faithfully,
Subhas C. Bose

M.A.H. Ispahani Esq.
Councillor
Calcutta Corporation
5 Camac Street
Calcutta

To Barada Babu

Presidency Jail
29.10.40

My dear Barada Babu,

On opening the papers this morning, my thoughts first of all went back to the late Babu Surjya Kumar Shome, who was not only a co-disciple of Deshbandhu Das but also a respected friend of mine. I can never forget how often I have partaken of the lavish hospitality of his Mymensingh home. During my last visit the vacant house extended its hospitality to me. Surya Babu's untimely death has left a gap which will remain unfilled in his own constituency.

Before I proceed further, I would request you to convey my warmest thanks to Sj. Majumdar, Sj. Neogi and Sj. Guha for generously withdrawing their candidature in my favour. I would like you to particularly thank Sj. Guha for his letter in the press this morning. I greatly appreciate the largeness of heart which finds expression in a statement ringing with sincerity and you may assure him that he will not find me wanting in generosity at any time.

Owing to my incarceration, it has not been possible for me to consult friends and co-workers whether I should stand for election to the Central Assembly and I shall not be surprised if some of them have wondered at this sudden decision. In a letter written from prison I cannot give vent to all the considerations that have weighed with me but I am sure that all politically-minded men will instinctively understand what has led me to such a decision and will heartily approve of it. I shall in this letter content myself with mentioning only one or two considerations. I could have communicated these to you at the next legal interview but that would not have been right or fair on my part. Hence this letter.

My election should among other things serve as a pointer to Moulana Abul Kalam and all those for whom he stands. Having been thoroughly discomfited in his assault on the B.P.C.C. and having thereby reduced himself to a ridiculous position, the Moulana thought that he would take advantage of our absence and deliver an attack on the Legislative Front, with a view to weakening our public position. Once again disillusionment is in store for him. His latest assault — his Vijaya gift as I call it — has already enhanced our strength and prestige in the country and exposed still further the real character of those who while paying lip-service to the ideals of truth and non-violence, practise in reality falsehood, violence and hatred.

In this connection the challenging letter of Sj. Santosh K. Basu, Ex-Mayor of Calcutta and Deputy leader of the Bengal Congress Parliamentary Party, should be read and reread throughout the country. I shall not at this stage say anything about my own bitter experience of the Moulana which I am reserving for another day. But it would be relevant to ask what the Moulana's following in the country is at present. Every leader worth the name brings with him a certain following into the Congress. What following the Moulana can claim — I wonder.

Our policy so far has been not to take the offensive in our relations with the Moulana and the Congress High Command and to that policy we shall adhere. But we must act in self-defence. Consequently for each attack there will be a strong counter-attack — let the Moulana beware of this. And the counter-attack will be all over the country, wherever we have friends and supporters. If the fight with the High Command is to be long and bitter we are quite prepared for it. We know our position in the country. Moreover we have youth on our side as well infinite patience and capacity to suffer persecution. We are therefore confident of success. We may nowadays be preoccupied with larger issues, but the Moulana should not think that because of that preoccupation, we shall fail to protect our houses from the ravages of the High Command.

My election should further indicate that I strongly disapprove of the policy of abstention from the Central Legislature. Probably because of this criminal neglect of public duty on the part of the Congress Party, the Defence of India Act could be passed in its present form and the people's voice has become virtually inaudible in the Central Legislature, needless to add that I shall not follow this suicidal policy of the Congress High Command.

To sum up, my election should along with other implications be taken as a symbolic gesture to indicate that we are fully prepared to meet the challenge of the Moulana and his caucus on every front and in every part of the country. We claim to be the true representatives of public opinion in India and we claim to be better Congressmen than those whose feet have begun to falter. We shall prove by our conduct if further proof be necessary that that claim is fully justified.

With kindest regards,

Yours very sincerely,

Subhas C. Bose

To Sardul Singh Caveeshar

Presidency Jail
Calcutta
4.11.40

Personal— not for publication

My dear Sardarji,

This morning I sent you the following telegram which I hope will reach you in due course:

'SARDUL SINGH CAVEESHAR
LAHORE
REFERENCE TODAYS PRESS REPORTS HOPE YOU WILL STRONGLY DISAPPROVE MAHATMA GANDHI'S FAST STOP LETTER FOLLOWS SUBHASBOSE.'

This morning's papers publish the news that Mahatma Gandhi has decided on a fast and that he has informed the Government to that effect. Prior to this, news appeared in the papers hinting that Gandhiji would in all probability go on fast again — consequently, nobody need be taken altogether unawares by this latest development.

I am writing this with the object of acquainting you with my views on this question, so that if you agree with them — as I am sure you will — you may take such action as you consider necessary in the circumstances, without feeling any doubt or hesitation as to what the reaction may be among members of the Gandhian fold.

After the debacle following the Rajkot fast, I thought that we had seen the last of the Gandhian fasts — but apparently I was wrong in doing so. Mahatmaji will not change even after his Himalayan blunders. What is this fast, if it is not moral coercion and why should the apostle of non-violence resort to it? The fact that he may see an inner light on the question of fast cannot change the character of violence. It cannot transform moral coercion or violence into non-violence. Our position is quite different. Our non-violence is not philosophical or metaphysical and we do not therefore rule out fast or hunger strike. As a matter of fact, I have been on hunger strike before and may resort to it again should I feel compelled to do so.

When Jatin Das resorted to hunger strike and immolated himself, the Mahatma had not a kind word to say about him. In fact, he wrote to a friend that if he did open his lips, he would have to say something uncomplimentary. But Mahatma Gandhi can himself hunger strike whenever it pleases him and we are to believe that in his case, moral coercion becomes sublimated into non-violence. There is surely some limit to our credulity. Even those who were once totally blind have begun to open their eyes.

My principal objection to this hunger strike of the Mahatma is that he is using it as a substitute for mass-movement after reducing the Congress to impotence through his assumption of sole authority. Personally in the matter of civil disobedience I would have no objection to his using this weapon for the vindication of honour and justice, whether personal or national as a supplement to the normal political method, but that would not involve substituting fast for mass-movement. We find that as at Rajkot, so also in this case, fast is to be resorted to when the mass-movement has been deliberately killed. The eyes of everybody may, by such a fast, be diverted from the movement or the cause which the public have at heart to the individual who fasts. Sidetracking the issue in this way cannot possibly serve the public cause, though it may enhance the individual's popularity or draw more sympathy for him. The situation would have been different if the fast had come naturally in the wake of a mass-movement as the result of the pressure of unavoidable circumstances.

Let us for a moment consider what Mahatmaji has hitherto achieved by his fasts. Suffering has no doubt an intrinsic ethical value — but apart from that, no objective benefits worth the name have accrued from his fasts. The Poona fast did bring some right to the scheduled castes, but even that goal was smothered by his implied acceptance of the Communal Award as a whole and by his partial acceptance of separate electorate in the case of the scheduled castes. Consequently, his record of achievement in the domain of fasting is practically nil. Nevertheless, no opposition was called for so long as fast did not replace mass-movement but aided it. Fast is now being employed in connection with sabotaging and killing of the mass movement with a view to replacing it by a substitute. Consequently, we, who believe in mass-movement, cannot give it our moral support. It should rather be our duty to openly denounce the fast — even at the risk of being misunderstood or abused in Gandhian quarters.

It would not be right for me to say anything publicly on this question even if I were permitted to, because I am not a free man. Nor should my name be dragged in this connection. But you have a great responsibility in the matter, being the President of the All India Forward Bloc in my absence and the public will naturally expect a lead from you. My further object in writing this is to assure you that on this question if you do what I would have done if I had been a free man, you will have my fullest support.*

With kindest regards,

Yours fraternally,
Subhas C. Bose

* One word more and I have done. M. Gandhi has often said that he did not want to embarrass the British Government. Will not this fast embarrass that Govt.? And will it not embarrass the people more than it embarrass the Govt., since at the time of the fast he will not be in prison?

With kindest regards,

S.C.B

Sardar Sardul Singh Caveeshar,
Chamberlain Road
Lahore

To Amiya Bose

By Air Mail

Presidency Jail
Calcutta
15.11.40

My dear Amiya,

I have not written to you for several months. Since my arrest I did not have anything particular to write, but I have been receiving regular news about yourself from letters and telegrams you have been sending home. May God keep you from all harm is my constant prayer.

Today I have something special to write to you — hence this letter. You have read in the Times the reply given by Mr Amery, Secretary of State for India, to the question tabled by Mr Sorensen about my arrest and imprisonment in the first week of July. It was then stated by the S.O.S. that I had been taken into custody in connection with the situation for the removal of the Holwell Monument in Calcutta. This is by no means the whole truth.

The fact is the that the Holwell Monument has since then been removed by Government. Except another friend and myself, all those who had been arrested in connection with H.M. Satyagraha have been released. Two and half months have elapsed since these releases took place. During this period I have been detained under Section 26 of D.I. Rules without trial and under Section 38 of the same Rules I am being prosecuted before two Magistrates for 3 speeches delivered some months ago and for an article in '*Forward Bloc*' weekly not written by me. This, you will realize is an unheard-of procedure. Government have not so far given me the faintest idea as to why detention without trial has continued after the liquidation of the H.M. Satyagraha and the launching of legal prosecution against me. To put Govt. to the test, bail applications were moved before the trying Magistrate and these were opposed by the Govt. spokesmen — thereby demonstrating that the Executive have been wantonly interfering with the process of the Law. Day before yesterday, one of the trying Magistrates openly declared that he would grant bail and he actually did so — but he added that until Govt. withdrew the order of detention under Section 26, his order re: bail would remain infructuous. No other explanation occurs to me except that I am the victim of a vindictive policy.

Now what I want you to do is this. I want you to bring these (and other facts which I am asking Mejdada to send you) facts to the notice of friends of the Indian League, Indian Conciliation Group, Swaraj League and Indian Political Group, so that they may inform our friends in Parliament and outside. I do not want you to waste any time over this or to divert your attention from your studies. You can have this letter typed out and forwarded to the above organizations and they will do the needful. Your task should end there. I know personally a host of M.P.s — mostly Liberal and Labour — like Mr Sorensen, Mr Thurtle (Lansbury's son-in-law), Mill Wilkinson, Col. Wedgwood, the I.L. Pers, Mr Vernon Bartlett, Lord Samuel, Lord Snell, Lord Listowel, Lord Faringdon — besides the Labour members of the Present Cabinet. I am also writing to Mr Arthur Greenwood separately. You may remember that Mr Greenwood presided over the meeting in Caxton Hall where I was given a public reception during my visit in 1938. Outside Parliament, people who would be interested and who know my personality are men like Prof. Laski, Sir Walter Layton, Mr Wickham Stood, Mr Basil Mathews and Mr Horrabin of London, Prof. Reddaway and Prof. Fay of Cambridge, Mr Bertrand Russell and

Prof. Lindsay of Oxford etc. All that is needed is to let them have the above information.

I shall not take more of your time — so I shall stop here. I do hope that this letter will be passed on to you. Even if it is not, I am sure that the news will reach England all the same through other channels. I am asking Mejdada to let you have more detailed information about my case of which I have given only a brief outline in this letter.

So long.

With love
Yours v. affly

Subhas

Amiya Nath Bose Esq.
(of Queen's College, Cambridge)
C/o, Lloyds Bank Ltd.,
6 Pall Mall
London S.W.

To Mr Greenwood

By Air Mail *15.11.40*

Dear Mr Greenwood,

I am sure it would interest you to hear how the Indian D.O.R.A. is being worked in this country. I shall herein deal with my own case.

Early in July last I was suddenly arrested under Sec. 129 of the Defence of India Rules and taken to prison. No explanation was given by the Government to account for my arrest until Mr Sorensen's question in the Commons elicited the reply from the Secretary of State for India, Mr Amery, that the arrest had been made in connection with the movement for the demolition or removal of the Holwell Monument in Calcutta. Thereafter, the Chief Minister of Bengal declared before the Bengal Legislative Assembly that it was the H.M. Satyagraha alone which stood in the way of my release.

Not long after, the Government of Bengal realized the reasonableness of our demand and ordered the removal of that Monument. With its removal, all those who had been clapped in prison in connection with the H.M. Satyagraha were set at liberty — except a friend of mine and myself. The order under Section 129 was replaced by another order Section 26 of the D.I. Rules providing for my permanent detention in jail without trial. This was accompanied by two prosecutions under Section 38 of the same Rules, for three speeches delivered by me several months ago and for a contributed article appearing in a weekly journal, *Forward Bloc*, of which I was the Editor. For this article published several months ago, the Government had already forfeited the security of Rs 500 without any warning and had taken a further deposit of Rs 2000 from us.

For the last 2½ months I have, thus, been detained without trial under one Section of the Rules and am being prosecuted before two Courts of Law under another section of the same rules. You can easily understand how unprecedented and improper such procedure is.

I can find no explanation for this except that I have been the victim of a vindictive policy and that Government are determined to keep me in jail by any means.

Government have been further guilty of interfering with the process of the law. When bail applications were moved on my behalf before the trying Magistrate, the Government spokesmen opposed the application at both places. Day before yesterday, one of the Magistrates declared that he was granting bail, but that order would be infructuous until the order under Section 26 was withdrawn by the Executive. It is to be noted that in the matter of working the D.I. Rules, the Bengal Government have not been carrying out the instructions of the Government of India.

Here in this province, astounding incidents have been taking place. If one happens to be a Muhammedan, the D.I. Rules have a different meaning for him. It is the non-Muslims who are being penalized. Several Muhammedans arrested and jailed under the D.I. Rules have been suddenly released for no other reason than that they professed the Islamic faith or were members of the Muslim League.

Towards the end of the last month I was elected unopposed to the Indian Legislative Assembly. In accordance with parliamentary practice, I demanded freedom to attend the sittings of the Assembly, but the demand for 'immunity' has not so far been fulfilled. Recently in the case of a convicted prisoner in Burma, the Burma Government allowed him to attend the sittings of that Assembly.

I have not indulged in any exaggeration whatsoever and have simply narrated the facts as I know them. From the above facts it should not be difficult for anybody to imagine what sort of injustice takes place in the case of people less prominent or influential than myself. What is the remedy?

The other day you were certainly shocked to hear that Pandit Jawaharlal Nehru had been sentenced to 4 years imprisonment under the D.I. Rules, but there have been thousands of cases in this province alone where people were detained in custody without trial from 1931 to 1938. I myself had to go through imprisonment and virtual exile continuously from 1932 to 1937. Pandit Nehru's case will, however, make it easy for everyone to realize what the fate of the rank and file is when a leader of his eminence and reputation has been treated in this fashion.

Would it be surprising if under such circumstances, we as human beings fail to see eye to eye with you on the problems of the present hour?

I am not writing this with the hope of getting any redress from above. I remember the case of Terence Macsweeney, Lord Mayor of Cork, who could not be released by the exercise of the Royal Prerogative because the then Premier Mr Lloyd George, stood in the way. And in the case of India, the very fact that men in the highest positions sometimes feel so helpless about remedying things serves to demonstrate that we are all up against a pernicious system. Until this system is altered, how can the individual have his birthright of liberty?

I have taken the liberty of encroaching upon your valuable time during such a crisis simply because I feel that since you know me personally, you may be inclined to put credence in what I say and that you may be able to see the other side of the shield even for one moment and thereby understand the predicament in which we find ourselves today.

With warmest regards,

Yours truly,
Subhas C. Bose

Arthur Greenwood, Esq. M.P.
Deputy Leader
Parliamentary Labour Party and
Member of the Cabinet,
Whitehall,
London, S.W.

To Arthur Moore

Personal

Presidency Jail
Calcutta
17.11.40

Dear Mr Arthur Moore,

This is a letter from an unexpected quarter. Circumstances have enabled me to read your paper more regularly than I could when I had little leisure outside. This is just to tell you that I appreciate greatly many of your articles on the burning topics of the day. You show therein an objectivity and critical faculty which are sometimes sadly lacking in these days. They give substance to what you write and thereby compel attention even when one does not agree wholly with a particular standpoint. Your attitude towards H.G. Wells and towards official communiques is but an instance in point.

I once told you across a luncheon table that I admired your articles on foreign policy and international affairs. I at least have no doubt that you were right in saying only the other day that events had justified your viewpoint and that therefore you were entitled to a hearing. But I wonder if you will get it.

I hope you have enjoyed your flight to the Middle East. With the greetings of the season,

Yours sincerely,

S.C. Bose

W. Arthur Moore Esq.
C/o, The Statesman
Chouringhee Sqauare
Calcutta

✉

To Mukundalal Sircar

CENSORED AND PASSED
Illegible
For D.C.S.B.

Passed
Illegible
Lt. Col. I.M.S.
Superintendent,
Presidency Jail

Strictly personal

Presidency Jail
21.11.40

My dear Mukunda Babu,

I am glad to have your letter of the 11th November which reached my hands day-before-yesterday.

I hope you are keeping well now.

When you interviewed me in jail, I was doing well. Since then I have had an attack of sciatica, or something like it. The attack is a mild one so far — and I am doing my best to check it. I still remember the bad attacks I had in the past and have no desire to repeat the experience.

How can I give you a message from jail for friends outside, when I am not a free agent?

I have received Sardar Sardul Singh's letter and I hope he has received mine. I would have been more happy if he had not mentioned me in the telegram to Gandhiji. One is liable to be misunderstood if one does not explain himself fully — which is so difficult while in prison.

After a great deal of hesitation I am offering you some advice. This is strictly for yourself and should be regarded as confidential and not meant to be communicated to others. If I had been free, I could have issued general instructions, But I cannot do so while I am here — for this might create misunderstanding. We do not take orders from Wardha. Consequently, no matter what Gandhiji may do, you should not feel obliged to jump into the movement and court arrest. You should carry on as usual. In the past, it is we who have toiled and suffered and others have reaped the harvest. But how long will this go on?

So long.

With cordial greetings,

Yours v. sincerely

Subhas C. Bose

Sj. Mukundalal Sircar,
37, College Street,
Calcutta

Index